Know Thyself

Know Thyself

Shankaracharya's timeless wisdom

Anandmurti Gurumaa

*"A book that has the power to liberate
you from all bondages and
awaken you to your enlightened self."*

FULL CIRCLE
HIND POCKET BOOKS

KNOW THYSELF
© Gurumaa Vani, 2009
First Paperback Edition, 2010
ISBN 978-81-216-1486-3

Published by
FULL CIRCLE
Hind Pocket Books Pvt. Ltd.
J-40, Jorbagh Lane, New Delhi-110003
Tel: 24620063, 24621011 • Fax: 24645795
or Post Box No. 3005, Lodhi Road Post Office, New Delhi-110003
E-mail: fullcircle@vsnl.com • *website:* www.atfullcircle.com

Designing & Typesetting : SCANSET
J-40, Jorbagh Lane, New Delhi-110003

Printed at Rakesh Press, New Delhi-110028

PRINTED IN INDIA
09/10/01/01/20/SCANSET/RP/RP/RP/NP250/NP250

Anandmurti Gurumaa

Mesmerising Persona
Piercing Eyes
A Crystal Clear Mind
Wisdom Personified
Anandmurti Gurumaa – A New Age Buddha

Anandmurti Gurumaa — a contemporary mystic master — is a beacon of light to those on the path of spirituality, meditation, love and wisdom. With her characteristic humility, Anandmurti Gurumaa says, "I have nothing new to offer in terms of words, but much to offer in terms of the understanding of the truth and its essence."

Anandmurti Gurumaa teaches all the important essential precepts that we must understand and internalise, if we are to progress on the path of spirituality. Anandmurti Gurumaa is an embodiment of love, grace, compassion, understanding and equanimity. At the same time, she is modern and dynamic in her thinking and outlook. Her pragmatic teachings empower the seeker with the wisdom to live with absolute harmony.

Redefining Spirituality

Anandmurti Gurumaa says: "The spiritual path is a warrior's path where you have to wage a war against your own darkness, your own ignorance — not to fight with your own mind but to understand it so as to transgress it. It is like the seed that is always there but flowers only in the right climate, rich soil and with the loving nurturing of a gardener."

Anandmurti Gurumaa is a constant source of wisdom and serves as a platform for inner transformation. "Things are difficult only up to the point where you do not wish to change," according to Gurumaa. The most amazing thing is that you may not wake up even after a lot of hard work, and yet for another, the door may open in a flash. This mystery cannot be understood by the mind, it can be known only through experience.

Anandmurti Gurumaa on Meditation

Demystifying the concept of meditation for the common man, Anandmurti Gurumaa has developed several meditation techniques that can be followed by anyone in day to day life. The art of meditation helps to connect with our inner bliss and to be peaceful, devoid of any past or future worries. The unique meditation techniques developed by Anandmurti Gurumaa encompass both, the timeless wisdom of the east and the highest technical approach of the west, helping the seeker enjoy the best of both worlds. Anandmurti Gurumaa conducts worldwide meditation camps where she personally teaches the art of meditation. The benefits of meditating in the company of a living enlightened master are enormous compared to meditating alone.

Anandmurti Gurumaa's crusade against the ills of society

With her mystic vision, wisdom, rationality and cosmic intellectualism, Anandmurti Gurumaa stands as a constant source of inspiration for one and all. She is working zealously towards the upliftment of women. Devoid of any fear and with great enthusiasm, Anandmurti Gurumaa through her divine utterances and 'Shakti' revolution has been waging a war against the exploitation of women, the ill-treatment meted out to widows, forced female infanticide, the dowry system and the prevalent discriminatory treatment of the girl child in our society.

Anandmurti Gurumaa motivates women to fortify their energy and respect themselves as women. In order to not confine her teachings to mere words, Gurumaa in her true crusader spirit has launched the project 'Shakti — An initiative to empower the girl child'. For more details, please visit www.gurumaa.com.

PREFACE

Every year, meditation camps are conducted by Anandmurti Gurumaa at Gurumaa Ashram and various other places all over the world. During the day, *sadhaks* are taught various meditation techniques. Care is taken that each is taught a method appropriate to his need and stage of spiritual development. In the evening, all aspirants gather for a *satsang* or spiritual discourse, which is conducted by Gurumaa herself. This is an interactive session which rounds off the day's proceedings.

One such camp was held at *Rishikesh* in the *Himalayas*. In this particular camp, Gurumaa spoke on '*Atmashatakam*', a classic work of *Advaita Vedanta*, written by *Adi Shankaracharya*. True to her style, she related real life incidents and anecdotes, connecting ordinary lives with Shankaracharya's great work and made high philosophical treatise into a feast for the listeners.

During this camp, Gurumaa deconstructed and analysed '*Atmashatakam*' word by word, revealing its true meaning and message, making it crystal clear to the *sadhaks* that God resides within each one of us and to realise the ultimate truth, one has to search within. Know Thyself is a compilation of these discourses.

ATMASHATAKAM
ADI SHANKARACHARYA

Manobudhyahankaarchittani naaham
Na cha shrotrajihve na cha ghraannetre
Na cha vyombhoomih na tejo na vayuh
Chidaanandroopah shivoham shivoham

Na cha praansangyo na vai panchvayuh
Na vaa saptadhaaturna vaa panchkoshah
Na vaakpaanipaadou na chopasthpaayuu
Chidaanandroopah shivoham shivoham

Na me dweshraagou na me lobhamohoh
Mado neiva me neiva maatsaryabhaavah
Na dharmo na chaartho na kaamo na mokshah
Chidaanandroopah shivoham shivoham

Na punyam na paapam na soukhyam na duhkham
Na mantro na teertham na vedaa na yagyaah
Aham bhojanam neiva bhojyam na bhoktaa
Chidaanandroopah shivoham shivoham

Na me mrityushankaa na me jaatibhedaha
Pita neiva me neiva maataa na janm
Na bandhurna mitram gururnaiva shishyah
Chidaanandroopah shivoham shivoham

Aham nirvikalpo niraakaarroopo
Vibhurvyapya sarvatra sarvendriyaanaam
Sadaa me samatvam na muktirna bandhah
Chidaanandroopah shivoham shivoham

CONTENTS

CHAPTER 1

LET THE TRUTH
SIMMER INSIDE YOU

Shankaracharya was born into a pious family. His parents were ardent devotees of *Shiva*, whom they worshipped as *Ashutosh* — 'the one who is easily pleased'. They lived a virtuous life practicing all the tenets of *dharma* — love, compassion, daily ablutions and piety. Their day would start with a round of meditation and *japa*, followed by *yagna* and would end with a round of prayers in the evening. In this way they started and ended the day.

After finishing the household chores, the husband, who was a learned scholar, often sat down to meditate; or else poured over scriptures for hours together. Those days it was considered the supreme duty of a *Brahmin* to acquire knowledge and then disseminate whatever he had learnt amongst others. Once he had acquired a fair degree of competence as a teacher, he was expected to set up an *ashram* and run it efficiently on the lines of *dharma*.

Shankaracharya's parents led a perfectly contented and peaceful life. Yet one little worry consumed them from within. They had no children of their own. Though it was against their natural disposition to harbour regrets, they often felt that it was only through a child that a couple could experience a sense of completion.

For a long time their extraordinary patience held them in good stead, but occasionally the desire for a son would surface in their hearts. They found that this desire would manifest unexpectedly — it was not really a desire — it was more of a suppressed emotion. They believed that with Shiva's blessing they could have a son, even if they were not destined to. Somewhere deep down in their hearts, this desire festered. Man is after all only human! He does not need to consciously awaken desire — it sprouts on its own, almost like the blades of grass.

The forest grass grows on its own, no one plants the seeds. It is quite a tedious affair to plant a garden in your house, you have to sift the soil, pass it through a sieve no less than four times; sift the pebbles and stones; mix the fertilizer made of cow-dung or burnt leaves; level out the ground, and then if there is still some wild growth, you need to weed it out. To protect your plants against canker, you add fertilizers made of *Neem* leaves. Only after such an effort, does the garden finally grow.

But who plants the wild grass mushrooming in the forest? Is it you or is it someone else? No one! Not our ancestors, nor you, nor me. Yet such beautiful trees, shrubs and grasses grow in the thick, green forests. If we fail to water a house-plant, in a couple of days it withers away and dies. And if by mistake, we water it excessively — it dies anyway. Plants are really very temperamental. They demand a lot of love and affection. They say, "Our real habitat is the forest. We belong to open spaces. Why have you imprisoned us in flowerpots?" Who wants to be imprisoned? Trees, fruits, flowers and vegetables are happy only if rooted to the soil.

Similarly, a man who is rooted to the soil is happy and contented. If someone tries to fly high, we immediately warn him, "You will fall flat on your face!" If you walk with your feet planted firmly on the ground and your eyes focused on the earth, you will never ever fall. If you look skywards and walk, you are bound to come crashing down.

After all, what does it mean to walk with your head in the clouds? When we allow pride, status and suffering to enter the portals of our being, we cease to be grounded. Only the one who remains grounded, truly deserves to be called man. It is only through contact with the soil that the trees, plants, flowers and fruits grow and blossom; sway in the breeze and laugh. When the wind blows, you should see the way the trees and flowers dance and smile!

Yes, it is a fact — trees smile! Trees break into loud guffaws of laughter, though certainly not as loud as man! Blossoming is their way of smiling. But when you uproot a plant with the intention of transplanting it, how can it be happy?

People who have researched plants say that if you shower the same love and affection on them that you do on your children, plants grow and blossom just as well in flowerpots. You may find this rather amusing — perhaps even intriguing — because often you find it difficult to be loving and affectionate even towards your own children. Sometimes you lash out at them; even refuse to talk to them properly. How many of you can claim that as parents you sit down with your children in the evenings and ask, "How was your day, son? How was your school or college?" How many of you want to strike up a friendship with your children? All the time mothers scare their children saying, "Do this properly or your father will come and beat you." Or, "Your father will give you a good thrashing. Let your father come today, I will report you to him!"

Often mothers instill such a fear in the mind of the child that the father appears to be more of a Hitler and less of a father. As a result, the child does not develop any love or affection for the father. He only shows respect or reverence, which must be shown anyway. But if your child only shows respect, I would say you do not deserve to be parents. In my opinion, the child must both 'feel' and 'show' love and devotion. But in most cases, the father's image is invoked only to strike terror in the heart of the child.

Once I was a guest at someone's house where the patriarch was a very stern man. We were all sitting around casually when someone suddenly exclaimed, "He has come!" All the children, who were till then sitting around playing, ran for cover! One minute they were sitting next to me and the next minute they just ran! I asked them where they were going but they did not even stop to respond. Opening their books hurriedly, they all sat down, as though they were neck deep in study. Only a while ago they were laughing and smiling; now all of a sudden they were silent, as if a hissing snake had left them paralysed with fear!

I asked, "Is he a father or a devil?" "We cannot do a thing without his permission," the children answered. "Do you laugh only when you get his permission?" *Gandhi* had instructed his disciples to laugh at least twice a day. The disciples, devoted to *Gandhi*, would look at their watch and say, "All right, it is half past nine. It is time to laugh. Ha, ha, ha!" And that would be the end of it. Sometimes people go to ridiculous extremes!

Now, what did *Gandhi* actually say and what was his intention in saying what he did? Only those who did not really understand his true intention coined the precept: we must laugh twice a day. As though you are expected to stay solemn throughout the day and laugh only twice, as if one has to follow a well-orchestrated routine which also defines the rules governing laughter. Just as we have tea at four, go for a morning walk at five, so must we laugh at a fixed time!

One should not fear or dread one's parents. Nor should one have only either respect or love for them. Love is not possible unless both children and parents enter into an alchemy of understanding. To understand each other, to show interest in each other, to be able to speak our minds — all of this should be possible in this relationship. But very often we neither ask nor tell — it is simply the father's writ that runs large.

On many occasions, I have had to interfere in the family matters of people. They were close to me and loved me; I thought I could take the liberty of interfering — and so I did. The children want to study something, but the father says, "No, you must study this!" I say, why burden them with your thoughts? It is their life, so let them decide. Even if they make mistakes, let them accept responsibility for their decisions. If a child does only what you ask him to, he will not forgive you all his life. He will always be scared of you; no doubt he may show respect, but he will never be able to love you. Try to explain things to him, but give him the opportunity to decide for himself. Give him the freedom to live life his way. Of course you must keep a watchful eye on him and must never let him go wild.

Now, it is quite natural for a man to develop a close bond with the ones who bring him into this world — his parents. When he grows into a young man and marries, a very natural human desire is born in his heart to have a child of his own; he too would like to be a parent.

In the heart of this *brahmin* couple too, this very natural instinct simmered. Then one night, they had a dream in which *Shiva* gave them *darshan*. Along with *bhava*, it is important to awaken *viveka* — the discerning intelligence as well. Our dreams spring from the deep recesses of our mind. Our mind is a virtual potentate. It is not weak at all! Our mind has the power to envision the future! It has the power to awaken the memories of our past lives.

Those ascetics, who are of pure disposition and always engage in meditation, are able to see each and every incident that may happen in their future lives. Very patiently, they wait for each moment; without rushing things; without hurrying the moments of happiness. They know it has to come, but they never hasten its coming. Even if you know that a moment of sorrow will come in the future, you cannot start crying over it right away!

You will wonder why, if we have the power to know our past and our future, are we not able to use it. Ordinarily you will not be allowed to use this power, until you have raised the level of your consciousness to extraordinary heights. Until then, the mystery of how this power is to be used shall not be revealed to you. But such a power is definitely there — present in all of us. It was this power that made the husband and wife see the dream. Remember, dreams are not always made of the same stuff.

Often in my discussions on dreams, I have explained that whenever you can, you must meditate on your dreams. If you see a dream at night, the first thing you must do on waking up in the morning is to reflect on what you saw in the dream. You must take stock of it at least once.

Now, why did both husband and wife have the same dream? Because both of them had the same desire — and the same desire led to the same dream! You could also say that when some great soul is to incarnate, it does not happen by accident or all of a sudden, but essentially by design.

Each time a *yogi* or a *guru* decides to take birth for the welfare of humanity, or opts to come back to disseminate wisdom, he chooses his own parents. Did you choose? No! What do you think? You chose the parents who gave birth to you? No, you were born just like that! But the one who knows the mystery of what happens after death, he alone knows how to search for the right kind of parents, and following all possible leads, reaches out to them. For, only a few *mahatmas*, great souls or *yogis* have access to this kind of knowledge.

The truth of the matter is that if you become a shining soul, only glorious souls shall be born of you. You purify yourself and pure children will be born to you. If your mind is always restless with sinful thoughts, you cannot hope to give birth to a *devpurusha* — a divine man — or a *devstri* — a divine woman.

It is just like going to some place and not knowing where to sit. You will sit only when you find a place appropriate to your station. For instance, if an I.A.S. or I.P.S. officer or a politician were to go somewhere, he would sit only when he finds a seat suitable to his position.

I remember one such person who came to my *ashram*. When he saw that everyone was sitting on the floor, he just stood waiting outside. Another person of a very high position, whom he was accompanying, just came and sat down on the floor. But that fellow kept standing aside. The *ashram* inmates said to him, "Why don't you go ahead and sit down?" He said, "No, no, I am alright here." When they requested him again he said, "Do you expect us to sit with the commoners? We are officers after all. Do you not know who we are? Should I tell you who I am?" One ashramite said, "We know. All right, I will get you a chair. You sit on that." He turned around and said, "Why? Everyone is sitting on the floor! You want to make me conscious by giving me a separate chair?"

Now you tell me! The poor inmate just did not know how to deal with him. "The chair should be appropriate to my station. It should be worthy of me. I will sit only if I find a seat worthy of me, otherwise I will not." This is the way an ordinary person thinks. In the same way, all ordinary persons simply come tumbling into this world. *Lalu, Pilu, Tilu* can be born anywhere. They in turn give birth to more *Lalus, Pilus* and *Tilus*.

But here I am talking about the pure souls — souls that shine bright with a divine glow. Here I am talking of Shankaracharya. And Shankaracharyas are not born to any *Lalu, Pilu, Tilu*. They look for an appropriate womb. After all, they have to live inside

that womb for nine long months. You will sit on a chair for a couple of minutes or a couple of hours, but the womb inside which the soul has to 'sit' for nine long months is always chosen by the all-knowing soul.

During pregnancy, whatever food the mother eats is also consumed by the child. Whatever the mother breathes, the child breathes. Whatever the mother thinks, the child thinks. Even the feelings that surge inside the mother leave an imprint on the child. Would you ever believe that a pure soul could live inside a cruel body?

I will give you an example. If a man is of pure disposition or has the heart of a saint, he cannot eat food cooked by any and every pair of hands. When I was studying in school and college, I had a real problem. If food cooked at home was given to me or sent to me in a tiffin, it was fine. But if somehow I left my tiffin home, or mother could not get it ready on time — because she hardly ever had time; she was always rushing off to *satsang* — I preferred to go hungry than to eat out. I would never eat anything from the canteen. Why? Who knows with what *bhava* — pure or impure — the food had been cooked?

Have you ever seen a *halwai* — a sweet shop owner — working? I have seen a *halwai* at work — he would make *puris* in the daytime and *samosas* in the evening. He made only a few sweets. Often I would walk through the same street to go to the temple for *satsang* (spiritual discourse). As soon as school was over, I would change out of my uniform, slip into a white *salwar-kameez* and rush for *satsang* in a rickshaw. That is where older women would be waiting for me. They referred to me as '*deviji*' — an angel. They would often say, "*Deviji* will come and start the *satsang*." So I felt awkward in cycling down to the *satsang* in my uniform. Handing over my cycle to someone, I would quickly change into another set of clothes which I carried with me in my school bag. Then I would go off to the temple. While going there, I would invariably pass through this street.

It was a congested little labyrinthine street and bang in the middle of this street was the halwai's shop. Around the time I would reach the temple, he would be getting ready to fry *samosas*.

19

He would not even wear pyjamas, just longish underwear and a *fatuhi*. By *fatuhi* I mean a kind of an undershirt, not like a regular vest, but a home-stitched one. I believe he is still around!

The *fatuhi* had a pocket in which he put all his money. Sitting outside his shop, he would fry *samosas*. Picking up one longish slice of dough used for making *samosas*, he would keep it on his naked thigh which was always full of grime and sweat! You can very well imagine the scene! Keeping it on his thigh, he would roll the dough and stuff it with boiled potatoes, fold it and slip it into a heavy bottomed pan for deep frying.

To put it another way, his thigh had become his workstation! And if while frying *samosas*, his nose started running, he would just blow it! It was as though he never felt the need to either wash his hands or clean them with a piece of cloth. Because the slice of dough would wipe them clean anyway! As I passed by his shop, I often witnessed this spectacle. Now, the whole world loved his *samosas* so much, that often those who ate them would keep licking their fingers!

Everyone knew that I did not eat anything from outside, so they always brought something for me — porridge or some such thing — from home. Crouching behind someone's door, I would eat it quickly, because then I had to rush back home. I always worried that if I failed to get home on time, my family would nag. So it was important for me to get back home on time. In spite of being headstrong and doing exactly what I felt like doing, being a girl I had a great deal of family pressure on me.

One day, a lady who had great personal affection for me spoke to me very indulgently, "Today I have brought these eats for you." I said, "What is this?" The moment I removed the handkerchief from the plate, I saw *samosas* there. I asked her where she had got them from? "Why?" she asked. "Did you buy them from that *halwai*?" She said, "Yes. People come from far off places come there just to eat his *samosas*." I said, "The whole world may love to eat them, but I cannot. How can I? It is just not possible, there is no way I can eat them."

After I left home, I came in contact with many saints who became rather fond of me. Most of my childhood has been spent in the loving care of saints. On many occasions, I have spoken to you about it. One particular saint had a lot of affection for me. I do not know who, but someone informed him that if I do not eat before leaving home in the morning, I prefer to stay hungry until late evening, as I am very particular about what I eat and where.

One day he explained to me. He said, "This is not good. This will make your body sick. How will you manage things then? You do not have any disciples to look after your health so you must take good care of yourself. This body is a kind of an automobile which will function only if you look after it well. So you should start eating and eat whatever you get. You should eat as and when you feel hungry." I said, "I do not feel hungry at all." "How would you? If you tell your mind once that you are not hungry, then you will not feel hungry at all. Hunger and thirst are connected to the steadfastness of our mind," he explained.

It was on the basis of this very firmness that *Bhagat Singh*, the revolutionary, was able to stay hungry for fifty-five long days. Now, he was not a *sadhu* or a *mahatma*, in fact he did not even believe in God. If I were to say that he was half a communist, it would not be entirely wrong. In order to bend the British rulers to his will, he went on a fast. Initially people felt that if *Gandhi* goes on a fast it has some impact, but what impact could Bhagat Singh's fast have? Bhagat Singh's response would be, "Only time will tell."

Gandhi's fast would last for four to six days. Whenever he wanted to have his way, he would proceed on a fast saying, "I will not eat." Almost like a child he would dig in his heels and say, "I will not eat." Then Nehru or Ambedkar would go running to him and plead, "No, no, please do eat." They all felt that if this old man stayed hungry, he would die. Not only did they respect him, they feared him too.

Gandhi's was a different matter altogether. He was a great leader of the nation. He had his own standing, his own position. But who knew *Bhagat Singh* then? Everyone felt that his fast would not last beyond ten days. When thirty days had gone by, the news spread like wild fire throughout the nation, that a revolutionary had stopped eating. Thirty days, forty days and then fifty days slipped by!

On learning about it, thousands of people who had developed a deep affection for him or were sympathetic to his cause also gave up food saying, "Until he eats, we will not eat". *Bhagat Singh* did not eat anything for fifty-five days. When you are fasting, the body does feel weak; it is but natural that this should happen. But, on the basis of a personal resolve, an ordinary revolutionary can also stay hungry for as long as fifty-five days.

Meerabai stayed without food for eighty-four days. She had taken a vow to eat only when *Krishna* — the flute player, gave her *darshan*. "Let the body die if it has to. Why preserve this body when it does not facilitate a meeting with my beloved," said Meera. So she went without food for eighty-four long days.

The activities of our body are controlled by our mind. So I said, "I do not know what kind of thoughts the fellow had when he made them. For all you know, he might have been terribly ill tempered and peevish. So how can I eat? It does not matter if the body is unclean, but if the mind is unclean then whatever a person cooks in that state cannot really have a beneficial effect on our body."

The saint started laughing and said, "Now you are far beyond the stage where other people's thoughts can impact you. Rather, whatever you eat, you must eat as an offering to *Shiva*. This will take care of everything." I accepted his advice, "If you say so, then it is all right."

What it means is that a monk or a mendicant is always very particular about these things. Often people say, "Kindly come to our house." If I accept the invitation and go along, they spread a rich fare before me consisting of various delicacies cooked by the servant. I am not saying that I will not eat whatever the servant cooks. But the question is, if you extend such a courteous and warm invitation, then why not take the trouble to prepare the food with your own hands?

Who knows, the servant may be in a foul temper for you may not have paid him his salary! Or you may have rebuked him for no reason. In that case, he will cook all right, but without pouring his heart and soul into it. Almost as if he just wanted to get it over with. He will not cook with love and affection. Why do you invite

me in the first place? To eat food cooked with love? Or just mixed with the servant's ill temper and bitterness? Is it just a duty you want to get over with?

It is as clear as crystal: when you offer anything to a saint, be it food, drink or a piece of cloth, it always 'speaks' to the saint. You just have to have the ears to be able to hear. It always says whether it is offered with affection or just a sense of duty; it also states the mind of the person offering it. All of this the 'thing' does speak!

That is why some people feel that if something is not prepared as an offering to God, it should not ever enter their body either. It is a well-known saying — 'the quality of food defines the quality of the mind.' It is what we eat that constitutes the stuff and substance of our soul. If we cannot eat the food cooked by anyone and everyone, how can a saint or a good soul incarnate itself through the womb of an ordinary woman? It does require a very special set of parents. Sometimes our *sadhana* and our *karmas* bless us either with one or both parents who are special. If both of them turn out to be great souls, it is so much the better. But one of them has to be an extraordinary person.

So both the husband and the wife had this dream. In their dream, they had *darshan* of *Shiva* who said, "You will be blessed with a son." Some people suggest that *Shiva* said, "I shall be born as your son for you have been my devotees all your life." When they woke up, it was early morning and the birds were chirping merrily. Feeling overwhelmed with love, gratitude and happiness, they both woke up reciting '*Shiva-Shiva*' — rather surprised to see that both were soaked in the same *bhava*. Once they started talking, they discovered that they had had the same dream. They were ecstatic at the thought; their joy was boundless.

After sometime, Shankaracharya was born to them, but soon the father passed away and the widowed mother brought him up single-handedly. When he was seven years old, he told his mother that he would like to be a *sanyasi* — a renunciate. Remember, this is what he said when he was barely seven! His mother laughed and said, "You must be crazy! How did this idea get into your head?" She thought that children are not to be trusted, they listen to all kinds of stuff and whatever they hear seeps into their mind.

A few days ago a teacher was talking to a child. She asked him, "What do you want to be when you grow up?" He said, "I will grow up to be a gangster." Surprised, the teacher asked, "Do you know the meaning of the word gangster?" He said, "Oh yes, I will be '*Munna bhai*'." There was a street *goonda* in their locality by this name. These days in Mumbai, *goondas* — goons, are referred to as *bhai*.

When those you call *bhai* have turned into *goondas*, what is the harm in calling *goondas*, *bhai*? So he wanted to be '*Munna bhai*', because he was known to be powerful and everyone was scared of him. No one dare challenge his authority. Seeing the kind of clout '*Munna bhai*' enjoyed, this child dreamt of becoming a *bhai*. When he was asked what he would be when he grew up, he said, "I want to be a gangster!"

When a child says that he wants to join the police or the army or become a pilot, it is perfectly understandable. If he says he wants to be a doctor or an engineer, even that is understandable. But to want to become a gangster! A child's mind is very sensitive and impressionable. Children hear all sorts of things, see all sorts of things and then, depending on their intelligence, they start imagining things.

But when a seven year old says, "I want to be a *sanyasi*", his mother thinks he must have been a *mahatma* or a *yogi* in another incarnation. After all he is only a child! So that must be the reason why he spoke the way he did. Soon though, the mother put it out of her mind. A year went by. During the year, he must have said at least a dozen times to his mother, "*Ma*, I want to be a *sanyasi*. Please give me permission. I want to leave home. I want to wear a sanyasi's dress and live in the forest." Had he been a little older, his mother would have explained things to him. But what could she tell a mere child? Can you imagine a seven year old talking in this manner?

One day, accompanied by his mother he went for a dip in the river. First his mother bathed and then she asked him to take a dip. He had barely removed his *dhoti* and stepped into the river, when a crocodile grabbed hold of Shankar's foot and started dragging him into the deep waters. The poor mother was old and helpless, what could she do? She started screaming and crying, but the crocodile continued to pull *Shankar* in.

The mother was certain that her son would be snatched by the cruel jaws of death right in front of her eyes. Seeing this, she was overcome with intense pain and grief. It was after great emotional turmoil that she had been blessed with a child; she just could not bear the thought of her child being killed in front of her eyes. The crocodile kept dragging the child into the deep waters. *Shankar* cried out, "*Ma*, now I am going to die, he will definitely kill me. Now at least give me the permission to become a *sanyasi*."

Imagine the situation: the crocodile had Shankar's foot in its jaw and was pulling him into the water; he could see the signs of death in front of his eyes. Still, he did not forget his mission — the fact that he had to become a *sanyasi*. He did not say, "*Ma*, save me from the jaws of this crocodile!"

After all, we are not talking about an ordinary child. *Shankar* said, "Give me permission." So what could the poor mother do? She was going to lose her son anyway. So she said, "All right son! I give you my permission. Go ahead and become a *sanyasi*." These words had barely escaped her lips when *Shankar* pulled his foot out of the crocodile's jaws and swam across to the riverbank!

What really happened? You may call it a miracle or whatever you want to. Some say that God had come in the guise of a crocodile, so that the mother could be persuaded to give her consent. There is one thing I would certainly like to add here. When I ran away from home to become a s*anyasin*, I did not seek permission saying, "Mother, may I go?" She would have beaten me up! Who allows you to go like this? But *Shankar* was adamant; he would not go without his mother's permission.

At the age of twenty-one, when I renounced my home, I had said that I would go to *Vrindavan* for a few days and then return. I had my true intentions conveyed to my family through a lady in Delhi who was known to them. When I met her at New Delhi station I said, "I am going on a pilgrimage. I will be back within a week." My family trusted her, but I had already made up my mind.

Somehow, once I left it was not possible for me to return. I had said I would be back in a week but four weeks went by. Then I wrote a letter saying, "Please do not wait for me now, I will not come back home. Just think that your daughter is dead. If you want, you may go ahead and perform all the rituals such as *shradh* etc and get it over with. Tell the world she is dead. Now I will not ever return."

I never sought permission! But *Shankar* sought permission. You could turn around and say, "Why tell us that he took permission? Why didn't you do the same thing? You too should have sought permission. Why did you hurt your parents so much?" My dear! *Shankar* is *Shankar* and I am I. A mango is a mango and a leechi is a leechi. How can a leechi be a mango? *Kabir Sahib* is *Kabir Sahib* and Meera is Meera. *Surdas* is *Surdas* and *Guru Nanak* is *Guru Nanak*.

Guru Arjan Dev agrees to die at the hands of his persecutors, but Guru Gobind Singh decides to raise the sword against them. How can they be the same? Every man has his own nature and disposition. Shankar's mindset sought permission, so he kept striving for it. It is only when the accident with the crocodile happened that his mother finally said, "It is all right son, you may go!"

Now his mother started crying, "When as a lonely widow I die, there will be no one to perform my last rites." *Shankar* who was barely eight years old at the time, made her a promise, "*Ma*" he said, "I give you my word of honour, that in your hour of death I will come back to you no matter where I am. I will not abandon you in your last moments. I will make sure you get a ritual cremation. I will perform all the rites and rituals myself. Do not worry about it at all? I give you my word. Right now, allow me to go with your permission."

On hearing this his mother was somewhat reassured. With tears in her eyes, she said, "All right son, now you may leave as I have already committed myself." If she wanted to, she could have gone back on her word. She could have turned around and said, "Now you have been saved and the crocodile has gone away. Now I will not let you go." But his mother was a woman of integrity, bound to her word by conviction — an ideal woman. It was not without reason that she had been chosen to be Shankaracharya's mother!

After this, for sometime *Shankar* stayed with his *Gurudev* in order to acquire knowledge. But surprisingly, the knowledge that others would take years to assimilate was something *Shankar* absorbed within a couple of months. It was almost as if he had crushed it all into a drink and swallowed it in a single gulp. Again, it is the same thing; here we are not talking of how much can be attained in the course of a single birth. *Shankar* was all knowing; already a realised soul; an enlightened one.

Once his education was complete, his *Gurudev* happily gave him permission to leave. Then he set off on foot, travelling across the length and breadth of the country, spreading the word of *dharma* everywhere. Wherever he went, he engaged in *shastrarth* (religious debate), only to emerge triumphant. Soon enough, the greatest scholars in the country had begun to acknowledge his superiority and his intellect as well. Though he still had the appearance of a child, once he started discoursing religious scriptures, everyone was stunned.

Shankar earned a great deal of respect, reverence and even a formidable reputation. Slowly he began to accept disciples — initiating only those who were amongst the most capable of his students. Under his strict and vigilant eye, he trained them and sent them on missions across the country. In the four corners of India — East, West, North and South — he set up *matths* (seats of knowledge), with a view to propagate the essence of the *Hindu* religion. The idea was that those who were keen on learning about the *Vedas* and *Vedanta*, should be able to come to these centres — to know, to understand, to meditate, or to gain knowledge. At Shringeri, *Badrinath*, Kanchi and Kaamakoti — four *matths* were set up. He entrusted each *matth* to the care of a capable disciple, instructing him to sit there and offer discourses on *dharma*.

I have spoken to you rather briefly of Shankaracharya's life. While expounding on the *shlokas*, I will try to talk of the special moments in his life as and when I can. Now let us proceed with the *shlokas*. The first *shloka* is:

Manobudhyahankaarchittani naaham
Na cha shrotrajihve na cha ghraannetre

Na cha vyombhoomih na tejo na vayuh
Chidaanandroopah shivoham shivoham

The four words that he has used: mano (mind), *buddhi* (intelligence), *ahankara* (ego) and *chitta* (sub-conscious mind), are four different ways of describing the *antehkaran*. There is no appropriate word in the English language to translate the word *antehkaran*. *Antehkaran* is that which lives inside, but works for the outside. *Mann* (mind) is inside but sees and hears things outside. *Buddhi* (intelligence) is inside, but tries to know and understand things which are outside.

Try to understand this a little. What is *mann*? It is not just another name for a gross material thing. It is not even another name for the heart. Many people think that there is no real difference between mind and heart. Sometimes when someone says that his mind is restless, it is thought he means that his heart is restless. The words are different and so are their meanings. Mind is subtle and heart is gross. Heart is the name of an organ, a part of our body. I will tell you something interesting. As the subject is serious, the discussion is bound to be serious. It might create problems for you, so I have to keep you in good spirits lest you doze off!

There was a man who was a habitual liar and one day his lie was nailed. Everyone started saying, "Oh! What a liar he is!" The people around him were waiting to pounce on him when suddenly, with his hand on the right side of his chest, he started screaming. When people asked what had happened he said, "I have had a heart failure." The people around him said, "At least keep your hand at the right place. The heart is not on the right side, it is on the left side." At that very moment, he shifted his hand to the left and said, "All right, now I have had a heart failure on this side." The people said, "Does it mean you have two hearts? First it was this side and now it is the other."

In our body the heart throbs towards the left side of the chest. What does it do? It supplies oxygenated blood to the body. Now, the heart is different from the mind. The heart's job is to supply cleansed blood to all parts of the body. All this is vital for one life. The moment the heart stops functioning, the body also stops functioning. When poets talk, they do not necessarily make this distinction and often use heart and mind as synonyms. You will recall the song from a movie:

Dil ke tukre hazaar huye,
Koi yahaan girra, koi wahan girra

My heart shattered into a thousand pieces
Some fell here and some fell there

Now tell me, is this a heart or a bag full of sweets? If a bag of sweets were to split open, some sweets would fall here and some there. If the poet's heart splits into a thousand pieces that scatter all around, would he be able to live and write about it? He will neither survive nor be able to write, leave alone sing about it! Here the poet is not talking of the heart but of the mind.

So, you should not use the two words, heart and mind interchangeably. Where the heart is a gross organ, the mind is subtle. All right, let me ask you a question. If the heart is here towards the left, behind the rib cage, then where is the mind? Where is the mind in the whole of your body? Is it in your finger, your arm, your head or in your legs? Where is the mind? We can say where the heart is, but not where the mind is. Someone says, "My mind is really sad, it is very dirty." The *sadhu* tells him, "All right, give it to me. I will wash it for you with soap." "But *maharaj*, the mind is not something you can hand over to another!"

The mind is subtle. But what does it do for us? All the time it is mulling over thoughts. It keeps meditating on what is experienced by our five sense-organs (the *gyanindriyan*), which are different from our five action-organs (the *karmaindriyan*). The mind reflects upon all those ideas, thoughts or sensations that we receive from the outside through the medium of the sense organs. Eyes, ears, skin, nose, tongue are the *gyanindriyan* — these are the doors from which cognitive triggers enter.

The eye catches a beautiful scene, the ear hears, the tongue speaks, the skin feels the solid and the supple or the hot and the cold. Even the tongue is one of the five sense organs. We experience a large variety of tastes through our tongue. When you taste something, you exclaim, "Oh, it is so sweet." Who tells you this? Is it the tongue that tells you the taste? It is not the tongue but the mind that tells you the taste. Who knows the taste? It is not the tongue but the mind that decides what the taste is.

A *mahatma* known to me spent a long time wandering in the *Himalayas*. He told me that a very special and unique herb is found in the *Himalayas* known as *rasakatini* — one that deadens all sensation of taste. You can identify it only if you recognise it. If you keep this herb on your tongue, after some time you will lose all sense of taste. Your tongue will lose its ability to distinguish between different tastes and become incapable of sensing any taste at all. The taste buds that help us identify taste become insensate for some time. If you place something sour on your tongue, you will not be able to taste it; if you place something bitter, still you won't know. All the six tastes — sweet, bitter, sour, salty, spicy and astringent — all become meaningless. Now, *Neem* is bitter, but if you were to keep *rasakatini* on your tongue, you would not know bitter from sweet. You will just not get any sensation of taste.

So this means that it is not the tongue that perceives taste. Through the medium of the tongue, it is the mind that perceives taste. Even when we eat, the tongue does not feel the hunger and we do not satiate the hunger of the tongue by eating. It is the stomach that feels the sensation of hunger. So, many times it happens that though we eat repeatedly to fill our stomach, our mind is not satiated. While the stomach exclaims, "You will die if you eat another morsel," the mind says, "No harm in eating a little more."

The stomach keeps pressing the buzzer inside, but the mind simply refuses to listen. It says, "Keep quiet! You do not get to eat a sweet-dish everyday. You are getting it free of cost. So why not polish it off." O dear! You must eat if it is being served free! But this free food is after all going into your stomach. And when it aches, it is your stomach that is going to ache, not anyone else's.

Once in my childhood, I attended a wedding. Those days women would carry huge purses or handbags — it was fashionable to do so. As the wedding was in our own mohalla, the tent had been pitched in our street. Though the wedding was taking place under a small tent, the bride's family had laid out a rich and lavish fare for the groom's party.

In every *baraat*, it is the custom for the groom's side to eat first. Now, whether it is old people or children, all of them have to wait for their turn. As per custom, they wait for the groom's party to finish eating before starting themselves. At that time breakfast was being served and the women accompanying the *baraat* were stuffing their plates, looking around surreptitiously to see if anyone was watching them. The moment they were sure that no one was looking, they would quietly stuff whatever they could not eat into their handbags.

As it is, they barely ate half of what was on their plate and kept stuffing the rest into their handbags. By the time the *baraat* had had its breakfast, the *halwais* declared that they had run out of stocks. Now everyone from the bride's side started wondering where so much food had gone? I had seen everything, but how could I open my mouth? But children are children after all! They watch everything and cannot help talking. So the little children present on the scene walked up to a couple of women and said, "Please open your bag!" "Why?" they asked. The children said, "Please allow us to eat the paneer you have stuffed inside." The children had only to try this trick and out came the secret. You will say that the children were not really well mannered. But would you say the women who stuffed their handbags with eatables were more cultured than the children? Now this is something even the hungriest of people do not ever do — except perhaps the greediest amongst the greedy!

The tongue does not ever know the taste, but the mind does. When, on feeling hungry you eat, who decides when you have had enough? It is the mind. Who is able to distinguish between joy and sorrow? It is the mind again. Who decides what the difference between an insult and praise is? Again it is your mind and not your body.

I will narrate to you an old story, some six or seven hundred years old. A man once travelled to foreign lands. After a very long journey he arrived in one country. It was a rich and affluent country. As he was hungry, he started looking for some eating joint and landed outside a restaurant. Now, he had not seen a restaurant in his own country. He did not know that you have to pay for everything you eat. So the moment he saw one he just walked in. As this was an affluent country, certain etiquette was practiced; after all affluence does make people cultured. And sometimes the affluent also start behaving as though they are actually cultured. The waiter came and greeted him with folded hands. Of course, he understood nothing of what the waiter said, except that he was smiling. He had no idea that this was the way he usually greeted all those who came to the restaurant. He was offered a seat and was also served food. After he had finished eating, he thought to himself what wonderful people they were! "They do not even know me, yet they first offered me a seat and then food. Not only this, they served the best of delicacies too."

Later when the waiter presented him with the bill, he did not know that it was a bill, and as it was, he had no money. He thought the people were offering him some certificate of honour saying that they were really grateful to him for visiting them! He took the bill, folded it neatly, put it in his pocket and walked out. Furious, the waiter started screaming. Still he thought, "Oh! I am being honoured." Now while the waiter was rebuking him, this fellow was laughing in his face. The waiter kept saying, "Take out the money," but all was lost on him.

Then it dawned on those people that he had not understood a word of what they were saying! On rummaging through his pockets, they found that he did not have any money either. Then they decided that there was no point in beating the stupid fellow, instead they should get a donkey, make him sit on it and parade him through the streets. When they made him sit on a donkey, he thought that they were extremely hospitable and lavished good care on all visitors. First they fed him well and now they were taking him out on a procession. So when they made him sit on the donkey he sat with aplomb. When the restaurant owner smeared his face, he thought they were putting sandalwood paste on his face, the way they put sandalwood in his country. "This must be their paste. This is somewhat like black mud, but they are trying to beautify me. This will take care of my fatigue. Now they will take me out in a procession."

When everyone was in splits looking at his face, he thought

they were praising him. He secretly wished someone known to him were around to see how he was being honoured. They were insulting him and he thought he was being honoured. Suddenly, on spotting one of his own countrymen in the crowd, he raised his hand as if to say, "Brother, see for yourself. You are standing there in the crowd and here I am going out in a procession." That poor fellow simply slunk away, thinking this man must have committed some serious crime to earn such a fate; he was more interested in saving his own skin. They were insulting him, but he thought he was being honoured!

Who experiences praise or insult? Our mind! The situation demanded that the traveller should have felt sad and insulted, but he was overjoyed. How you react to the situation around you, the world around you, is something only you can decide. *Krishna* says that though your circumstance may be happy or sad, how you react to them depends on the state of your mind. If you are detached, neither happiness, nor sorrow will have any impact on you and you will gain freedom from the effects of both.

Who experiences joy or sorrow? Your mind! Reflecting, thinking and assessing a situation are also some of the functions of our mind. When the thoughts and ideas of this mind are established through acceptance and conviction — then this happens due to *buddhi* (intellect). What is the intrinsic nature of *buddhi*? Our *buddhi* does the job of sifting and settling our ideas, convictions and beliefs.

Now, all of us have a mind. But *buddhi* is available only in a small potential measure. Psychologists are of the view that even the best of bright men use less than ten percent of their total potential intelligence. That means we are unable to use ninety percent of our intelligence! Why is that so? Because most of the time we are preoccupied with our body — 'I' am a body — with sense organs! The mind says, "Let me enjoy all the worldly pleasures through these senses." Most of the time man is lost in such delusory thoughts and is unable to make optimum use of his intelligence. What does intelligence offer? Determination! *Sankalp*! *Shakti*!

Let me give you an example. Once on a dark night a young man saw a figure walking towards him. It was very dark and he was with his friends. When he saw the figure approaching from a distance, he thought it was a woman. Her *sari* was fluttering in the breeze. As they were all young and strong, they got excited at the very thought of a woman. This very thought awakened all kinds of sensual desires in them. Now they started speculating, "What kind of a woman is she, walking the streets at such a late hour? She cannot be from a respectable family." While they were still busy talking in this vein, the shadow came so close to them that they could recognise it. And the moment that happened, they burst out laughing. For it was not a woman but a *sadhu* whose *dhoti* was fluttering in the wind. His long hair was flowing and so was his *dhoti*. Seeing this, they had mistaken him for a woman. But when the shadow came closer, they found it to be a man. The moment *buddhi* decided that it was a man, the flight of mind ended in a sudden crash.

The mind can throw up all kinds of images and projections, but it is *buddhi* that discriminates, determines and decides. Like this, so many thoughts surface in our mind, whether we should do this, that or the other. Finally, what is it that we decide to do? Whatever our *buddhi* decides is what we end up doing.

Someone known to me once said, "Sitting with my family one day, I said that I wanted to wake up early to do *dhyana*, as you had told us in *satsang* that the best time for *dhyana* is early morning. So I thought the right time would be four-thirty or five. I decided that come what may, I would definitely wake up. I set the alarm for four-thirty, but somehow I felt it would be too late. So I set it again for half an hour earlier. After setting it for four o'clock, I went off to sleep. When the alarm rang at four, I switched it off. I felt that as I was to get up at four-thirty, half an hour would not make such a difference! So I went back to sleep again and woke up at ten-thirty!"

Man's mind is fragmented in such a way, that often we decide for and then against the same thing. We do not know what we really want, because we do not know who we really are. The mind says that you must wake up in the morning, but then the same mind brings forth another thought, "Never mind, sleep a while longer and get up in half an hour." So you go back to sleep. When you wake up, it is nine o'clock. So you forego the *dhyana* and worse still, you cannot even make it to college on time. Indecisiveness is the nature of the mind. It is the intellect which guides one out of dualities.

So all kinds of thoughts splash around in the mind, but we end up doing only what our *buddhi* decides. It is the function of the mind to throw up alternatives in terms of ideas or convictions and it is the function of *buddhi* to discriminate and decide. It is this decisive power of the *buddhi* which finally rescues us from indecision.

Now, what is *chitta*? It is our memory bank — the store-house of all information. *Chitta* is the 'storekeeper' of all our experiences. That which stores all our memories is called *chitta*. Shankaracharya says:

Manobudhyahankaarchittani naaham

'I' am not mind; 'I' am different from mind. 'I' am not intellect; 'I' am different from intellect. 'I' am not *chitta*; 'I' am different from *chitta*. 'I' am not *ahankara*; 'I' am different from *ahankara*.

Na cha shrotrajihve na cha ghraannetre

What does *shrotra* mean? It is a word from the *Sanskrit* language which means ears. 'I' am not *ghraan*, meaning the nose. We have five sense organs: eyes, ears, nose, tongue and skin. Shankaracharya says that 'I' am none of these; 'I' am different and separate from all of these, all these are gross — the body is gross and so are the sense organs — the nose, eyes, ears, tongue and skin. He says that 'I' am not any of these; 'I' am none of these; 'I' am separate from all of these.

Na cha vyombhoomih

I am not bhoomih (earth), either. 'I' am not earth. Now everyone knows that our body is made out of dust. What does it mean — 'I' am not *bhoomih* — it means that the body is made of inert elements and earth is one of the components and 'I' am separate from it. Now just think of it, where did all the food grow that your father and mother had? Where do all the vegetables, fruits, corn, wheat and rice we eat grow — on the earth? All the food consumed is assimilated in the body, in the form of nutrients. This is what helps in the formation of the ovum in the mother and the sperm in the father. It is the combination of the ovum and the sperm that gives rise to the formation of a child.

Whatever a mother eats — grain, milk or fruits — during her pregnancy, helps in the formation and growth of the foetus. Often a pregnant woman is told that she is not eating for one but for two. Now, if she were to eat fruits, vegetables and milk, it is all right. But in our country, they often make the mistake of telling a pregnant woman that she must have lots of *ghee* as well. Dear, do you want to kill her! *Ghee* is meant only for those who walk five kilometres a day! *Ghee* is certainly not meant for those who do not walk or exercise. In the olden days, there were no cars, scooters, buses or trains. So you had to walk everywhere. There was no mixer-grinder or washing machine for household chores. You had to do everything with your own hands. So whatever *ghee* you ate was easily digested. But now all kinds of machines are there and all kinds of food choices are there too. What you did earlier is what machines do now, so what will happen to the heavy stuff you eat? Where will it go? It will surface as a disease, as an ailment. So the food makes our body — and food grows on the earth.

Shankaracharya says, 'I' am not *bhoomih*. This he has explained in a very poetic manner. 'I' am not *dharti* (earth); 'I' am not *vyom* (sky); 'I' am not *agni* (fire), either. This entire creation is the product of five elements — earth, fire, ether, water and air. These five elements constitute our body as well. In other words, Shankaracharya is saying: 'I' am neither body nor the five elements of which this body is made; 'I' am not water; 'I' am not fire; 'I' am not ether; 'I' am not earth; 'I' am not air. And 'I' am also not the body made of these five elements. Then who am I?

Chidaanandroopah shivoham shivoham

'I' am *Shiva*. The word chida means pure consciousness. 'I' is *anandaroopa* or ever blissful being. First we need to understand how 'I' am not a body. This pint-sized body is for you what a car is to a driver! The driver sits in the car and drives and when the destination comes, he stops the car and steps out. In the same way this body is a car, a machine!

Does the bicycle rider not know that he is different from the bicycle? If the cycle gets punctured or the tyre is deflated, he just parks the cycle and says, "Oh! The cycle has got punctured!" And the day the breath, the cosmic energy leaves the body, will you be able to say with the same degree of detachment that the body has died but not the soul?

If someone known to you dies... and of course you too will die, or won't you? Well, what do you say? What is your programme? Will you or won't you die? In remote villages, when someone dies the villagers say he has gone bust. Now, what does it mean to go bust? The only difference is that when someone else dies, we just shrug our shoulders and say, "he has gone bust." But when death arrives at your door, will you be able to make fun of it and say, "well, now this body is going bust?"

A few days back one of my disciples called me. She was crying on the phone. Doctors had diagnosed cancer. I said, "What is the matter?" She said, "Doctors have diagnosed cancer and tomorrow is the operation." I said, "What then?" She said, "I am a little scared!" "You are not a little sacred, you are scared a great deal, but answer this question, 'Who are you? What is your essence'?" The moment she heard this, it was as though *viveka* was awakened inside her and the essence of knowledge suddenly dawned on her.

Chidaanandroopah shivoham shivoham

I said, "Now say it again." She said, "I am just realising my fault in identifying so strongly with the body. I have to work on it, but for now my fear is gone."

This is true for all. You have to remember that you are neither this body nor do you own this body. A major problem with people is that they think that just by listening they have acquired knowledge. No way! Knowledge is attained only when you go deep into it and lose all false identification with the body, mind and intellect. And then in this inner space you find your 'self' and realise what 'self' really means. Then you never lose this revelation. You cannot lose it for you can never lose your 'self'!

So if this car develops a snag, what do you do? You go to the garage, show it to the mechanic and ask him to look into the problem and set it right. The radiator is leaking, or the battery is down — you just ask him to check it. When your car develops a problem, you do not come back home and start crying, "Oh, our poor radiator has sprung a leak!" Do people come rushing to your house to condole and say, "Oh, it is so sad your car has gone to the service centre? It is really very bad." Does it ever happen like this? You leave the car in the garage and when the problem has been looked into, you bring it back home.

Now, the car and the driver are two separate entities, but it is not the same with 'I' and the body. This is due to the association with the body being so deep rooted, that you feel as if the body and you are one. That is why this feeling, that 'I' am the body, 'I' am the mind, 'I' am the *buddhi* is so deeply ingrained in us that it just refuses to go away. But body is separate from you and this is the truth!

Remember, the only way to experience peace is to detach yourself from your body, mind and intellect. Whenever you get restless, it is only because somewhere you have identified yourself with your body or your mind or your *buddhi*. That is the real cause of your unhappiness. It is only when you think of yourself as a 'body' that you say, "Oh! I am so unwell!" Can you really be unwell? Think this over. Disease happens in the body, not in you. So how can you be unwell!

Once a man, who had a disability came to meet me. He had had a road accident in which his spinal chord was severely damaged and he was in a wheelchair. The first time he came to me, the family members accompanying him were feeling helpless and had pain writ large on their faces. "Gurumaa! Please bless him. Do something to cure him." I said, "I will definitely bless him, but I do not believe that my blessings can cure him. Yes, I shall try to cure his mind."

So I sat with him, talked to him and by the time our conversation ended he was feeling lighter. Now, the situation is that his body is still as diseased as it was, but his mind became strong. He often writes to me saying that initially he used to feel that he was a patient, very ill and dependent upon others. But now he felt like a sovereign monarch! Now he did not feel that he was ill. At first when he sat in the wheelchair, he used to be depressed, but now when he sits in it, he feels as if he is sitting on a throne!

I had told him, "Look, only big people go out in a royal procession. And this is your royal procession. Others are there, to wheel you around. When the bride goes in a palanquin, someone has to lift the palanquin, isn't it? The bride just sits inside and looks around and enjoys the ride. So just believe that this is your palanquin or your royal procession, whatever you like. Why say it is a wheelchair? Let others look after you; let them shower their love on you. The day they refuse to push it around, something else will work out."

The wheel of life keep rolling forever
They never stop, never stop
For anything or anyone

I am ailing, I have cancer, I will die. If all the time you keep crying like this, you might end up in a psychiatric ward. Do not punish yourself. The body can be healthy or sick; in some circumstances you cannot even do anything about it. In this state, if you are ever able to apply the knowledge:

Na cha vyombhoomih na tejo na vayuh

'I' am not the five elements, nor the body constituted of the five elements, then you will be able to find peace within yourself. Life will turn into a drama where you see and experience all the joys and sorrows of the body from a distance. You become a spectator and enjoy the show. When you become a seer of the mind, then it will not cause you any sorrow, nor will the mind agonise.

'The real essence of God is *Sat* (Truth), *Chetan* (Consciousness), *Ananda* (Eternal Bliss) and *Vyapak* (Omnipresent). All your life you have been praying to God, "You are my father and my mother." And if this 'I' is the child of God and God is *Satchidananda*, then how can his child be anything but Satchidananda? You are truth, you are pure consciousness, you are the ever blissful one. You are omniscient. But the day this false 'I' dies, a new 'I' is found which is ever glowing.

39

Biologically, a man's offspring will be a man, an animal's offspring an animal, a bird's offspring a bird. What else? Have you ever heard of a cow giving birth to a bird? No! A sparrow will give birth to only a sparrow; a parrot to a parrot; a man to a man; a monkey to a monkey. As the parents, so the offspring. If we say that *Paramatma* is our parent — our mother as well as our father — and your parent is *Satchidananda* — blissful truth, then how can you be any different? How can you be *jara* (non-sentient), *asat* (untrue), dukharupa (form of sorrow)? You are *Satchidananda* — Eternal bliss and truth.

But somehow man has forgotten all about his own reality. Because of ignorance he has begun to believe that he is no more than a mere body. Therefore, whosoever talks in this vein — 'I' am a woman; 'I' am a man; 'I' am old; 'I' am unwell; 'I' am healthy; 'I' am strong; 'I' am weak — is talking of the body alone. Always remember that such a person can never know happiness in life, as the body is changeable, and sickness, old age and death will occur. Nothing can stop this from happening. We can ensure good health with the right diet and exercise, but can we ensure that this will prevent death? You may acquire a multitude of possessions, but if you do not have this knowledge, if you do not have the knowledge of who you really are, your *chitta* shall never be free of *dukha* and *Klesha* — sorrow and suffering. And you will constantly be racked with conflict and pain.

You must reflect on this question — 'Who am 'I'?' From the time of its conception to its present age, the body is in a constant flux. As the changes are gradual and subtle, you are absolutely unaware of them. The body grows through various stages but something within remains unchanged. Who or what is that?

During his student days, *Sri Rama* lived in the *ashram* of his *guru Vashishta*. One day, in the early hours he went to his guru's home and started knocking at his door. *Vashishta* asked, "Who is it?" *Rama* did not utter a word, he just kept quiet. Again a knock was heard. Again *Guruji* asked, "Who is it?" Again *Rama* remained silent. Then *Vashishta* got up to see who was at his door so early in the morning. The moment he opened the door, he saw his dearest disciple *Rama* standing there. *Vashishta* was somewhat surprised.

But on seeing *Rama*, he smiled pleasantly and asked, "*Rama*! What are you doing here? Why were you not answering? You did not even respond. Why so?"

Sri Rama prostrated himself on the ground and said, "*Gurudev*! In fact, this is what I have come to ask you: Who am I?" *Vashishta* responded, "Your body is the son of *Dasharatha* and *Kaushalya*, but you are beyond the body. The real you is separate from the body, senses, mind and the intellect. But as long as the attachment to the body is there, you will not be able to understand what I am saying. *Rama*, those who can remove the veil of ignorance from their mind, to them alone is this truth revealed."

Rama is considered an ideal human being. He is regarded as an incarnation of *Vishnu*. Such persons are born evolved, with a heightened consciousness. In spite of being an *avatar* and the wisest amongst the wise, he chose to have a *guru*. This was to explain to mankind, that even an incarnation needs a *guru*, leave alone ordinary mortals. Every human being should seek the truth about his true identity and must go to his *guru* to seek knowledge. Only by gaining knowledge can this *agyana*, this ignorance — which is the cause of his *dukha* be removed. And that is how *Rama* plays the *leela* — the cosmic play. The life of *Rama* is said to be a *leela*. Those who live life as a *leela* are called *avatar*.

It was with this great reverence, dedication and fervour, that *Rama* approached his *guru* and said, "You tell me! Who am I?" *Guru* said, "You are not mind, *buddhi*, *chitta*. You are not *ahankara* and you are not this body constituted of the five elements. Reflect on this, meditate on this." Your mind is always engrossed in mundane futile things, but never reflects on what your true essence is, or from where you have come and where you will go after death.

> **O mind, why do you search for your Self outside**
> **You are Ganga, you are Yamuna and the Pure Stream**
> **You are full of positivity and you are the abstract**
> **You alone are beyond all forms and in the forms too**
> **You are the Creator, the Preserver and the Destroyer**
> **You are the giver and the taker, you are the basis of all**
> **Why do you look outside, why look outside, O mind?**

What you wish for is there within you, with you
Just dwell in silence and let the song be sung!

Knowledge which binds you is not true knowledge. True knowledge is the knowledge of the 'self'. This is what *Brahmangyana* (knowledge of the Supreme) is all about. Anyone who has understood the secret of this *Brahmangyana* is able to liberate himself from the eternal cycle of life and death. Only those who delve deep into the knowledge of the 'self' are able to cross 'The Great Ocean of Life'.

Who are 'you'? Shankaracharya says, **'shivoham, shivoham'**. This is all that you have to remember:

Chidaanandroopah shivoham shivoham

While sleeping, waking, walking, talking and eating — this idea, this thought, should never go away, that in fact, 'I' am not a body. But somehow this falsehood that 'I' am, has been so deeply ingrained in us, that now it appears to be true. Knowing your real 'self', you must allow this truth to seep deep into your mind.

The word '*Shiva*' that I am using here is not synonymous with *Shankar*. The word '*Shiva*' means *anandaswaroopa*, vyapakswaroopa, satyaswaroopa. '*Shiva*' means one who is benevolent and aham means 'I'. This 'I' is in no way different from the pure form of *Shiva*. **Satchidanandaswaroopa** is my real essence. Except this, whatever I believe about this 'I' is patent falsehood. We have to liberate ourselves from this very falsehood, this very ignorance.

CHAPTER 2

DESIRE ALONE BREEDS SORROW

**What was in the mind, remained buried in the mind
Neither prayed nor went on a pilgrimage
The pinnacle remained unclaimed**

The ordinary man who floats on the ebb and flow of desires is always on a ride. Desires rise and fall in the mind, as a result of which sometimes he is happy and sometimes sad. If things are favourable, his mind rejoices. If things are unfavourable, his mind slides into depression. Sometimes we start applying these whimsical ideas of the mind to our spiritual pursuits as well. When you bring this same habit to matters of spirituality, you will experience the same rise and fall; the same principle of the fulfillment of a desire will make you happy and unfulfilled goals will bring pain.

As a result of these tidal waves of desires constantly chasing the mind, man remains oppressed. There is no end to the turmoil in the mind. Sometimes when such individuals come to the *guru*, they seek fulfillment of their desires. If the *guru* fulfills these desires then he is great, a know-all and capable of miracles! And if he does not? Then, is he a *guru*? What does he know? In a way, we drag *gurus* and even God into the web of our desires. When you are not able to fulfill your wishes on your own, you want to use a miracle-maker — a *guru* — one on whose shoulders you can complete your journey. But whether this can really be done is a matter for reflection.

Someone wrote, "I want to be a *sadhak*." What does *sadhak* mean? First you should try to understand this. Whatever be the nature of the desire, it will bring unhappiness. A desire is a desire, whether it is of this world or of the spiritual world. It is not that worldly desires alone cause misery. The desire to achieve *nirvana*, the desire for *samadhi* too brings restlessness. You think that only the worldly desires should be given up and not the spiritual desires. Well, the question arises: Why do you want something? Desire brings anxiety and anxiety invites tension and frustration.

If a desire, whether small or big, is not fulfilled, it will cause misery. A small desire will bring less grief and a bigger desire will cause greater pain. If a desire is fulfilled, it gives rise to another desire and so on and so forth. The cycle goes on and on. That is why a *fakir* once said, "O *Khuda*! Do not ever fulfill anyone's desires in this world." Every desire fulfilled will provoke man to greater desires. Now, someone might feel that this *fakir* is a real sadist. Why does he want everyone to remain buried under a huge burden of wants? But he is actually voicing a profound truth. The fulfillment of every desire awakens new ones.

In *Hindu* mythology, there is a story of *Devi Durga* who kills a demon named Raktabeej. *Durga* fought a pitched battle with him and finally she chopped off his head. But as soon as his head was cut off, several demons sprang up from every drop of blood that fell to the ground. It was as though the blood itself had become the seed for sprouting new demons! Since it was getting extremely difficult for her to slay this demon, *Durga* herself evolved into nine forms and instructed them, "Do not allow the blood of Raktabeej to fall to the earth." The moment his head was chopped off and the blood flew out; it was contained in a vessel and drunk. This is how *Durga*, through her nine different incarnations, succeeded in killing the demon Raktabeej and his progeny. In this story, somewhere your own story lies concealed. Ignorance is the demon which you have to kill. You are divine and you are *Durga* yourself! So who is the demon? The desires springing inside your heart are the demons. As long as these desires are in the mind, you can never experience peace. You cannot get peace by satisfying desires alone. You have to kill the source, the ignorance, and only then can ultimate peace be experienced. Every desire brings a trail of emotions with it —

sadness, pleasure, anxiety, anger, lust. A mind that experiences these emotions in their full range can never be at peace.

I have heard about a gentleman called Harish wished to buy a posh car. But his income was not sufficient so it was not possible to buy it with his own resources. He started thinking — "should I borrow money from the bank or the financer? What should I do? Should I take a loan or try a lottery instead? Or should I raise a loan through some other source?" Now, if someone is thinking things through at such a hectic pace, how can his mind rest easy? Finally he thought about his in-laws, but they too could not help. So he vented out his anger on to his poor wife and abused her. Seeing this, her whole family suffered silently. Now this man was leading a perfectly contended life till he saw someone else's car and it fired a desire within him. The flames of his desire torched several other hearts. What is at the root of all this misery? Relatives who refused to part with money? Or his mind that gave birth to this desire? No one is responsible for your pain and anger but your reckless and mindless desires. When you run after money and the things it can buy, it blinds you. It is not that money is bad or a car or a bigger house is bad. But if you buy a car with your hard-earned money, you deserve it and you will be able to enjoy it as well. But if, for the fulfillment of your desires, you inflict pain and suffering on others, or drag yourself or others into a dragnet of hostility, then how can its fulfillment bring happiness to you? Understand the difference between desires and needs. Ask yourself, are you earning to fulfill your needs or desires? If the answer is needs, fine! And if the answer is desires, then know that you can never be at peace.

If you are doing your *karma* in a natural spontaneous manner and it brings riches — fine! And if it keeps you hand to mouth, know for sure that material things cannot give you joy. You have to understand, that even to fulfill your needs, you have to remain calm and collected. Sometimes we are not able to see the difference between needs and desires. The borderline is very thin. This creates conflict and one runs after things, mistaking them for one's needs. This brings pain and suffering to your mind. And then you unknowingly pass it on to others. How can you ever be happy and how can your family be happy?

To put it another way, after so much conflict and pain, even if you ultimately get the desired object, will it be able to satisfy your desires? It certainly will not keep your desires in check; rather the mind will start hankering after other objects. It is as though desire knows no end, no fulfillment. This demon of desire keeps your mind on tenterhooks and you try to appease it by fulfilling it. Please do not be delusional. Desires cannot be eradicated by fulfilling them. You do not have any control over your desires and there is no point in suppressing them. What you need is wisdom and awareness. Be aware of every thought, every desire — and live accordingly.

Now we shall digress a little from the main topic. I would like to comment on something that happened a few days ago. I met a sage I had known long ago. In my life I have met all kinds of sages — good, bad and excellent ones — and have had a sweet-sour interaction with all of them. This particular sage was troubled by the fact that he was not as famous as he wanted to be. He continuously compared himself with me. He would often pull rank on me saying, "I am much older and so I should be respected more." He was troubled by the fact that my disciples loved me and he was not respected even by his own. You can perhaps force others to respect you, but you cannot ever force anyone to love you. He would even fight with me saying, "Why do they love you so much. They should love me instead, I am older."

I do not know how I can call him a saint, but still, that is the way I must refer to him. If someone is looking for worldly fame and respect and is also jealous of those who get it, how can such a person be a saint? Though I have not met him for eighteen long years, he still publicises himself as my master! Wow! I had a good bunch of *sadhus* who were eager to make me their disciple, but I was not interested in any of them.

I have met scores of *sadhus*, sages and *rishis*, but I speak on the basis of my own experience. For most people, the desire for fame is not as strong as the desire for another person's disgrace. In other words, it does not matter if you do not make any profit, but the competitor must suffer losses. So the mind flows in two different directions. On one hand the mind constantly worries about seeking one's fortunes, fulfilling one's desires, proving one's own worth and superiority, and on the other, it also struggles to discover newer ways of humiliating others and inflicting pain on them.

I am saying this because sometimes people are misled by a sadhu's dress or by his speech. I must make one thing very clear — speech alone does not make a *sadhu*! Even the saffron dress does not make a *sadhu*. The one who is still of mind, has no emotions of jealousy or hostility — he is a real *sadhu* — regardless of whether he is a householder or a renunciate. Remember, if your mind is constantly afflicted by the twin emotions of *raag-dvesha* (attachment-hostility), then you will never be able to attain the heights of *gyana*.

Desire blinds you. When the tidal wave of desire surfaces in your mind, you simply flow along with it. You are unable to separate yourself from this flood of emotions. For instance, you buy a beautiful watch; the watch is very impressive, looks extremely good and you admire it dearly. There is no harm in admiring something that looks good. But to make a habit of looking at it at all times, talking about it, showing it to people, is an attachment that is called raga. If you lose or misplace it, you will be seething with anger and everyone around you will have to bear the brunt of your anger.

When you tie a leash around the neck of a dog, the dog is forced to walk besides you even if it does not wish to. When you force the animal, the rope begins to tighten around its neck, and in order to loosen the stranglehold of the rope the animal walks. In the same manner, the moment we tie our mind to a person or a thing with the rope of attachment, our mind gets dragged behind that person or thing. The fear of losing them arises, and with it come insecurities and dependence.

Say, if you lose your expensive ring or watch, can you remain calm? You will turn the whole house upside down. "Where has it gone? Where is it? Has someone taken it or stolen it?" So you will blame one person or another and in the process, go through a great deal of pain and suffering yourself. You begin to treat everyone like a thief. You will go to the police, lodge a complaint and start interrogating your poor servants. At night you will toss in bed with exhaustion. So you may remove the bed-cover and find the watch dangling from a thread in your bed-sheet! You did find your watch finally! But throughout the day you suspected so many people of stealing it. Throughout the day you remained uneasy. Throughout the day you kept shouting abuses and kept inflicting your discomfort on others. Finally you found it in your own bed! So what should be done now? Shouldn't you apologise to all those you suspected, blamed, accused or cursed?

This is how material possessiveness works on a man. This is how the possessiveness of relationships also works. Whether it is your brother, father, husband or wife, you cannot rest easy until you have seen them. You always feel that they are yours! The first mistake is to think that this body is mine and the second is to think that all the relationships connected with the body are also mine. All the time, our mind is trapped in this *Mahabharata* of 'Me and Mine'! The man who is forever caught in this syndrome of 'me, myself, and I', can never understand the meaning of these sutras of the *Atmashatakam*.

I want you to take time off and sit in solitude. Do not try out any of the techniques of meditation. You do not have to recite any *mantra* either. Do not even focus your attention upon a deity. Just sit and watch your own mind. Just look at the thoughts as they flow through your mind. Do not sift or judge whether or not such thoughts should arise in your mind. Just sit or lie down or walk, whichever way you feel comfortable. Try to open your mind. Slit open the layers of your thoughts and study them, to see exactly what is going on in your mind.

When we relax our control over the mind, its real face begins to show up. You will find all kinds of vague, useless, idle thoughts appearing in your mind — thoughts that make absolutely no sense and have no co-relation whatsoever with your circumstance. You wonder about yesterday's unfinished work and work still to be done tomorrow; who was to come yesterday and who will come tomorrow; whether I was to go to his house or had he to come to mine; what she said to me and what I will say to her; how she harmed me and how I will harm her; how she benefited me and how I will benefit her!

Such vague thoughts often float in our mind unnoticed. The moment you relax your conscious mind, you will find that scores of thoughts begin to surface. No wonder then, it seems to people that if they meditate they are troubled a great deal by the mind. If you think that your mind is silent you are mistaken. Just relax your mind and witness the thoughts. There will be a flood of thoughts. Have you ever been to a place where water freezes? In Kashmir, the Dal Lake freezes in winter. Though it might be frozen on the surface, water continues to flow underneath. In the North Pole, the Atlantic Ocean freezes to a depth of fifteen to twenty feet and yet the water below flows smoothly.

The animals and the vegetation that survive underneath, continue to live and breathe. Seals can survive on the surface of snow for sometime, but when they feel cold or breathing becomes difficult, they burrow a hole in the snow and dive into the water. On the surface is the hardened snow and deep down you find hundreds of seals swimming. Sometimes lakes freeze and become a hard floor of ice on top, but if you hammer a nail or dig a hole through it, you can see the water underneath. Then, before you can show it to another, right before your eyes, a thin crust of ice is formed and within minutes, the surface crystallises into hard ice once again.

In exactly the same manner, beneath the calm surface of your mind, a raging storm of thoughts is always waiting to break forth. Often *sadhaks* come with the query that whenever they sit down to meditate, many thoughts besiege their mind. The truth of the matter is that it is not the process of meditation that triggers off your thoughts — rather it is only when you are calm that you see the tumult of thoughts raging deep inside.

It is like looking at an area or a spot and finding it spotlessly clean, but the moment you run a broom through it, you discover a thick layer of dust — on an apparently clean surface! Where did this dust come from? It was there right from the beginning but it was not visible to the naked eye. The broom only unsettled the layer of dust. In the same way, the flow of thoughts and desires inside your mind continues unabated. They flow so effortlessly that you rarely ever come to know of their movement. You will wonder how this is possible. How come we are unable to see the thoughts raging inside our mind? But really, we are never quite able to see them.

The house I was born in was close to the railway tracks. It was hardly seven or eight hundred yards away. In the summer we slept on the rooftop. And whenever a passenger or a goods-train passed by, the vibration could be felt in the entire house. If it was a goods train, then the vibrations were much stronger. So whenever any relative came to our house for the first time, he would be restless. Once, someone came to visit us from Delhi. We offered him tea. He had barely settled down with his cup when a goods-train went by. It created such a vibration that he got scared and said, "There is an earthquake." I told him to just keep sitting quietly as this was no earthquake but just a goods-train speeding off!

So the trains would speed by every now and then. Every few hours, whenever a train went past, it was like an earthquake for him. He could not sleep throughout the night. Each time the train went by he would wake up. He asked, "How do you sleep?" I said, "We have got used to it and the trains do not bother us at all."

When I first visited *Badrinath* in May 1984, I stayed in an *ashram*. At night, I felt as though heavy artillery fire had opened somewhere. Being restless, I could not sleep throughout the night. In the morning I asked a *brahmachari* (celibate) if war had broken out during the night? He started laughing but did not utter a word. I said that there had been so much commotion that it seemed as if heavy firing was going on. He said, "No, no! There was no such thing. At night you can clearly hear the sound of the Alaknanda river as it flows into a deep gorge and the sound just reverberates in the air."

The first night, I could not sleep thinking that a terrible battle was on. So I just sat up all night. When the situation in Punjab took a turn for the worse, I was still living there. The sound of firing was a common enough occurrence. So I felt some such thing must have started here as well. Who knows? After all, China is not too far away! Of course the next day the terrible sound of the river had not subsided, but the knowledge that this was only the sound of the river, helped me sleep through the night. And I slept without any trouble, without a thought about the sound of the river.

This is how we get used to the idea of living with a conflict-ridden mind. The conflict rages in our mind and it continues unabated. Furious storms of desires keep brewing inside. And we remain completely oblivious, completely unaware of this perpetual conflict of *raag-dvesha* in our mind. We do not even realise how many waves of anger, greed and attachment arise in our mind.

But when some *mahatma* talks about it, we feel good. If it happens to other people's mind, it must be happening to our mind too. But that is it — all we do is listen and then forget about it. We never try to probe our mind on our own; never try to find out whether or not these things arise in our mind too.

Let me ask you a question. Have you ever tried to search for your mind? Have you tried to look at your mind? Do you ever look at it? Are you ever able to anticipate a wave of anger arising within? The wave comes; you are swept away and end up abusing or cursing someone. After the fight is over, someone points out, "You really have so much anger bottled up!" On hearing this, you just turn around and reply rather thoughtlessly, "There is no anger inside me. That person said such a provocative thing that I had no choice but to retort. *Sri Krishna* also says….." And why do you have to drag poor *Krishna* into it? Of course he is the one who said, "You must fight! If someone deprives you of your rights, you must fight to preserve them. Do not suffer injustice in abject silence!" He was the one who urged *Arjuna* to fight. "We too shall fight like *Arjuna*." You claim to be *Arjuna*, but you have no consciousness of the thoughts sinking and floating in your mind. Endless and fathomless is the flow of thoughts arising in your mind. You may ask, "How does it matter? After all these are just thoughts, they come and go. How can these thoughts harm anybody?" Of course you do not harm another, but you do end up harming yourself — not just a little, but a great deal. You do not ruin just one life, but several lives!

Have you ever wondered why you were born in the house in which you were? Have you ever wondered why you were born in this family and not in some other family? Husband and wife fight, mouthing the same dialogues which remain unchanged.

The moment they enter into an altercation, the wife says, "I was to be married into that family. Your relatives begged my parents for this alliance. But you will never know how to appreciate me." The husband says, "My alliance was fixed with that family. Such a beautiful girl! They were giving me a car as well. But somehow your parents trapped us."

Now that you are trapped, why cry? First you walk into the trap and then start complaining. Whenever a couple has an altercation, you hear this dialogue. If for some reason they do not have the courage to say this to each other's face, they say it behind each other's back. They do not say it to each other's face as this may create further complications.

Once a wife told her husband, "We must give to some charity." The husband said, "Oh yes! I married you, is that not charity enough? Marrying you was a great act of social service! Who else would do such a good deed?"

Often strange thoughts surface in the mind. Your mind changes at an unbelievably rapid rate! You may call your husband all kinds of names — 'good-for-nothing', 'mama's boy', 'pumpkin' — but if someone else abuses your husband and calls him these very names, you flare up in an instant. "How dare you say even a word against my husband?" You may say it yourself, but if someone else were to say the same thing, you get angry.

One moment it is raga and the next moment *dvesha*. One moment you say, "They are all mine!" And the next, "None is mine!" The person whose mind vacillates all the time has all the more reason to guard it.

When you practice *mantra*, chanting, or *japa*, the mind goes into a daze. It may seem that the chattering of the mind stops when you chant, but the truth is that it is just one way of making the mind dull. Our mind gets bored very easily, so if you repeat a *mantra* again and again it dulls the mind. You might think that the mind has calmed down, but the truth is that the mind has gone into hibernation. The mind cannot be tamed by reciting *mantras*. You need to keep a vigil. And keeping a constant vigil over your mind is something that is a tough task to accomplish. Only if you can keep a constant vigil, will you be able to guard yourself against

the tidal wave of emotions flooding your mind. Now, what is the advantage of keeping a vigil over your mind? The biggest advantage is that it prevents you from slipping into doing a wrong act.

Let me share with you a precept that should become the guiding principle of your life: "Whatever you do, give it your hundred percent". Until you drown yourself deep in whatever you do, that act cannot really fructify. Whether big or small, when you drown yourself in an act wholeheartedly, you do manage to check the flow of unregulated thoughts in your mind.

As long as we do not check the flow of our thoughts, we cannot perform a single act in a righteous manner. The advantage is that once your thoughts are held in check, then even a relatively small act becomes an act of meditation. The only condition is that whatever you do, drown yourself fully in it.

You will be surprised to know that in Japan, tea making is considered a great ritual, akin to meditation. You will wonder what the connection between meditation and making tea is. In Zen Buddhism, making tea is an act of meditation. For them, meditation has become an integral feature of their social life.

The woman who makes tea sits quietly and people around her too sit quietly and watch her. She sits in the centre and others sit in a circle around her. They all sit in vajrasana — a yogic posture, their hands resting upon their knees and their eyes focused exclusively on the woman making the tea. They sit quietly and serenely and keep watching every move of the woman. The woman also takes special delight in preparing the tea. In a very quiet, confident and self-conscious way, she looks at herself in the process of preparing tea, just the way a spectator does.

You people create such a commotion when you select a utensil to make tea, make all kinds of noisy sounds as you pour water into it. You do everything in a tearing hurry, as if you are only half-conscious of it. But that woman picks up the kettle as though it is not an object but a living thing — as if it has life in it. She does everything in a simple, natural and conscious manner. All this is done in absolute silence without a word being spoken.

When the water begins to boil and she adds the tea leaves, all her movements are slow and graceful. She holds the kettle as if it is alive and not a dead object. Nothing is dead, everything is alive, but we are unable to see the divinity in objects. Our eyes and our mind are not trained to see that. In this tea ceremony, everyone in the room sits in silence, all of them in quiet repose. Everything proceeds in a quiet manner. After some time, her picking up the cup and pouring tea into it also happens in an equally simple, spontaneous and beautiful manner — ever so slowly. Then the tea prepared thus is offered to all the guests with acute awareness and devotion. Those who receive the tea accept it in silence. In a state of complete wakefulness, everybody sips the tea meditatively.

This is an ethereal experience. Even the ordinary act of making tea is transformed into an act of meditation. This is just an illustration to show that you do not need to sit alone to be able to concentrate or meditate. If you become 'aware' of what you are doing in the course of the day, that work will be transformed into meditation. As such, if you meditate for an hour and then sink in the tidal waves of the mind for the rest of the twenty-three hours, you can never claim to be a *sadhak*.

Once someone asked Rinzhai, a Zen Master, "When do you meditate?" He said, "I do not ever meditate." The person who had asked the question was puzzled and said, "What kind of a reply is this? You are a famous Master and yet you say you never meditate? I do not understand. There is a whole tradition of meditation named after you. Your presence and your words have transformed millions of lives. And you say you do not meditate?"

Rinzhai said, "I said that I do not meditate — it happens and I merely witness it. I do each task with complete wakefulness and this awareness is *dhyana* — meditation." If this wakefulness is missing, how can you meditate? The word *dhyana* means "complete awareness". If you are not aware, but sit with your eyes shut, it is not *dhyana*. *Dhyana* is not the name of a process or a ritual, it means "complete awareness". To be in *dhyana*, you cannot really meditate, the only thing that you can do is to simply 'be aware'.

Right now you are listening to me. Are you listening in a state of 'awareness'? Are you fully conscious of what you are listening to? Or are you just sleepwalking through it? What state are you in? The question is not whether you are physically present here or

54

not. The real question is: what state of mind are you in? Only if you drink in each and every word in a state of complete awareness, does real listening take place.

If you listen to a couple of words in a state of awareness and the rest are drowned in the sweeping currents of your mind, you are not listening fully. The currents that flow in your mind sweep you off your feet and you have absolutely no control over them. This goes on all the time and it becomes an endless spiral. It is just not enough to listen to *gyana* — ultimate knowledge, but how you listen to it is equally important.

Guru Nanak Sahib used to sing. His disciple *Mardana* would play the *Rabab*. So, he used to sing the lord's praises. His songs are not ordinary songs. They reflect his love, his depth and his devotion. Guru Nanak's singing was meditation. His heart, mind, and soul were all synchronised in a wonderful rhythm. Someone asked me, "What kind of *sadhana* did *Guru Nanak Dev* do to attain God? What was his path? *Gyanamarga, bhaktimarga* or *Yogamarga?*" The only path he knew was that of singing. He did not do any *sadhana* as such; he was born enlightened. He just expressed his state in his songs.

How did he propitiate God? Only through his singing! The song itself became his *sadhana*. If someone is singing to impress others, to out-do others in a competition, to win a contract from a music composer — then it is not true singing. When one sings from the heart, then the song gives as much joy and bliss to the singer, as *sadhana* gives to an aspirant. This is an established fact.

I used to travel by train frequently. In the second-class compartment, often people enter with a hand-held drum and start singing. Some of the street-singers would have rings on their fingers with which they would beat a perfect rhythm and would sing along. I vividly remember one such singer. He wore large wooden earrings. Both his ears were pierced and wooden earrings were dangling from them. His dress was of a saffron colour — more like a *baba*'s. Perhaps he had not bought a ticket, so he did not take a seat. He kept standing and once the train had chugged off, he broke into a song. Now, he was not a beggar. A *Dafli* lay dangling against his shoulder. He kept tapping on it for a long time and then suddenly broke into a song. His voice is still resounding in my ears — I have never heard such a soulful, piercing voice.

There are scores of wonderful singers in India who are well trained and sing exceedingly well. But his voice had a mesmerising quality. The magic of that baba's voice was simply ineffable and I was floating along with the *bhavas* of his deep melody. The *bhava* with which he sang was so powerful that it simply swept me off my feet. His song was not an ordinary song.

When we are aware, it is the awareness that tells us of the difference, the separateness between our mind and us. Only in awareness are we able to see how we are distinct from our body. Only in a state of awareness can we see that the eyes are seeing and that 'I' is watching the act of 'seeing' being performed by the eyes.

Right now you are seeing, thinking that 'you' see. But it is the eyes which are seeing and not you. When the 'eyes' see and 'you' know that 'you' are not the eyes that are seeing, then the whole drama changes. 'I' am also not the 'scene' which the eyes are watching; this breaks the identification with the body. 'I' am separate and different from these 'eyes' and from the 'scene' that they are watching. The scene changes, but the seer remains the same — eternally unchangeable.

The sense of attachment with the body is so deep, that we have taken this body to be 'me' and not just mine. But this body is neither 'me' nor 'mine'. The raga — attachment with the body is so strong that it takes a lot of effort to finally come out of it. This will not happen if understood at the intellectual level — real-time experience is required. Now, *raag* and *dvesha* are so deep-rooted that your mind is humming the song of *raag-dvesha*. And even if somehow you move away from worldly attachments, you still manage to bring this attachment to the *ashram*, getting attached to the *guru*, to your image as a seeker, to your achievements etc. This tendency of the mind to fall into the trap of *raag-dvesha* is embedded deep in the sub-conscious mind.

Sri Krishna says in the *Bhagavad Gita*: "When our mind interacts with the world through the doors of the senses, it drags itself into the net of *raag-dvesha*. Only if you can learn to remain unattached, can you indulge in this world and yet remain a renunciate — untouched. The world cannot bind you; it does not have the power to do so. It is our mind which creates the bondage of attachments. The senses are ruled by the mind and the mind is ruled by the intellect. If only we could understand that 'I' am the seer of the senses, the mind and the intellect! 'I' am the witness of the mind! Remaining in this wakefulness, you can rule the world and yet remain untouched by all the flair and glare of *samsara*.

Just look at what *Adi Shankaracharya* has said:

Manobudhyahankaarchittani naaham

Right now you feel that 'I' am the mind, 'I' am the *buddhi*, 'I' am the *chitta* and 'I' am the body. It is only when you use the sword of eternal vigilance to cut through this chord of attachment tying you to your body and mind, that you are able to experience ultimate freedom. You identify with your body, you have become attached to your body, or so you believe. Once this belief is trashed and once you wake up, you will know that you are not and you cannot ever be a body even if you so desire.

The entire journey is to move to the core; from the body to the senses; from the senses to the mind; from the mind to the *buddhi*; from the *buddhi* to the *chitta* and from the *chitta* to the *ahankara* — ego. Finally you reach your 'self — the pure self. Witnessing is the method and awareness is the tool. Once you have these, nothing can stop you.

Keep the sword of awareness with you and severe all ties with the mind and the body. These ties are not even real ones. Ties are illusory and so are your bondages. You are chidananda and you will remain that. Nothing can change your being. Be in the being and know that you are the truth. You do not have to do anything to achieve truth — you are the truth! So how can you attain yourself!? What can you do to know 'you'? Just wake up and see. The whole journey is the journey of waking up from this sleep.

Manobudhyahankaarchittani naaham
Na cha shrotrajihve na cha ghraannetre
Na cha vyombhoomih na tejo na vayuh
Chidaanandroopah shivoham shivoham

I am *Shiva* always. Eternally I am *Shiva*. Even when I did not know this I was *Shiva*. The one who has not heard this *gyana* is also *Shiva*. But he will not enjoy his being *Shiva*. And the one who has realised it, enjoys it immensely. Every moment becomes a celebration. It is not that you alone are *Shivaswaroopa* and others are not. The essence of *Shiva* is everywhere, it is omnipresent. And if it is omnipresent, then how can you not be a part of it? But you have forgotten your true essence and are just oblivious of it. You regard yourself as the 'body', but this 'body' is not you. You are neither anyone's brother, nor anyone's sister. If this body is not you, then how can anyone be your brother or sister? You are neither a man nor a woman; neither a child nor old. These are attributes of the body. Your essence is not this body — it is chidanandaroopa.

After becoming a *sanyasi* — renunciate, some people are christened with new names beginning with the title of *Swami*. *Swami* means lord, or the one who has known '*swa*' — the self. So everyone is a *swami* even without taking *sanyas*, without getting the head shaved and without performing rituals. I know a *swami* called Chidananda, a pretty common name amongst *swamis*. He became Chidananda after becoming a *sanyasi*, but you have always been one. What else can you be apart from it?

But is it not strange? I have to do all these calisthenics just to help you discover your true '*swaroopa*'. And your mind too has to perform these jigs. You say, "How can I be *Shiva*? I do understand how I can be a *bhakta* — a devotee of God, but how can I be God himself? How is that possible?" You might as well get this straight. What is the *swaroopa* of *Paramatma*? That he is present everywhere. That he is omnipresent. And if he is in everything, then how can he not be in you? He is in you as well. The one who is omnipresent, how can he not be present in your heart? He is there as well!

Sri Krishna says in the *Bhagavad Gita*, "Among trees I am the *Pipal*; among animals I am the *Kamdhenu* cow; among rivers I am *Ganga*; among words I am *Om*; among Gods I am *Indra*." Now this does not mean that 'I' am only in these and not in others. If the *Krishna* consciousness is present in the cow, does it mean it is not present in other animals? *Krishna tattva* is omnipresent. And how can something that is omnipresent be restricted by the limitations of time, space or corporeality?

The one who is everywhere and is eternal, is also the one who is never born, never dies and is present in my 'I' too. But somehow our vision is blurred. We are so inextricably tied up with our body! The attachment with the mind is so strong that we are blinded by it. When the mind is immersed in joy, you are joyous and when the mind sinks into sorrow, you are sorrowful. If a sinful thought steals into your mind, you begin to look upon yourself as a sinful being and if a pure or good thought comes into your mind, you begin to treat yourself like a pious person.

In fact all this *raag* and *dvesha* is taking place inside your mind, but you are not the mind. Because of your ignorance, you are not able to understand this separateness and have mistakenly identified with this 'I'-ness. And so you continue to float or sink in the currents of joy or sorrow that sweep through your mind. But the truth is that you are neither this mind, nor this *buddhi*, nor this *chitta*.

You are not your senses; you are not the five elements either. Then who are you? You are Chidanandaroopa. I can see signs of tension and anxiety. Your mind is getting bogged down by thoughts. What is she saying? Do not get worked up, be attentive, this will take sometime to settle in your intellect. As you listen to all this, even if your mind is ravaged by doubts, be patient and keep listening.

I had told you earlier as well that this is higher knowledge. And I know that your mind does not have the capacity to receive this knowledge. Why is it impure and riddled with desires and lust? The scriptures say that these are blockages — I know it only too well. But I believe you should still listen to this as it may act like a wake up call and you stop this reckless race of running after sensual satisfaction. Once this knowledge strikes at the mind, everything will change. Worldly pursuits will seem like a dream.

Now, do we need to keep repeating these words — 'I' am not mind, *buddhi, ahankara, chitta*? If earlier we used to recite, 'Srikrishnasharnam,' do we now need to recite — 'I' am not mind, *buddhi, ahankara, chitta*? No, we do not need to start parroting anything. There is no need to keep repeating these words. Then what is to be done? You have to maintain a vigil, live in *drashta bhava* and keep watching the flow of your mind. The best way to watch the mind is to not pounce on it directly; to begin with, watch your breath. Every second be aware. When you wake up, do not say, "'I' am waking up". Know that the body is waking up. You just be aware and watch the body walking, eating, talking, resting. Every moment, every step that you take, be aware. Awareness is the *mantra* to attain *nirvana*. You are *nirvana*, this knowing, this knowledge is *nirvana*.

Slowly, you must allow this consciousness to grow. This is something I cannot do for you. This is what you will have to do on your own. Had it been within my powers to help, I would have helped. Had it been within my powers, I would have given you enlightenment, but the truth is that no one can give you enlightenment — **you are the light**.

When someone takes a dip in the holy *Ganga*, they can also take a proxy dip for someone else. *Brahmins* fool people saying that the *shastras* — our holy scriptures — say that you can take a dip in the name of your mother or father — dead or alive. You can thus get the *punya* — good virtues, of this holy bath. It might work in the outer *Ganga*, but not in this *gyanaganga*. Here you have to step in and get soaked. If you take a dip in this *gyanaganga* once, then there is nothing else left to do. There is no duty greater than this, no *karma* greater than this and no *yagna* greater than this.

Krishna says:

Namey hi gyanen sadrasham pavitra meeh vidyate

There is nothing that can be as pure as this ***gyana.***

CHAPTER 3

THE LAST JOURNEY

This is an ancient story: Once different parts of the human body — the sense-organs, the motor-organs, the mind, the *buddhi*, the *chitta*, the *ahankara* and the *prana* — had a debate to decide which one of them is the most important and superior of all — whether *prana* is superior or the eyes, ears, nose, tongue, touch organs are superior; whether the hands, feet and the two orifices are superior, or mind, *buddhi*, *chitta* or *ahankara* is.

The story goes like this: The eyes said to the ears, "We are superior as without us the body cannot see, so it cannot function fully." The feet said to the hands, "We are superior, for without us man will not be able to walk, so how will the body move?" The tongue said, "If other parts are present but I am not, then man will not be able to speak or know the taste of different things. So of all the different parts of the human body, I am the most superior." Then the mind said to the senses, "You may have everything, but without me you cannot function. Eyes, feet, tongue — every organ functions because of me. You do not have the ability to feel and experience. Without me the business of the *gyanindriyan* or *karmaindriyan* cannot be transacted, so I am superior to all. I am responsible for all convictions and beliefs."

Chitta said, "No, I am superior to you as whatever you think or reflect, believe or trust, is what I gather for you. If the treasure house of memories is not there, nothing is possible and you will not be able to do your job." With the help of the mind we know things, discover them, feel them and *chitta* stores all the information. You do not ever forget your house or your name because your memory bank — the *chitta* — always remembers it. You do not have to make a special effort to remember it. You learn to drive, cycle and swim. Whatever you learn, whatever information is gained through the windows of the senses and the mind, it is all accumulated and this information is stored in the *chitta*. When someone goes insane, what does it mean? It means that his mind is able to feel and experience but his *chitta*, the store-keeper is not functioning properly, as a result of which the person is unable to assess things correctly. His wife may be right there in front of him, he can see her, but if his *chitta* — this peculiar device that stores things becomes dysfunctional, then he is unable to recognise her. Memory lapses, partial or full amnesia, Parkinson's, are a few conditions in which a person loses his grip on his memory. *Chitta* is the store-keeper, where all our memories, present and old ones are stored.

If I translate the word *chitta* into English, it will be 'sub-conscious mind'. The other deeper layer of the mind is the 'unconscious'. When you see with your eyes you perceive a colour as red, yellow or green. The memory of the colour is stored in your sub-conscious mind. So the moment you see colour, the *chitta* transports this information to the mind and you recognise it. This whole mechanism is so smooth and quick that we remain unaware of what a great complex activity has occurred in our sub-conscious. Whatever gets into our sub-conscious mind, begins to control and dictate the entire behaviour pattern of our life.

There is a difference between *buddhi* and *ahankara*. One of the ways of looking at *ahankara* is to treat it as a synonym for 'ego'. But the word *ahankara* as used in the context of the mind — *buddhi*, *chitta*, *ahankara* — certainly does not mean the same thing. Here *ahankara* is conviction and knowledge of that which I know. For instance, if I ask you, "What is the colour of my robe?" your eyes can see the ochre colour and this gets confirmed by *chitta*, and then you reply, "It is ochre." This conviction comes from *ahankara*.

I wish to say something about this ochre colour. I am digressing a bit, but this is important. The *sanyas* that Shankaracharya eulogised so much, has been thoroughly disgraced by some people in saffron robes. So much so, that now this colour arouses more revulsion than reverence. *Sadhus* have raped their women disciples and even cheated disciples of money. At places they have entered into a nexus with politicians and created an upheaval in the country. They have even tried to run the politics of the country. Men in saffron have also been responsible for triggering off a whole new cycle of violence in this country! I feel repulsed by this colour as it is increasingly associated with goons, rapists and sick politicians. Though I love this colour, the need to always wear this colour has somehow weakened over the years. Now I do not have any special preference for this colour. I have worn the ochre colour with love, but now it is time to move on, so now every colour is welcome. Black, red, white, blue, all are wonderful now. I have jumped to the next level of *sanyas* — renunciation of the ochre colour!

Swami Ramtirath, who often called himself 'Ram Badshah' — an emperor, had taken *sanyas* after leaving his home town, Lahore. He gave up his professorship, his wife and children. His head was shaven. He wore a sanyasi's dress — a *dhoti* and an *angavastram*. He travelled extensively and later on settled in Uttar *Kashi*. In his last days, he gave up his saffron dress and started wearing white. People were shocked by this act. But he said, "I had worn the ochre colour for a purpose and now when that purpose is served, why should I carry on with this colour?" When he breathed his last, there were no saffron clothes on his body, only white.

Sanyas was just a medium that helped in the fulfillment of a goal. Now that the goal has been realised, what is the use of the medium? There is a huge pride in being a *sanyasi* too. First you were an ordinary householder, then you gave up everything and became a *sanyasi*. Every other type of pride or attachment has been left behind, but this new found status is bigger than any social status. It is hard to find a humble *sanyasi*, most of them are walking mountains of ego.

When I took *sanyas* it was for a purpose and now I find myself in a different state. So I have dropped the ochre colour. Now I have liberated myself from all kinds of bonds. If being a householder is a bond, being a *sanyasi* is also a bond. Now I have liberated myself from all kinds of attachments. Once a *sanyasi* is truly liberated, why would he remain in the bondage of a particular colour? You are in bondage when you insist, "I shall not wear any other colour." This is stubbornness. I have liberated myself from this stubbornness as well. So you see what different types of bondages we live with.

Now I am more like these clouds floating across the sky — the clouds are just there. They carry no label whatsoever. I have become somewhat like the birds that carry no label. No hold, no attachment remains. I am neither a *brahmachari* nor a householder, neither a *vanaprasthi* nor a *sanyasi*. I have liberated myself from that bondage as well. Who am I? All I can say is, 'emptiness — *shoonya!*'

I am reminded of an incident from Baba Bulleh Shah's life. Once, Bulleh Shah was sitting in his *dera* — ashram, in *dhyana*. It was winter and his disciples were basking in the sun. Those were the days of roza. A couple of mullahs were passing by with royal soldiers. When they saw that men sitting in the *dera* were munching carrots and radishes, they were shocked. What kind of a *dera* is it? What sort of *fakirs* live here that even during the roza, they are eating? So they came inside and asked, "Who are you? What kind of people are you? For if this is a *dera* and you are all *Muslims*, then you should be fasting and not feasting." They said, "We are the disciples of *Baba Bulleh Shah*." Once it was confirmed that they were all *Muslims*, the soldiers started beating them with shoes and sticks, saying, "You are worse than infidels. You live in a *dera* and call yourselves *Muslims* and you do not observe roza!"

Fanatics like them always impose their own will on others. They do not give the freedom of choice to others. When these disciples were being beaten up, the *maulvis* saw Bulleh Shah. One of them came inside and asked, "Hey, who are you?" Bulleh Shah kept quiet. He did not utter a single word. Again they asked, "Are you a *Hindu* or a *Muslim*? Who are you?" Again he kept quiet. The third time they said, "If you do not respond, we will beat you up. Who are you?" Then Bulleh Shah lifted his hand and shook it to indicate 'neither'. They felt he must be some crazy fellow. Either he is dumb or is out of his mind. Then leaving Bulleh Shah alone, they again started beating his disciples. The men were thoroughly beaten, like animals, but their master who was also eating was spared!

Once the soldiers had left, all of them came to their master and asked, "Pir Sahib, we were beaten up so badly. How come you were spared?" Bulleh Shah said, "Tell me, what did they ask and what did you tell them?" "They asked us who we were and we replied that we are *Muslims*." Bulleh Shah said, "That is why you were beaten up, because you chose to put a religious label on yourself. They came to me as well and asked me the same question, 'Who are you?' Now what could I say? There was a time when I was only a man. Then the time came when I became a syed. Then I became a *haji* (one who has done the pilgrimage to *Mecca*). Then the time came when I became a disciple. Then my murshid (master) gave me knowledge, showed me the light, and after receiving that knowledge *Bullah* ceased to be *Bullah*. That was the end of Bullah's existence, his ego, and his identity. Now when there is no *Bullah* left, what could I say? I remained silent and thus escaped the beating."

In Sufism, *fakirs* scale great heights of spirituality and drop all labels. On being asked who he was, Bulleh Shah just chose to remain silent. Silence is the answer — the only true answer.

Someone asked *Kabir*, "Have you attained enlightenment? Have you experienced the grace of God?" *Kabir* remained silent. The one who had raised the question pestered him saying, "Please say something." All that *Kabir* said was:

> **Crazy am I if I say I have found Him**
> **And a liar if I say I have not**
> **Neither have I found nor lost anything**
> **I am in fullness complete**

How can I say I have found God? When did I lose Him? How can I say I had lost Him? He is available to me all hours of the day. And if someone is available all the time, why do you need to find him? How can you ever be separated from the one who is always there, every hour of the day? Then how can I say that I have found God now or had lost him earlier? I have neither found nor lost him. In the process of articulating this I will get trapped. That is why I am unable to speak a word. Now I have removed all the labels.

Now I return to what I had started off with. If I ask you what colour this is, you might say it is saffron. Are you sure that it is saffron and not orange, red or maroon? Where does this knowledge come from? It emerges from your *chitta*. The mind can contemplate the colour the eyes are seeing. According to the hues, the names are different. Now this is where your mind gets involved. The mind starts debating whether it is saffron or red and it is your *buddhi* — the intellect that settles this question conclusively. In this situation, each one's *buddhi* will decide for him. Someone says, "No, it is definitely red." Someone else says, "It is a deeper tone of saffron." So the *buddhi* is capable of arriving at its own independent decision. Whatever information is stored in your *chitta* comes up to the surface of the mind and on the basis of that your *buddhi* arrives at a particular conclusion. And then *ahankara* takes over, pronouncing that this is indeed the colour.

Modifications appear in the mind and the *chitta* supports it with its bank of knowledge and information which it has gained from all the external impulses. The intellect's work is to come to a decision and *ahankara* puts the final seal on this. The mind and the *chitta* work together and the intellect and *ahankara* work together. Mind, sub-consciousness, ego and intellect support one another and as such they are inter-related.

So in the story, the mind said, "In this body I am the superior most." *Buddhi* said, "No, you just throw up alternatives. Ultimately, I am the one who resolves issues." *Chitta* claimed, "No, I am superior to all of you. After all, I store all the knowledge you gain in this world." The *chitta* is very important — it is our hard disc where everything is stored in the computer.

The entire behaviour pattern of your life is controlled by your *chitta*. If a virus enters your computer, it will crash. Now who is called a mad person? A mad person's mind also functions; when he eats he puts food in his mouth and not in his ears. He has the necessary *buddhi* to know that it must go straight into the mouth. But the integration of all information does not happen. This is the function of *chitta* and intellect. The link between the mind and the *chitta* gets muddled. The ability to synchronise information goes haywire.

A few days back I read a story about a mad man. He was treated in a hospital for several years. Finally he was cured and the day came when he was to be discharged. In his state of madness, he would just pick up stones and start breaking all the windowpanes he could set his eyes on. He was given all kinds of treatments: shock treatment, sedatives and tranquilisers. Finally when the doctors felt that he was much better, they decided to discharge him. They called him and asked, "Please tell us what you will do when you are discharged from here?" He said, "I will go home." The doctors thought that he was on the right track. "And what will you do when you go home?" He said, "I will meet my wife and children." They said, "And then?" He said, "Then I will bring all of them here and ask them to smash all the windowpanes in this hospital. Right now I am alone. Then I will bring everyone and together we will smash all the windowpanes!"

Once a gentleman came to meet me. In the course of our conversation, every two minutes he would say, "Earlier I was mad, but now I am alright." I thought he must have recovered, after all people make all kinds of confessions in my presence. After five minutes, he again said, "Earlier I was mad, but now I am alright." Then again after two minutes he repeated the same thing! Then again after five minutes! Then his family members who were with him, intervened saying, "He hasn't really recovered so far." I said, "Well, I can make that out!" He was properly dressed. The way others removed their shoes outside, so did he. The way others offered me *pranam*, so did he. In other words, his *buddhi* was obviously doing its job well. Then what really went wrong? If the *chitta* that stores all information doesn't function properly, then the whole system of the body can go haywire.

The story continues. *Buddhi* said, "Everyone has spoken and now it is my turn. Let me clear things up for all of you. I am supreme; neither the mind nor the senses are superior. If other things remain the same, but I do not function, then nothing can work." *Prana* sat through it all quietly but finally said, "This isn't solving anything, now we will do this: the sense organs should leave the body, one by one. Then let us see whether or not this body can function without the sense organs."

So first the vision left the body and blindness struck. But the body continued to function. Then it was the turn of the ears and they discovered that the deaf also manage to survive. Then the sense of smell left and thereafter the sense of taste. But the body continued to function. One by one all the sense organs left the body but it made no difference to its functioning. Of course it created its own share of problems here or there, but the body was still alive. Then the mind left, then *buddhi*, then *chitta*, then *ahankara*, but the body still functioned.

In sleep your mind and *buddhi* do not function. When your body is asleep, your mind and intellect get submerged. When you go into a state of *samadhi* through *yoga*, then *buddhi* and *ahankara* disappear but *chitta* remains. And yet the body survives. With the light of knowledge you dispel the darkness of *ahankara*, remove the ignorance of *buddhi* and submerge your mind in *dhyana*. Still the body continues to live and breathe.

When all the five *gyanindriyan* (sense-organs) were separated from the body, it still continued to function. When all the five *karmaindriyan* (motor-senses) left the body, it still functioned. Then mind, *buddhi*, *chitta* and *ahankara* also deserted the body. Yet it did not stop functioning. But the moment *prana* left the body the entire system came to an abrupt end. *Prana* is supreme in the body; it runs this body. On one hand *prana* is energy and on the other it supports the body systems. Now, when I say *prana*, it does not mean the breath. Breath is not *prana*. When you breathe in and out, whatever goes in or out is not *prana*. *Prana* is the life force. This life force is present inside the body all the time. So what is the most precious thing in this body? It is *prana shakti*. Ordinarily, in our language we make no distinction between *prana* and breath. Though both mean the same, yet in their behaviour they are not the same. So what is the most precious thing in the human body? *Prana* is the power. If *prana* is not there in the body, then the body is a corpse. What is the difference between the living and the dead? The living has *prana* in them, but the dead do not.

In the Hindi language, human beings are called *prani*. Both *Kabir* and *Guru Nanak* have used the word *prani* extensively in their writings. I would say the word 'human' is a very impolite expression; the correct expression is *prani*. This life force surges through our entire body, makes the different organs function, controls our breathing pattern, our blood supply, our thoughts and the functioning of our eyes and ears. All the major and minor body functions are controlled by *prana*.

Just come to think of it, how indifferent we are to our own body! All the time we are worried about which leader has joined another party, who has done what, who said what! We are so obsessed with all this that we debate these issues all the time. We always make an effort to gain as much information as we possibly can, on things like which actor is going around with which actress. We want to know what is happening in the state or national politics, or what the foreign policy of our country is. In a way, you have not even succeeded in formulating your domestic policy, but of course you must offer your comments on the foreign policy. What does George Bush think, eat or drink? How much time is wasted in gathering this useless information! But we remain hopelessly oblivious of what is going on inside our own body. To put it another way, you can somehow manage to drive the car, but you do not know your own car. It is only when we try to understand this entire process that we gain knowledge about it. Don't we?

We know about our breath, but not about our *prana*. Breath is not *prana*. In this body, *prana* is the most precious of all. In the subtle body, *prana* is the most vital component. It is this *prana shakti* that provides the subtle body a passage from one corporeality to another. Now, let us proceed to the second *shloka* of Shankaracharya's *Atmashatakam*. In this *shloka*, you will find him discussing *prana*.

Na cha praansangyo na vai panchvayuh
Na vaa saptadhaaturna vaa panchkoshah
Na vaakpaanipaadou na chopasthpaayuu
Chidaanandroopah shivoham shivoham

Shankaracharya says, "'I' am not *prana*; 'I' am different from *prana*. 'I' am separate from this vital energy, this life force. 'I' am different from this life force that surges through the body at both the levels — gross and subtle." In the first *shloka* he said, "'I' am not the mind, 'I' am not *buddhi*, 'I' am not *chitta* and 'I' am not *ahankara*. 'I' am not the eyes, 'I' am not the ears, 'I' am not the tongue and 'I' am not the nose either." Then talking about the five elements he says, "'I' am not the earth, 'I' am not water, 'I' am not ether, 'I' am not fire and 'I' am not the air either. Then what am I? And who am I? 'I' am separate, different from all these."

In the next *shloka* he says, "I am not *prana* either." The *shastras* say that the *atman* is not *prana*. In the *Bhagavad Gita*, *Krishna* uses the word '*atman*' extensively and freely. *Krishna* says, "*Atman* cannot be soaked in water, nor can it be burnt and weapons cannot destroy it. *Atman* is invisible, ineffable and defies description. The body is visible and *atman* is invisible. *Sri Krishna* says to *Arjuna*, "Before you acquired this corporeality you were invisible. And as long as this body was not born, you and I were invisible. When this body dies, again we will be invisible."

What is your true essence, visible or invisible? The answer is: invisible. It has not been referred to as even *atman*. The word used is — invisible. Every time *Sri Krishna* refers to himself in the *Gita* he says 'I', but while explaining to *Arjuna*, he says '*atman*.' "Hey *Arjuna*! This is your real roopa (essence), this *atman* cannot be killed with weapons and fire cannot burn *atman* to ashes. Hey *Arjuna*! This *atman* is your real roopa! Do not think of yourself as just a body."

Shankaracharya has condensed the *tattvagyana* into these *shlokas* of Atmashatakam. In the ninth chapter of the *Gita*, *Krishna* talks about what happens when this *Jivatman* leaves the body. In the second chapter however, he talks of how this *atman* is imperishable and cannot be destroyed with weapons. So whatever *Krishna* has said in the *Gita* in various contexts — about the nature of the *atman* — is what Shankaracharya has woven into a single rosary so beautifully. Shankaracharya has brought to us the distilled wisdom of the *Vedas* in a clear-cut way. Shankaracharya has presented the essence of the *Vedas* in this poem. Clarified butter is present in milk but we have to run the milk through various processes and only then are we able to extract it. From the milk of the *Vedas*, he has extracted this wonderful essence — Atmashatakam.

Expounding on the nature of 'I', Shankaracharya says, "'I' am not mind, 'I' am not *chitta*, 'I' am not *buddhi*, 'I' am not *ahankara*, and 'I' am not *prana*. After the death of the body, sometimes people say that his *atman* has not found a resting place or that

his soul is unable to achieve freedom and a *yagna* will have to be performed for the liberation of his soul. Such expressions are inept and inappropriate. From a logical point of view, this argument does not hold any ground. But in common parlance we often say, "his *atman* has not found a resting place," or "that particular house is haunted by someone's *atman*."

The *atman* never gets restive, nor do you have to perform *yagnas* for its peace. The *Vedas* say:

Avinashinam Nityam Ya Ainam Ajam Avayam

The *atman* is eternal and present everywhere; it is unborn and invincible.

The *Gita* says:

Katham Sa Purusha Paartha Kam Gatyati Hanti Kam

O *Arjuna*, *atman* does not go anywhere after death and no one can destroy it.

In the Hindi language the word for suicide is *atmahatya*. Now the logical question arises, can we kill *atman*? The answer is no, so it can be said that no one can ever commit *atmahatya*. The only thing that can be killed is the body. Even your subtle body is deathless. *Atman* can never be killed. It is not within your power to kill either your own *atman* or anyone else's. Actually no one can be killed and no one kills. This does not mean that you go out and kill someone! I am not giving you a licence to do that! What I mean is that even when the body is killed the *atman* remains invincible.

I simplify this very word '*atman*' and refer to it as 'I'. In the language of the *Shastras*, *atman* is Chidanandaroopa, but I just say 'I' am Chidanandaroopa. Those who have read the *Bhagavad Gita*, but have not understood it properly think that there is an *atman* in our body which is invincible and imperishable. They speak as though *atman* is something distant and far-off. The *atman* simply means 'I' the pure self. Just by parroting *Sanskrit shlokas* you will not gain anything — you have to delve deep into it.

Let us understand *prana*. It is of five types: *prana, apana, vayana, udana, samana. Prana* governs the area between the larynx and the top of the diaphragm. It is associated with the organs of respiration, gullet and speech, together with the muscles and nerves that activate them. It is the force by which the breath is drawn in. *Apana* is located below the navel region and provides energy to the large intestine, kidneys, anus and genitals. *Samana* is located between the heart and the navel. It activates and controls the digestive system — the liver, intestines, pancreas and stomach. *Samana* also activates the heart and circulatory system and is responsible for the assimilation and distribution of nutrients. *Udana* controls the area above the neck, activating all the sensory receptors such as the eyes, nose and ears. It also harmonises and activates the limbs and all their associated muscles, ligaments, nerves and joints. *Vayana* pervades the whole body regulating and controlling all movements. It acts as a reserve force for the other *pranas*.

If there is an imbalance of any kind in any part of our body, that part gets afflicted with disease. This is caused by the improper functioning of the *prana*. Now, in medical science, they understand the value of oxygen. If for some reason — an accident or an injury — oxygen does not reach your brain, you will suffer brain damage. Or if a vein bursts inside the brain and the oxygen supply is cut off, the brain stops functioning. The entire science of acupressure and acupuncture is based upon this principle of *prana*.

Prana is present in the whole body. Blood pressure, cardiovascular diseases, cancers, tumors — all kinds of diseases occur due to imbalance of *prana*. The *pranas* circulate throughout our body in a uniform manner. If there is any disruption in their circulation to any specific part of the body, that organ stops functioning.

Now I would like to talk about the Chinese therapy popularly known as acupressure. There are centres of 'pressure' present in different parts of our body, especially in our hands and feet. On the tip of the thumb is located the nerve centre of the pituitary gland. If this gland in our brain functions properly, then the thyroid gland also functions properly. If the thyroid gland functions properly, then our other systems of digestion etc. work properly. There are major pressure points in the hands and feet that deal with most of our problems. Apart from the hands and feet, pressure points are also present in other parts of the body.

If *prana shakti* does not circulate in the body in an even manner and a particular part of the body is somehow deprived of it, that part gets afflicted with a problem. Acupressure therapists can diagnose your disease just by checking your pressure points. They will tell you at that very moment, whether it is your liver or your pancreas or your lungs or your eyes that have a problem.

For a long time these techniques of acupressure and acupuncture were ridiculed in the west. They would say things like: "What good are these needles?" But now medical science is beginning to recognise it as an alternative therapy. Even in hospitals where they otherwise use allopathic drugs, these therapies are now being recommended with much enthusiasm. They have even started departments to promote these therapies in hospitals.

The entire science of acupressure and acupuncture is based on the laws of *prana*, but they use different terms; they do not call it *prana* but chi. Just look at your body — the kind of machinery God has created. Each and every organ, every limb is a marvel of engineering. The life force — *prana* keeps it alive. When *prana* functions in harmony, the body remains healthy. The five types of *prana* run this body perfectly. One helps in your digestion and excretion. The second gives you breath and therefore life. The third regulates the functions of all the organs of your body. The fourth releases the toxins and the fifth assimilates the nutrients.

Who says that *dharma* is just another name for faith? It is an advanced mystical science. In order to explain these different types of *vayu*, the *yogis* must have first made a scientific study of each and every limb of our body. Even now, the allopathic doctors have no concept of this panchvayu. They only speculate and keep on experimenting. But *yogis* understood the mechanism of the body by *tantric* means. *Ayurveda* talks about how the *prana* controls our body. When the body gets polluted due to the malfunctioning of *prana*, it begins to give rise to several diseases. Much before Shankaracharya talked about it, several other sages had made similar observations. Sage *Patanjali* has written extensively on *prana* in his scripture, 'The *Yogasutra*'.

The human body is a magnificent work of architecture, where electrical and mechanical energies function. Look at the way nature has created this beautiful system; but poor God never got any Nobel Prize for his creation. Can there be a more worthy claimant of the Nobel Prize than God? Can there be a more effective invention than this? In his ignorance, man keeps fighting with him saying, "I do not have this, I do not have that." You keep fighting for the fulfillment of your trivial desires. But have you ever thought how precious this machine he has handed over to us is?

If your mind does not function properly your life will be a total waste. If your *chitta* does not function properly your life will be a dead loss. If a small part of the brain becomes dysfunctional, no Ph.D. or M. Phil degree will be able to save you from going crazy and wandering aimlessly in the streets. I remember a mad man who used to sit in front of our house, stark naked, that too in severe winter. People often beat him up in an effort to force him to wear clothes. In the chilly winter, he would just keep lying naked. He was an educated fellow from a reasonably good family. But once he lost control of his mind, his education was of no use. He would call every passerby a *goonda* (scoundrel). People got irritated, but they also pitied him because he belonged to a family that was known to be cultured and was well respected. But what could they do?

God is so kind to us. It is because of his benevolence that all the parts of our body function properly. If different parts of our gross body do not function properly, then the body gives us trouble. And if different parts of our subtle body do not function properly, even then it gives us trouble.

Na vaa saptadhaaturna vaa panchkoshah

'I' am not *prana*; nor am 'I' panchvayu. *Dhatur* means mineral. The human body is made of seven *dhatus*: Rasa (Lymph), Rakta (Blood), Maans (Muscle), *Meda* (Fat), Asthi (Bones), Majja (Nervous System) and Shukra (Reproductive Cells). But in obese people the *meda* is excessively nourished and the remaining *dhatus* are malnourished. *Kapha* (humour) gets accumulated and when it increases to abnormal levels, the fat metabolism is hampered and the person becomes obese.

You will be surprised to know that if somehow we are able to extract these seven minerals out of our body — though we cannot ever do that in actual practice — but if we were to, they will not be worth more than five odd rupees!

Na vaakpaanipaadou na chopasthpaayuu

Shankaracharya says, "'I' am not *vaka* (speech), nor *panipado* (hands and feet). Na cha *upastha payuh* — 'I' am not the organs of procreation or excretion either. I am not any of these." *Atman* has no gender. *Atman* is neither a man nor a woman. The difference between a man and a woman is that of gender.

I am not man or woman — the self is beyond the distinction of gender. Naming each organ and limb one by one, Shankaracharya says that 'I' am none of these. 'I' am not the hands, 'I' am not the feet, 'I' am not speech, 'I' am not the ears, 'I' am not touch and 'I' am not the nose. 'I' am none of these. Then who am 'I'? 'I' am:

Chidaanandroopah shivoham shivoham

This 'body' is not the hallmark of my identity. What do you regard yourself as being? In fact your faith, your belief and your conviction is — 'I' am a man and this is my name. This is so deeply ingrained in your mind, that if someone calls out your name when you are in deep sleep, you will wake up with a start, realizing that your name is being called. If ten people are asleep, only that person wakes up whose name is called out. You have to break this excessive attachment with the body. 'I' am not this body; 'I' am not this body composed of five elements.

People only recognise the shape of this body. If someone goes to get a licence or a passport made, they stick the photograph of this very body. Therefore you have to say, "Yes, this is my licence." But the fact is that this is not your true identity. We must reflect deeply on this. The path of knowledge says that you should not just repeat the name of *Rama*, but if you really want to know *Rama*, then you must first try to know who you are. As long as you do not understand yourself in the true sense of the word, how can you ever understand *Rama*?

Suppose I decide to visit you, but when I come to your house you are fast asleep. If I sit in your house for a while and come back, would you ever know that I had visited? God is right there in your house but you are asleep, so no meeting takes place. It is even possible that while I am in your house, you are dreaming of me and yet you will not know that I am already sitting in your house.

Kabir Sahib has rightly said, "You are sleeping and your lord is wide-awake." How can someone who is sleeping meet someone who is wide-awake? Now, here sleeping does not mean the physical sleep but the sleep of the mind. Here sleeping means forgetting who you really are. When someone loses his true sense of identity — when he becomes oblivious of his atmanswaroopa — this is sleep.

Every soul is a traveller and if a traveller halts and sleeps at some place it is alright. To rest a while is alright, but if the traveller pitches his tent permanently and forgets all about the journey, then definitely there is something to worry about. Mystics give the call, "Arise and awake!" Before this birth, there was another birth. Before this body there was another body. The journey of your life goes on endlessly! In every birth you set up your house, family and friends. In every birth you say, "this is my body" and accept this claim as the truth. In this vicious cycle of 'mine and yours', you spend your entire life. But this world does not become yours just because you claim it to be yours. As long as the *prana* is there in the body, this 'me-mine' syndrome continues. The moment the *prana* leaves your body, nothing is 'mine' any longer.

Arise and awake! The lord is wide awake; *Bhagwan* is awake and you are still sleeping. When you use the word '*Bhagwan*', it does not refer to a person. It does not mean that we are talking about *Rama*, *Krishna* or *Shiva* and saying that they are awake and we are asleep. We are talking about the ever blissful, conscious, omniscient being. It is an expression used for the same cosmic force, the same *Satchidanandaswaroopa* that is omnipresent. The one who has woken up is called an awakened, realized being.

The world is transitory and mortal, and so is your body. *Kabir* says, "After death, the shroud shall cover the body, it will not be on 'me' but on my body. There is no sheet in the world with which one could cover 'me'. No sheet can spread as far as 'me'. This sheet can spread as far as this body but it cannot ever reach 'me'."

Kabir is simplifying it for the benefit of the people he is addressing. In order to create a sense of detachment in the hearts of these people, he says, "These very people, for whom you often worry to death, shall not lose any time in covering you with a shroud and packing you off to the funeral home. It is strange how in their foolishness, people often politicise this simple ritual too. When someone dies, his family members keep discussing things such as: "When so and so died, there wasn't even a single person to put a sheet over his dead body, but when our father died, the whole town turned up to offer shawls." While you are alive, you remain mired in attachment, affection, love and pride and even after death it is the same attachment that makes you say, "How lavish my funeral will be?"

You will be amused to know that an American billionaire put in the false news of his death in the newspapers. His secretary was the one who dictated: "He died last night." Over breakfast the next morning, he was sipping his tea and enjoying reading who had said what about him. Then sitting in his house, he was watching the entire program of his own funeral on a close circuit television and wondering, "So this is what my ex-girlfriend or my wife has to say." Even his wife and children did not know that he was alive. Only he knew that he was alive — or his secretary knew that he was not dead yet!

There on the close circuit TV he saw big businessmen vying with one another to issue all kinds of statements. When his worst detractors also started praising him, he laughed till his sides split. He said to himself, "All my life I could not get them to say even a single word of praise for me. Am I really hearing right?"

People were paying tributes to him and he was sitting there listening to it all. When everything was over and the empty coffin — of course the coffin was empty — had been buried, he announced in a press conference that he was alive. It left all the people who knew him quite stunned, even nervous. They asked, "What is this all about? Why did you do it?" He said, "Look, I have to die one day, but I wanted to see how much respect you will show me when I am gone. I wanted to actually hear all the good and kind words my wife, children, family and friends would say after I am gone. Because once I am gone, the game is really up. How will I know who is doing what behind my back? That is why I enacted this little drama. But now I am satisfied that I do mean a lot to people around me."

He is the only person in the world — who, while still alive — saw the spectacle of what his death and funeral would be like. Often the ignorant *chitta* engages itself in such trivial pursuits. And man often gets involved in such foolish acts. How many people shall praise me after my death? The people who offer a shawl over your dead body are your own people after all! They are the ones who bring you to your funeral tied to a wooden plank!

How many days do we mourn someone? We grieve for a couple of days and then return to our usual business. In the good old times, the mourning would continue for twenty-one days, before that forty days and prior to that, for three months. That is it! There is a limit to mourning as well. How long can you sit and mourn? After some time the family members start telling each other that the one who had to go has gone — why mourn for him now; those who go once do not ever return; you better get a hold on yourself. Then the more practical considerations take over — do not drown in your sorrow; you better take charge of your responsibilities; all that you say for others today will be said tomorrow by someone else for you. The ultimate truth of this body is death. But a bigger truth is that only the body dies. 'You' never die.

'You' are forever. 'You' are never born and 'you' will never die. How can he who is not born die? But as long as you have tied yourself up in the various bonds of attachment, all this shall simply flow over your head. But this is the only truth. And this truth is worth introspection, even meditation.

Step by step, I am initiating you into this method of self-knowledge that Shankaracharya has outlined in his *Atmashatakam*. Step by step, Shankaracharya is assisting you in climbing the stairs leading to the discovery of the 'self'.

CHAPTER 4

LOOK INSIDE

This body is mortal and you a Witnessing light
An extension of five elements in space and
You the drashta, the knower
You live in every grain of life and
Yet you are a Witnessing Light
Arise and awake, it is but a dream or an illusion
Your fears soar because you have forgotten
Being a master, why choose to be a slave
You be your own Witnessing Light
It is your fault, you alone should expiate
'I' am an unattached witness, you convince yourself

The final liberation from the cycle of birth and death is to see yourself as a 'Witnessing Light'. Everything in this world can be divided into two categories — perishable and non-perishable — those that go through cycles of change and those that do not change at all. There is no third category! One category is that of truth and the other of falsehood. One category is of the sentient and the other of the non-sentient. So everything is either sentient or non-sentient, truth or falsehood, perishable or non-perishable.

We become whatever we connect ourselves with. If we connect ourselves with the perishable, we become perishable. What is perishable? Whatever comes to an end, whatever changes and whatever has change as its basic essence, is perishable. Can we change nature? No, we cannot do that.

The intrinsic nature of things cannot be changed. You in

your core are immortal and imperishable, this cannot change. It is extremely difficult, almost impossible. The perishable cannot become imperishable. And the imperishable cannot become perishable. You cannot make something eternal, if by its very nature it is transient. And whatever is immortal can never die.

Now the question is, where do you position yourself? In the category of the 'imperishable' or that of the 'perishable'. Among those who change or those who do not? With what can you be associated — falsehood or truth? Do you see yourself as one with the non-sentient or the sentient? If someone says, "I associate myself with the perishable, but I wish to be imperishable," then there cannot be a greater fool than him. It is in the nature of matter, the body and the world to change. Matter has to change.

Water at room temperature is liquid; in freezing temperatures it becomes solid ice; when it is heated, the same water turns to steam. These are the three states of water — as a liquid, as a solid and as vapour. When water is liquid it can assume the shape of any vessel as it is itself shapeless. If you freeze it then it assumes the shape of the container in which you freeze it. So the form of water keeps changing. Earlier I had mentioned that there are places such as the Arctic, the *Himalayas*, *Kedarnath* and *Mansarovar* that remain snow-bound through the year. If you climb up to these high altitudes, you will see a different spectacle altogether. There are areas which are covered with snow for some period and then the snow melts. When these areas are snow-bound, you feel as though a white sheet has been spread all around. But when this very snow melts because of the rise in temperature, you get to see the peaks clearly. When the snow melts, the seeds buried in the ground begin to sprout. Then you feel as though a carpet of flowers has been spread out.

There is a place in the *Himalayas* called the 'Valley of Flowers'. For nearly six months in a year, this 'Valley of Flowers' remains buried under a thick layer of snow. But with the return of summer, the snow melts and the entire valley starts blooming with greenery. In that green valley, various seeds planted by 'God the gardener', begin to blossom into multi-coloured flowers. And then you feel as though a carpet of flowers has been rolled out everywhere. The whole valley begins to bloom with flowers.

The areas of *Kedarnath* and *Badrinath* remain snow-bound for nearly six months, but when summer comes, the ice melts forming beautiful little lakes and waterfalls. Various kinds of flowers bloom in these lakes. These flowers are not seen in the winter, it is only in summer that they bloom.

When water solidifies it becomes ice; when ice melts it turns into water and on being heated, it becomes vapour. These are the three states in which water exists. Now, if you were to tell water, "You must not change your form and always remain liquid," it is just not possible for it to obey. Even if water wants to, it cannot stay that way, because change is inherent to its nature. When the temperature rises in summer, it evaporates into steam. And when the temperature falls in winter, it solidifies into ice. These are the only three states possible for water.

Man's body is made of matter. Now, the nature of matter is that it has to change. What was your weight when this body of yours was conceived in the womb of your mother? At that time too you had a weight, no matter how little it was. Even if it was one millionth of a gram, still it could be measured. *Guru Ravidas* has put it so beautifully, "You are born out of one single drop of semen. Why be proud, what for?" So the next time when you are tempted to tell anyone, "You do not really know who I am", you must remember that you are no more than a mere drop, that is it.

At the time of conception the body was a mere drop. In the womb the weight was in micromilligrams. What is the weight of a sperm? And even when it meets with the egg, it still has a very miniscule amount of weight. If only medical science were somehow able to measure it, you would know that as you kept growing your weight also grew. After your birth, this process of change was accelerated. Soon enough, a child who is less than a foot first grows to one foot, then two feet and then three, five and can even grow up to seven feet.

In India, the average height of people is five and a half feet. In Denmark, the average height is six. In Holland you will not come across anyone less than five and a half feet. When some Dutch fellow comes to meet me, I do feel good. Do you know why? Because in India, I often come across men or women who are not that tall and in order to speak to them, I have to tilt my head considerably. I am five feet seven inches in my heels…!

It is a fact that at the time of conception, we all weigh the same. The average weight of the foetus is the same. But later on, due to the genes of the parents, the shape of the body, the colour of the eyes and the skin, the weight and height of everyone changes. If a Chinese man or woman marries a person of their own race, their children would still have small beady eyes and a flat nose. You cannot change that. In America and in England, a good number of young Indian men and women marry people from other races. A lot of people object to it saying, "This is not right. This is against the principle of racial purity. They should marry within their own race and caste." Forget about another race, in India marriages have to be conducted within the same caste too!

But if you ask me, the only way to save humanity is to encourage inter-racial marriages. Otherwise politicians are hell-bent on destroying the peace of the world. Just to satisfy their greed and power, they are ready to divide people and provoke them to fight, kill, hate and persecute in the name of religion and race. Their grip is tightening on man's mind. God knows what our future will be! People want to be patriotic; they want to love their country, but this love is at the cost of hostility to another country. In times of war, everyone turns patriotic. One country turns hostile toward another and both go to war. When a man fights another man, his hatred will have little effect on others, but when a nation fights against another nation, this hatred is magnified.

There is no dearth of such people in any country who are ready to go to war. But the geographical conditions are such that if India or Pakistan decides to explode a nuclear bomb, the impact will not be confined to the enemy area, but will spread across thousands of kilometres. Destruction will be of an unimaginable scale. The threat of nuclear warfare is looming large over our heads, and politicians — fanatics — are holding humanity to ransom. What kind of stupidity are people indulging in? They nurture hatred against each other, but when war breaks out, the common man will face the brunt. "My country is greater than yours, my race is superior to yours, my religion is greater than yours." These statements are

not of evolved human beings. Ignorance is the root cause of such approach. As such, right from the lowest rung to the highest, almost everyone is busy destroying their country through bribery, corruption and dishonesty. The only difference is that people at the lower rung are easily caught, whereas those at the highest get away with the worst of crimes. No one can even touch them. But the moment war-like conditions are created, this hatred — like a demon — begins to raise its head.

That is why I say that there should be more inter-nation marriages. Once you have relatives in another country, the whole game of exploiting religion for the sake of politics will end. Man imprisons himself within a belief system and suffers from complexes or gives complexes to others. Man lives with so many complexes and self created problems that this wonderful life changes into a dreary drag, a burden. Where it is possible to live with love, awareness and sharing, we are fighting for nothing. The end of the day is the same for everyone. Everybody comes from dust and goes back to dust. The material things which you label as expensive are left behind for others who will lay claim to them. The truth of the matter is that nothing is yours.

Once thieves barged into Mullah Nasruddin's house. Now what was there in the house of *Mullah* to steal? The thieves started searching for valuables in the dark. On hearing all kinds of sounds, *Mullah* got up and started lighting the lantern. When the thieves heard the commotion, they were immediately alerted. As they were about to leave, the *Mullah* shouted, "Wait a while! I am lighting this lantern only for you. Search thoroughly, for you may just find something valuable in this house. I do not want you to go out and say that not even a broken canister was found in Mullah's house. Wait! Just hold on!" The thieves were surprised to see this kind of a reaction. They had seen and met all kinds of people who either shouted at them or ran after them the moment they spotted them. And if once they laid their hands on them, they beat them up thoroughly. But never had they seen a man who offered a lantern to them saying, "Go, look for whatever valuables there are!" But the thieves turned out to be more stubborn than *Mullah*, they just ran.

On going a little distance, they felt someone walking behind them. They turned back and asked, "Why are you coming along?" *Mullah* said, "These trunks are the only property I had and you are taking them away. Now there is nothing left in the house. I am just a lonely old man, so why leave me behind."

I have shared this story on a number of occasions earlier and here I narrate it all over again. Once a couple of friends went to attend a wedding. As the wedding was in a village across the river, they went in a boat. They tied the boat to a tree on the bank and went to the house where the wedding was being organised. They wined and dined through the night and then it was time to leave. When they went back to their boat one of them said, "We will row the boat and surely we will reach home soon." All night they paddled the boat and as dawn broke and light spread, they saw that they had not moved even an inch from the bank. They had forgotten to untie the rope and the boat remained tied to the tree!

If you remain tied to your body, you may keep performing all kinds of spiritual practices, but you will not reach anywhere. First, you must untie the ropes that you have tied yourself with. Someone's mind is tied to a shop, someone's to a house. You need to learn the method of untying yourself from worldly attachments. These material things are for you no doubt, but you have become their slave. Use things by all means but do not let them own you and your spirit.

Tenderness, love, compassion — these words are talked about so much, and yet man's heart is devoid of these emotions. These words have become meaningless. Especially when spoken by politicians, they get sullied. In place of the heart, they must have an organ which is similar to the heart, but is not the heart; just an organ which pumps blood. Lucky are those who are in the company of evolved beings, for they have a great and genuine concern for others. Selfishness, greed and lust for power have become the motivation of life today. *Gyana* teaches us how to come out of this swamp.

It is only with the sword of knowledge that you can cut through these ties. Thus the importance of *tattvagyana* and of the giver of *gyana* — the master — is immense. The master loves you unconditionally and becomes a catalyst of change in your life. One

learns the art of giving from the master. The master's heart opens your heart with the warmth of pure love. The glow of love purifies you and all negativities are washed away. The guru's heart will make your heart bloom like the lotus flower. Slowly the master fills you with his colours. But, if you do not surrender yourself to the master, how can he work? You cannot fight with the lotus flower insisting that it open up and bloom at night. The sunflower opens only with the first rays of the sun and closes with the last. There is no other way it can possibly bloom. Be true to yourself and surrender to your master. He will pour divine wine into your heart.

Once a *sadhu* came to me and said, "Either help me enter a state of *samadhi* or kill me. Or else I will kill myself." I was surprised at his urgency. I explained to him that this may happen in a moment or it may take years. How can I give a guarantee or a promise that I can do this? Just be available, listen, meditate and this magic light may shine any time. He was not just desperate, but an egoistic person as well. He stayed in the *ashram* and promised, "I will surrender to you, I will do anything, but help me get enlightened." He would walk in the *ashram* with pain, anger and ego written on his face. One fine day he again started blabbering, "Make me enlightened or I will kill myself." I said, "Fine, kill yourself." Do you know what he did? Well nothing, he did not kill himself! Then one day his letter came asking when his *agyachakra* would open? One evening all the *sadhaks* were sitting in meditation. He was also there. Suddenly he started beating his forehead saying very loudly, "Open up! Open up!" He was screaming, as though his words alone would help open up his third eye. For a good fifteen minutes he kept repeating, "Open up! Open up!" Then it must have opened up! The next day he started telling everyone around, "I have had the awakening. Now you sit and I will give you *gyana*."

This mind is such a devil that it wants to don the mantle of a *guru* much before it can even become a true disciple. It wants to be known as a *gyani*, without acquiring any *gyana*. Without finding the secret of brahmagyana, it wants to be known as a brahmagyani. It is *tamas* — the negativity of the mind — that you are not even a disciple but are dying to be a *guru*. Give up your *Khudi* (ego) and you will become a *Khuda* — God. But you say, "I would much rather protect my ego and still be a *gyani* or a *guru*." But I say, "You give up your ego and become a *Khuda*." You have to give up this false 'ego' or 'I'-ness.

You should lead an unencumbered life. Learn dispassion and live in this world, then it will not bind you. It is our mind and not things that bind us; untie yourself and fly in your inner space. Do not be ruffled by trivial matters, break the habit of making a mountain out of a molehill.

In order to climb the ladder of *gyana*, you need to experience *vairagya* (detachment). Do not delay! Wake up now! Why are you lost in this magical world? You have forgotten yourself and due to ignorance, you are inflicting pain on yourself. You are responsible for your own miseries. We keep losing sleep over little things. This is all due to attachment to our body and mind. It is like Newton's law of gravitation that can never change. Whatever you throw up in the air must return to earth, owing to the principle of gravity. In the same way, *yogis* have evolved the fundamental principle: whosoever is deep into worldly attachments, can never ever live in peace or attain happiness.

Vairagya is the foundation of *sadhana* — in its absence you cannot proceed on the path of knowledge. Once you have disassociated your mind from the world, the mind will be still. The mind which is still and calm can grasp knowledge and then enlightenment is not far away.

Attributes like detachment, compassion, forgiveness and reflection have to be developed. *Sufis* have said, "Just as a woman without make-up is unable to attract the attention of her husband, in the same way, the mind that is not bedecked with the attributes of love and *vairagya*, shall not be able to please God. In order to meet our beloved God — the one who is beyond all shapes and attributes — you have to decorate the bridal chamber of your mind. This will create a power that will impel us to be re-united with him.

There was a great saint called Yaari Sahib. Not much is known about him, but whatever little he has written — not many of his writings are available — and whatever little I have read of him tells me that each and every word he has crafted is packed with

crystallized and distilled wisdom and *gyana*. As long as this longing is not born in the heart, this seed of *tattvagyana* will not find the right kind of soil for its fruition. One must prepare the soil, water it, add fertiliser and then plant the seeds. If you just scatter the seeds on the open land they will not grow.

The seeds of *gyana* will sprout in the mind which has been cleared of all desires; 'all' desires have been removed, the rubble of attachment has been removed and the mind has been watered with dispassion. The seeds then sown will definitely germinate and grow into a strong and healthy plant.

This body is perishable and you are imperishable. You are *drashta* — an observer of the body, mind, senses and objects of *samsara* too. But you have bartered away your freedom for petty and trivial pursuits and have thus become a slave of the mind. If you are born to be a master, then why not continue to be a master? Not only have we forgotten this fact, but have also forgotten that we are the master of all masters — God! Separated from God and mired in this ignorance, we continue to wallow in our misery and unhappiness.

A vital question arises: If I am the observer, then how come I forgot my true self? When and how did this ignorance enter my mind? It is very difficult to say exactly when this ignorance entered the mind. It is not easy to say on which day or date you fell into a state of ignorance. But this ignorance can certainly be dispelled. All right, I will give you an example. You tell me, when did I get this wristwatch that I am wearing? Can you tell me for how many days, weeks, months or years this watch has been in my possession? Did I buy it or was it gifted to me? Tell me? You wonder how you are supposed to know all this! After all, you came to know about it only when I mentioned it.

So you cannot really say for how long you have been ignorant about the watch. Still, it is possible to give you information about it — how this watch came to me, when it came, who brought it. Of course all this can be talked about. But do you have an answer to this question? Since when have you been ignorant about the watch? Once I give you the information about the watch, your ignorance ends. Similarly, when you attain *gyana*, then *agyana* is dispelled. So your emphasis should be on *gyana* alone.

I want you to fly across the skies, but you want to crawl on the earth like insects. Crawl if you must — well, that is your choice! Everyone is free to choose! I am teaching you how to be liberated, so that you experience the freedom of the skies, but you want to remain tied to this earth. I will go on talking to you, hammering your mind. Let us see how long you can remain ignorant.

My love for you is boundless. I can wait for you. Take your time. How long can you remain static? You have to wake up and see for yourself that your bondage is just an illusion.

CHAPTER 5

FROM DEHOHAM TO SHIVOHAM

There are three stages and three states in which you can be, or in which you are right now. And these are: *dehoham, jivoham* and *shivoham*. *Dehoham* means: 'I' am a body, 'I' am this body made of skin and bones and apart from it, I am nothing. Because 'I' am a body, therefore 'I' should eat, drink and keep this body happy — this is *Charvaka* philosophy that has been popular for ages. There is a sutra in *Charvaka* which says, 'Rinam Kritva Ghritam Pibet'. *Charvaka* says that even if you have to borrow *ghee* to satiate yourself, you should just go ahead and do it. You may or may not have the power to return the *ghee* to the person from whom you borrowed it. This statement reflects the epicurean philosophy: 'I' am only a body. This body is God. We must worship this God. All those who claim, "Eat, drink and be merry for tomorrow you may die," fall in the category of Charvaka's followers. All of them subscribe to the notion of *dehoham*.

If your understanding is that 'I' am only a body, then you will keep this body happy by feeding it properly and will savour all the flavours that your palate can relish; see all the good things with your eyes; listen to all the lilting tunes with your ears; experience all the lust you can. Why have only one woman or one man, why not go in for multiple partners? Anything and everything which can titillate your senses — is the stage of *dehoham*.

'I' am a body, and so the relationship with the body is superior to all other relationships. Whichever way it is possible, the body and senses must always be kept happy. The people who indulge in dishonest practices, are the people for whom money is a ticket to pleasure. So without blinking their eyes, they indulge in it, without any guilt. Only that person can accept a bribe and spend his ill-gotten money on his family, who regards himself as a mere body.

But the one who knows that even after this body perishes, the *jiva* — individual soul, shall continue to live on and that this *jiva* shall be reborn in another body and then shall have to repay for past deeds; he tries to remain eternally vigilant and alert. He does not do any wrong, at least not consciously. He neither earns money through wrongful means nor does he do any injustice to others. He takes good care of this body, knowing fully well that it is only through the body that he will be able to achieve great heights. He knows that his body is an asset entrusted to his care, through which he may be able to discover his real self. It is not a mode of self-gratification; it is not an end in itself. Body is a means, not an end.

Guru Nanak Sahib says in his works: Just as the *Hindus* consider eating beef a great sin and the *Muslims* regard even the thought of consuming pork a great sin, in the same way, spending money earned through dishonest means should be regarded as a great sin. If you are a *Hindu*, you should consider it to be equivalent to eating beef and if *Muslim*, then for you it should be equivalent to eating pork.

Guru Nanak Sahib says, "Do not spend money earned through dishonest means. How will you settle the account of the money you have earned thus?" One who regards himself only as a body is not prepared to listen to such words. He says, "Why should I bother about what will happen after my death? Who knows where we go after death? To *Dharamraj* — the God of death, or to someone else? Has anyone ever returned from the land of the dead to narrate his experiences? Has anyone ever received any communication from there?" People often weave a complex web of arguments around themselves. But the principles do not change. Or do they? You may or may not recognise them. If the laws of science are unalterable, then how can the regulations and principles of nature be subject to change? *Dehoham* — 'I' am merely a body, so I am perishable.

The story of my life began with the birth of this body and shall end with the death of this body. The person who believes that 'I' am no more than a mere body, often disregards all notions of good and bad. His philosophy is that if inflicting pain on others or depriving others of their rights contributes to his personal happiness, he should try and attain it anyway.

After *dehoham*, the second stage is *jivoham*. I am a *jiva*. What does *jiva* mean? *Jiva* means the self that is still under the layers of *koshah*. *Koshah* means a sheath and it is of five types: annamaya (physical body), pranamaya (cosmic energy), manomaya (mind-body), vigyanamaya (intellect or ego) and anandamaya (causal blissful body).

Now let us understand what a *jiva* is, in somewhat greater detail. You must pay attention to it. This is a very complex and subtle subject. You will not be able to grasp it very easily, so you need to be very alert and vigilant.

Let us presume that there is a pitcher full of water. When we keep it under the open sky at night, the reflection of the moon is seen in the water. Now, there are four things involved; the pitcher, the water, the reflection of the moon in the water and the moon in the sky. As long as the water is in the pitcher, the reflection of the moon will be seen in it. Once the pitcher breaks and the water flows out of it, the moon's reflection will no longer be visible. So the moon's reflection will only be visible as long as there is water in the pitcher. If the pitcher breaks, where do you think the moon's reflection will go? Where can it go? It will just not be visible any longer! So if it has to be visible, the essential pre-requisite is that there should be water in the pitcher. If the water is shaken the reflection also shakes. Now if the reflection is shaking, does it mean that the moon is also shaking? It makes absolutely no difference to the moon.

If you pour that water into another pitcher, what will happen? The other pitcher will begin to reflect the moon in the water. If you pour that water into a *surahi* (a narrow necked pot), you will be surprised to see that the same reflection is now visible in the *surahi* too, though it has a much smaller opening. You might wonder how the moon could enter this *surahi* which has such a small opening. But it is there all the same! The reflection of the moon is present there as well.

You can keep changing the pitchers. You can pour water into this one or that one; the reflection will always be there. If the pot changes, the nature of the reflection does not change. So this is how it goes, from pitcher to pitcher, from *surahi* to *surahi*, from *surahi* back to the pitcher and from the pitcher to the ever-flowing river.

Now, this reflection is floating in and out of these pitchers. If the pitcher is broken and somehow we manage to stop the flow of water and immediately pour it into another pitcher, the reflection remains unchanged. In the midst of all these changes taking place in the pots, the moon in the sky is still. It does not undergo any change. Have you been able to follow this? I will extend this analogy to help you understand better.

In this story our body is the pitcher. The water inside the pitcher is our subtle body which has as its constituents the mind, the senses, the intellect, the *prana*, the *chitta* and the ego. And the reflection you see in the water of that God-like moon is what we call *jiva*. The reflection of the moon is related and connected to the moon and not to the pitcher or the water. And what is the pitcher connected to? To the earth! And the reflection of the moon is connected to the moon in the sky.

Let us presume that while you were still looking at the reflection of the moon in the water, the clouds suddenly passed over and eclipsed the moon temporarily. Now reflect on this. Do the clouds pass over the moon or over your eyes? The clouds invariably cover your eyes. And your eyes are unable to see the moon. No cloud can ever dare to eclipse the moon. The clouds are far below the moon. When the reflection ceases to be visible, what do we say? That the reflection has died or that it has returned to the moon? The reflection neither dies nor does it go back to the moon. Similarly, our body is connected to the five elements and the individual mind is connected to the collective macro mind. **And *jiva* is connected to *Brahman*.**

Almost 95% people live in *dehoham* — they think and believe that they are only a body. They consider themselves to be just a

body and they die in that *dehoham bhava*. In every birth you have had a new body, but the same old mind, the same old *chitta* and the same old intellect.

Alright, now suppose that the reflection of the moon starts pondering over these questions: Where have I come from? What is my source? And some wise men try to explain that it is connected neither to the pitcher nor to the water but to the moon. If the reflection understands this, all its fears related to death will disappear and we can say that the reflection has got enlightenment! This is the whole process — you see yourself as a body and you fear death — *tattvagyana* removes this darkness and once this ignorance is dispelled, you surpass all fears. Once it has been realised that 'I' never dies because 'I' is the reflection of that which never dies, then all fears die. As long as the moon is in the sky, its reflection will stay. As long as the kingdom of *Brahman* is intact, the kingdom of *jiva* shall also remain intact. In order to wipe out the kingdom of *jiva*, first the kingdom of *Brahman* has to be wiped out. But that kingdom is simply imperishable.

So what is the *swaroopa* of *jiva*? *Jiva* is imperishable, yet conditioned by time. *Jiva* has no power of its own. But *jiva* is time-bound and has limited powers in comparison to *Ishwar*, but like God, *jiva* too is imperishable and is truth.

If you stand in front of the mirror, your reflection will be cast in it. Your reflection in the mirror is conditional and remains there as long as the mirror is there. If the mirror breaks, you will not be broken. In the same way, the reflection of the moon is seen in the pitcher of water. And the reflection is of course inseparable from its source. If this truth remains unknown to the reflection, then it will keep crying all the time.

Due to *avidya* (ignorance), the reflection often begins to identify itself with the pitcher. It begins to believe that 'I am this pitcher'. And sometimes it identifies with the water too. Due to ignorance, *jiva* identifies itself with the body. But know this well, that when the body dies, 'you' do not die. The one who is in *dehoham bhava* always says, "When the body dies, I also die." But the fact is that even though death has happened to your body, 'you' do not die. The body dies, but you live on. During sleep there is a temporary death of the mind. The mind does not think or dream about anything in deep sleep. In the same way, 'you' experience temporary death when the body dies. When you are in a deep sleep, do you realise where you are — at home, in *Rishikesh*, Delhi, Mumbai, Ahmedabad or Pune?

While commenting on memory, I had told you that our *samskaras* (deep impressions) live at the bottom of our subconscious and unconscious mind. In our sleep, we lose the consciousness of our beliefs and convictions, as in this state our mind and intellect also suspend their operations temporarily. But in that state 'you' are still there. 'You' do not wither away. That is why, wise people have drawn this parallel between sleep and death. Sleep is similar to death; it's very close to the experience of death.

If someone dies in his sleep, the family members will not even know what has happened till they try to wake him up. What is death? Death is the separation of the subtle body from the gross material body. To put it in the language of *koshah*, death is the separation of the vigyanamaya, manomaya and pranamaya *koshah* from the annamaya *koshah*.

In other words, the jiva's position is transferable. The *jiva* regards each 'body' given to him as his own or as an expression of his 'I-ness', which is essentially foolish. He begins to own the home he is born into. All the awakened ones have the same thing to say: This body is neither yours nor mine. 'I' am a body — this is a statement that reflects total ignorance. *Jivoham* is the state of those people who have some degree of interest in religious matters. They know that this journey will continue even after this body dies. Your journey was there before death and will continue after death. 'I' was there before death and 'I' will remain. Everything else will be left behind.

So *jivoham* is the second stage. When this stage comes, the *jiva* starts contemplating: So who sired me in the first place? *Paramatma* is my source, and 'I' am his reflection. Then he starts worshipping. It is only in the *Jivabhava* that the worship of God really begins. Devotion takes place between *jiva* and God. Love is the binding factor; all major works of saints are based on devotion.

Out of a hundred thousand *Vedic mantras*, nearly eighty

thousand deal with the *karmakanda* i.e. how the Gods and Goddesses have to be placated, how they have to be worshipped. Why is it so? Why should there be eighty thousand *mantras* dealing with the *karmakanda*? This is interesting. How come such a huge volume of *mantras* is devoted to rites and rituals alone? The reason is that there are a large number of *Hindus* who are living at the level of the body. They know neither about *satsang* nor meditation. They do not even go to a *guru* and listen to his *gyana*. For them religion is all about wish fulfillment alone. They have no interest in knowledge, peace or *samadhi*. This higher wisdom is beyond the capacity of many humans who live obsessed with their body and senses. They worry only about their physical gratification. Out of the twenty thousand *mantras* left, sixteen thousand are for worshipping different deities. These *mantras* teach us how to concentrate on the deities.

Most of these *mantras* talk about the means and methods of purification of the mind. Devotion is the perfect path to teach the mind to be more introverted and concentrated. There are only four thousand *mantras* on *tattvagyana*. *Tattvagyana* is the only one that gives us rare insights into life by opening our third eye. The realisation of the true self is *shivoham*. On realising that 'I' am *Shiva*, the reflection says, "I am neither a pitcher nor water." In the *Atmashatakam*, Shankaracharya's sutras resonate this very truth — 'I' am not mind, 'I' am not intellect, 'I' am not *chitta* and 'I' am not body.

Jivatman is a combination of two elements: *antehkaran* (mind, *chitta*, *ahankara*, intellect) and *atman*. The existence of *jivatman* is a falsehood, the way the reflection in the water is an illusion. Once we cut through this sheath of ignorance with *gyana*, once we break the myth of jivatman's existence, once we step out of this falsehood, then all we are left with is the pure soul. And this pure soul is *Shiva*. This third stage is *shivoham*.

So far you regarded yourself as a body and believed: 'I' am a body. Even if you join me in reciting 'shivoham, shivoham', you will not move into that state automatically. Unless you elevate yourself from the physical level, how will you enter into *atmabhava*? Only if you see yourself as separate from the mind, *prana* and body will you be able to experience the *bhava*: 'I' am Shivaroopa. It cannot happen only at the intellectual level. It has to be experienced, lived.

I am going to respond to a question sent to me. The question is: We understand how we are all a part of *Ishwar*, but we do not understand how we are *Ishwar* ourselves. If this is true then who should we worship? Who do we contemplate on? Who should we pray to? All this is very confusing. We had come to learn about devotion and prayer, but you say, "You are *Bhagwan*." Now what do we do?

Try to understand this very carefully! As long as you regard yourself as a *jiva*, you cannot understand *shivoham*. There is no doubt that *jiva* and *Ishwar- jiva* means reflection in the mind and *Ishwar* means reflection in the collective mind-are two separate entities. *Jiva* and *Ishwar* cannot become one. *Atman* and *Brahman* are one but not *jiva* and *Ishwar*. As long as you are trapped in the sense of being a *jiva*, the *Ishwar* element too is there — and duality shall persist for they are different. *Ishwar* is one — omnipotent, all powerful. *Jiva* are many, has no power and is an ignoramus.

Let us take the example of a drop and an ocean. *Ishwar* is the ocean and *jiva* a drop. But both are forms of water. Now you do not know what to do. You are trapped in your form, in your individuality and then you wonder, "How can I be an ocean?" If you are trapped by your sense of being a drop, how can you ever become an ocean? A single drop is not the ocean but both are made of water. Water is the one common factor in the drop and in the ocean. You cannot bathe in a drop, but hundreds of elephants can in the ocean. If we compare the forms of the ocean and the drop, then they are different. But if we see the water in them, it is the same. The drop has to give up its limited view of being a drop, only then will it know what it really is. In the same way, the *jiva* will have to elevate itself from being a mere *jiva*. Only then will it be able to enter into the *bhava* of Shivaroopa.

There are three paths in Indian philosophy: *bhaktimarga*, *Yogamarga* and *gyanamarga*. Now what is *bhaktimarga*? Worshipping *Rama*, *Krishna*, *Shiva*, *Durga* and other Gods and Goddesses; reciting *mantras* to propitiate them, remembering them; visiting their pilgrimage centres — are all different methods of the *bhaktimarga. Bhaktimarga* purifies our heart and soul. What does *yoga* do? *Yoga* teaches the eight-fold path of *yam, niyama, asana, pranayama, pratyahaar*, dhaarna, *dhyana* and *samadhi*. This is a methodological path of evolution. *Yoga* means joining of *Shakti* and *Shiva*. The major focus is on preparing the mind for *dhyana* (meditation). *Yama* and *niyama* are the ethos of life which prepare the base for pratyahara, that is withdrawal of the senses — which on its maturity becomes *dharana* (concentration). Dharana's completion is in *dhyana* — it is only in the state of *dhyana* that the mind achieves a degree of purity and now it can understand the secrets of gyana's dictum — 'I' am *Brahman*.

Now, these are the experiences of the *jiva*: You are a lamp and I am a wick, you are a forest and I am a peacock, you are the moon and I am a *chakor*. This relationship between the two is the product of *Jivabhava*. Duality is the basis of the devotional path. There have to be two between whom this transaction takes place — one is God and the other is the soul. And then prayer begins; prayer cannot happen in Brahmanbhava as in it there are no two entities. And when there are no two, then who will pray to whom? This game of prayer cannot happen in the non-dualistic stage. That is the reason why I say that the awakened one does not pray. To whom will he pray? In the *Ramayana* there is this beautiful analogue:

Jiva is an inseparable part of Ishwar and is imperishable
Conscious, pure and naturally happy
But when Jiva becomes a captive of Maya
He scampers around like an impish monkey

I have already told you that in the *bhaktimarga*, the entire play is of the inter-relationship of *jiva* and *Ishwar*, where *jiva* is small and *Ishwar* is great. *Jiva* beseeches *Ishwar*, "I am nothing without you lord, you are my God and saviour. We make mistakes, every day we commit sins, but you keep forgiving us. You have a pure heart and soul." All these couplets that I am reciting here are of *Jivabhava* and not of *atmabhava*.

Bhaktimarga, the path of love, is nothing but prayers and wooing God, thinking that God is different from us and he is the protector and creator of this world. In the *gyanamarga* — the path of wisdom — *jiva* removes the wall of ignorance through *gyana*. He understands that 'I' and 'God' are not two different things but one.

It is the same as the drop realising that it is not different from the ocean. The same water that is in the ocean is in the drop too. When the drop awakens to this understanding, then we say that it has entered into the zone of truth. As long as the drop says, "I am a mere drop and you are the ocean", *Jivabhava* persists.

In the state of *dehoham*, no spiritual prospects are sought, so involution is not possible. We can say that it is the lowest rung in the spiritual ladder and millions of people live and die in this very ignorant state; never going deep within the heart, never seeking the truth of the self and always thinking of the mortal body.

Blessed are those who move on the path of devotion, on the *bhaktimarga*. In the practice of this path, you learn that you are not a body but a *jiva*. In the state of devotion, he says out of love, "Hey *Prabhu*, O lord! You alone can save me! Hey *Prabhu*! Help me move from darkness to light." There is a beautiful *shloka* in the *Vedas*:

Asatoma sadgamaya
Tamso ma jyotirgamaya
Mrityorma amritamgamaya

From falsehood to truth; from darkness to enlightenment and from death to immortality — lead thou me on.

Devotion and meditation cleanse and purify the mind, whereas the practice of *yoga* helps it attain a high degree of concentration. Only that mind is worthy of hearing *tattvagyana* that is pure and focused. *Tattvagyana* gives you the knowledge: 'I' am not a body, 'I' am not *jiva*, 'I' am atmanswaroopa — and this *atman* is nothing but *Shiva*.

Now the problem that most people face is that they are not even able to understand themselves, then how can they be expected to understand the difference between *jiva* and *Ishwar*. Tell me what if the pitcher starts saying, "How do I re-establish my relationship with the soil?" You tell me, what should the pitcher do? Should it worship the soil? Should it sing 'Soil! Soil! Soil!'? Will its connection

with the soil be re-established? No, this is not required at all. You just have to remind it, "O pitcher, you are made of the soil, you can never ever be separated from the soil!"

What about the shape of the pitcher, is it true or false? It is false! The potter pounds the soil with a stick, mixes some water with it, kneads it and then gives it shape. This shape can always be changed. Regardless of what shape you may choose to give it, it remains what it essentially is — a part of the soil.

I will give you a different example. What should a gold ornament do to establish its relationship with gold? Do push-ups or *pranayama*? What should it do? It needs to do nothing of the sort. The ornament simply has to be told that it is gold! All it has to do is to wipe out the thought that it is just an ornament and is different from gold.

In the same way, what should a *jiva* do to be re-united with *Brahman*? Well nothing! *Jiva* is already *Brahman*. But *jiva* will understand that 'I am *Brahman*', only if it is able to rise above its own limitations. Otherwise it is not likely to understand this reality. It will know only when it rises beyond its ignorance.

I have already said that seventy or rather eighty percent of the religious scriptures enunciate the *bhaktimarga* — whether it is the *Qur'an*, the Bible, or the *Gurbani* — verses of *Guru Granth Sahib*, the *Gita*, or the *Ramayana*. But these scriptures have a fair amount of *tattvagyana*. The general readers do not have the vision to understand the higher knowledge, hence they are not able to recognise the real gems which are hidden in them.

Kabir says:

**Hum tum beech bhayo nahi koi
Jinka pyara bahar hai,
bhatakte dar-ba-dar phirte
Hamara pyara hami mein hai,
humko dar-ba-dar jane se kya?**

Now, nothing stands between the two of us. Only those people wander about in the world whose beloved is in a far off place. But my beloved is in me, why would I wander here or there? For those who think that their loved one is far off, let them wait. But

99

my beloved is right here, why should I wait for even a second to meet my beloved? When the *Brahman* is present in my own *atman*, then what should I do to meet God? All I need to do is to understand the *gyana* that the *guru* imparts and realise that my lord and I are one.

Now the next *shloka*:

Na me dweshraagou na me lobhamohoh
Mado neiva me neiva maatsaryabhaavah
Na dharmo na chaartho na kaamo na mokshah
Chidaanandroopah shivoham shivoham

I wish to say this once again: What kind of a mind is able to receive this *gyana*? The mind that fulfills two conditions — it should be free of all garbage i.e. desires; it should not be restless. Now, it is for you to peep inside your heart and see whether or not your mind fulfills these conditions.

Na me dweshraagou na me lobhamohoh — Raga means possessiveness, the urge to own. *Dvesha* is jealousy, *lobh* is greed and *moh* is attachment. And all these happen in the mind. The question arises, why do these negative emotions arise in the mind? And the answer is: because the mind is looking for joy and mistakenly thinks that it can be attained by sensual gratification alone. You are jealous of all those people who have things which you believe can give great pleasure. You wish to have all those things which can give you joy. Therefore the rat race begins and once you attain the things which give you pleasure, you associate yourself with those things. This is attachment and it gives rise to possessiveness. You begin to hate those people who somehow come between you and the object of gratification. Attachment, lust, greed and jealousy are all inter-related. The root cause of all this is *avidya* (ignorance). The day you learn the eternal truth from the master — that all things are temporal, mortal and perishable, your focus changes. Your gestalt of thinking changes, you begin to reflect upon the self and realise that 'I' am not the body, the mind or the senses and you begin to cultivate awareness from that day onwards. As the mind turns inwards to the self, the external race of the mind ends and the desire to possess diminishes. Now, why would *raag*, *dvesha*,

lobh and *moh* bother such a mind — one that is not seeking joy from anyone or anything? Attachment and hate cannot defile a mind which is illumined. The fascinating truth is that even when the mind was polluted, the self was beyond all impurities.

Shankaracharya says, "'I' has no *raag, dvesha, lobh* or *moh*." When he says this, he is not speaking about himself alone. He is saying that all of you are also free of *raag, dvesha, lobh* and *moh*, but you do not seem to understand this fact because you are not aware of the distinction between 'you' and the 'mind'. Whatever is happening to your 'mind' is being misunderstood as happening to 'you'. It is a strange kind of identity crisis that you are facing.

An identity crisis is the dilemma you are facing. I was reading about the time when the World Cup Football tournament had just got over. It had generated a strange kind of mania all around the world. India too went through some of it, though it wasn't all that strong here. When England was playing, some fifty thousand spectators had come to watch. People cheered only for the team they had immense attachment and affection for. David Beckham is an extremely popular British player. He is so popular that a couple of weeks back, when he was taken ill, the Queen herself went to pray for his speedy recovery saying, "He is a hero of our country. He should get well soon. The World Cup is approaching." Those people almost worship David Beckham, just the way they worship Sachin Tendulkar in India. For cricket-lovers he is almost a God.

When a cricket match is on between India and Pakistan, all Indians turn into die-hard patriots. And if by chance India loses the match, cricket lovers get depressed and dejected. They tend to feel that the defeat of their team is their personal defeat, and their team's victory too would mean a personal victory.

If it is Sachin Tendulkar who is declared the man of the match, he gets some five-ten lakhs into the bargain. And sitting there you feel ecstatic, even though you do not get a single dime. You light crackers and distribute sweets. Why? It is an identity problem. You unknowingly associate yourself with players, actors and politicians. Their defeat is your defeat and their victory is your victory. It was indeed surprising when India lost one of the matches and two or three youngsters just went ahead and killed themselves!

This is how we too have created an identity problem for ourselves. We are not the mind but we regard ourselves as the mind. The association is so deep-rooted that it seems difficult to see the fact that the mind is just a tool. Why? Because we look upon ourselves as a body and a mind. The upshot of all this is that the body changes and so does the mind. A child's body is growing every second and an adult's body is decaying every second. The child grows into a young man and then into an old man, who is first healthy and then becomes ill. Once you understand this, you begin to see the body as 'the other' and not as 'I'. Now, if the body is ill, you feel and say, 'I am ill'. Once you break this wall, you will feel that the body is ill and it is not you but the body which is suffering the illness. If you are separate from this body, then tell me, are you young or old? If you are not the body, then you are neither young nor old. You are beyond the body, beyond the senses and beyond the mind.

All these differences lie at the bottom of the mind. The mind has been conditioned to believe that you are a *Sikh*, a *Hindu*, a *Buddhist*, a Jain or a Christian and once you alienate yourself from the mind, then you drop all these labels and experience a new kind of freedom. If you do not consider all these labels of caste, religion and language, they drop off in a split second. 'I' am not the mind — then the joy and sorrow experienced are also not mine. 'I' am only a witness. Attachment and hostility, greed and affection — every feeling occurs within the periphery of the mind.

Once you understand this, you gradually begin to climb the ladder of spiritual growth. You start with the thought that 'I' am not a body and slowly, with the power of observation, you begin to see the difference between the mind and the self. Whatever conflict of interest you had with others, whatever hostility you nurtured in your effort to provide more pleasures to your body, slowly begins to loose its meaning.

If you are not a body, then why would you have any fear? All fears drop! Then there is a perfect balance in your actions and thoughts. Then you eat just enough to satiate your hunger. This seems surprising, but yes, people eat for all the wrong reasons. They are unhappy, so they eat. Their eating is for the mind and

not for the body. It is the mind which is empty, but they fill their stomachs. This is the root cause of obesity, which is spreading like an epidemic in developed countries. People are starved in their minds but do not realise this. To get a sense of fulfillment they fill their stomachs. So you need to understand the difference between eating food to satiate hunger and eating food for emotional fulfillment. Be vigilant when you eat. Enjoy every morsel, see the food, taste it, smell it and relish it with all the five senses. Once you adopt this new style of eating, you will eat less and you will eat light food. As a result your body will be healthy, fit and energetic.

Mr Singh's wife said one evening, "It is raining and I am dying to eat *samosas*." Mr Singh said, "All the roads are waterlogged. Where will I get *samosas* for you? My scooter will stall in the water." She said, "I do not know all that. Why did you marry me if you cannot even get me *samosas*?" The husbands who preen around twirling their moustaches in the world outside, lower their moustache the moment they enter their home. After all, the wives wield a lot of clout. Poor fellow went out in the rain to buy *samosas*. Half way through, his scooter broke down. He was stranded in the middle of the road with the drivers of cars, buses and trucks constantly honking, as though to say, "If your scooter was not in a working condition, why did you leave home at all?" All kinds of abuses rained down on him. He dragged his old scooter through the dingy streets and reached the shop. On reaching there he realised that the *samosas* had already been sold out! He had to wait for a good hour or so. Finally, after an hour he got the *samosas*. His wife was very pleased and eating them, she said, "Aha! Now I am at peace! Mr Singh you are such a wonderful person." Peace was conditional. This time it was food, next time it will be something else. And after that, still something else. There is absolutely no guarantee of peace and happiness as long as there are conditions.

You tend to lay down conditions in your mind. Only if I get this will I be happy. Only if I marry that man or woman will I be happy. It is a fact that these very conditions give you turmoil and suffering. These desires are deeply ingrained in your *chitta*. Often in your effort to give pleasure to your body, you hurt yourself and others, as you are willing to go to any length to satisfy your desires.

Tulsi Das was so overpowered by the desire to make love to his wife that he left home on a dark stormy night. Fearing that if he entered the house of his in-laws from the main gate, people may gossip, he chose instead to climb the wall of the backyard to go to the rooftop. You must have heard of a rope being mistaken for a serpent, but here he mistook a serpent for a rope and climbed up. Waking up his sleeping wife, he said, "Look, I have come all this way only for you." The sexual urge was so deeply etched in his *chitta* that he wanted to get pleasure from his wife's body. The body is just a bag of skin and bones. But lust makes you see the body as wonderful. Seeing her husband entering her parent's house in this manner, Tulsi's wife was irritated. She yelled, "You say you love me so much. If only you had such fiery love for God, you would have become a saint by now." This insult changed him forever. Well! Indeed no man can take an insult from his wife anyway.

There are three states — *dehoham*, *jivoham* and *shivoham*. As long as you do not go beyond the confinements of this mind, you will not be able to understand *shivoham*. Right now, you are in the state of *dehoham*, but you have to reach the state of *shivoham*. From body to self, it seems like a short journey, but in reality it is a long path, a really long one. This *tattvagyana* is somewhat like doing your post-graduation. I know very well that most of you are still at the nursery level, only a few have made some progress.

My effort so far has been to facilitate your passage from *dehoham* to *jivoham*. Whatever you see in this whole world is not true. Nothing belongs to you and this body is not yours. Your connection is only with *Paramatma*, so you should look for *Paramatma*. *Paramatma* does not mean God, but truth. I conclude every time on this very note, so that I can ignite the fire in your heart; so that I can awaken the urge to seek what is beyond this transitory world.

It is this urge in your heart, though mild in nature, which has actually brought you so far. But the question is, are you at peace with yourself? Whatever little restlessness was there inside you, has only increased and not lessened after listening to my discourse. This restlessness alone will pave the way for you to the path of self discovery. It is this urge that made you think, and has finally brought you here as well.

Now when I see you ready to commence this journey, why won't I tell you everything that I know for sure is as true as pure gold? Why will I keep any secrets from you? Look, *Arjuna* was standing in front of *Krishna* and crying. He was crying out for attachment and love. Then *Krishna* had to explain to him the difference between *kshetra* and *Kshetragya*. "Hey *Arjuna*! This mind, body and senses are the *kshetra* — the observed and you are the *Kshetragya* — the observer." He also explained what it means to be a witness or a spectator and that this world is nothing but a spectacle, that the mind, senses and the body and the whole world are also spectacles. And you who watch this spectacle is a *drashta* — a seer.

Arjuna asked him questions and *Krishna* provided the answers, expounding on the different paths of knowing the truth — *gyana*, *yoga* and *bhaktimarga*. If in one chapter of the *Bhagavad Gita*, he expounds on the *tattvagyana*, in another he tells us how to be initiated into the process of *yoga*. In short, the quality of the guru's sermon is directly linked to the nature of the disciple's curiosity. Even in the *Upanishads*, the sermon of '*tatvamasi*' is encoded. The *guru* explains that *tat* means reality, *Brahman* and *tvam* means you. Now, this *tvam* does not mean body or mind but the individual self — *jiva*, and *tvam* is not God but *Brahman*. The seers of the *Upanishads* state that you must rise above *jiva* and know that this pure consciousness is your real roopa. If you were to take away the godliness from *avatars* or whomever you refer to as *Ishwar*, say *Rama* or *Krishna*, they too will be left with pure consciousness. Ultimately you have to come to the realisation that you are just the way *Shiva* is. *Shankar*, *Krishna* and *Rama* are all similar to what you are. There is absolutely no difference in the core. Whatever difference is there is at the level of the mind and not in the *atman*. Now, this is something really profound. I am not even hoping that you will be able to understand it in a single sitting. You need to listen repeatedly. You need to meditate over it. Only then will the mystery unravel.

What really happens is that when I am explaining something, you just catch one thing and then your mind starts mulling over it. In the meanwhile you lose the thread of what I am saying and miss a great deal. Listening to a discourse too is an art. Everything is an art; to cook in the kitchen is an art; and so is singing or playing a musical instrument. Creating a musical composition is as much of an art as listening to it or appreciating it. It is not possible for everyone to enjoy classical music.

Once a very well known musician was singing raga *bhairavi*, during a musical evening. He had just about started the *alaap*, when a villager sitting at the back started crying. The person next to him asked, "Why are you crying?" He said, "This fellow is going to die very soon." "What do you mean?" He said, "My buffalo cried like this for two hours before she died. When this fellow started making all kinds of weird sounds I was reminded of my buffalo. I am feeling sorry for this singer. And I am surprised that no one in the crowd seems to be worried about it. They are all sitting and cheering him. He is dying and they are cheering him."

So it is an art to sit through an evening of classical music and appreciate its nuances. In the same way, it is an art to listen to *tattvagyana*. Sometimes people think that I am really a very harsh *guru*. Well, I simply expect total attention and nothing less. Is that too much to ask? The truth is that if a person knows something very precious, he does his best to pass it on to those he loves.

Let me tell you a little incident from the life of *Mullah Nasruddin*, an amazing *fakir*. There are many stories connected with his life and many more of a purely speculative nature, have been added to that repertoire by different orators and writers. But what I am going to tell you is a true incident. *Mullah Nasruddin* once told his son, "Get hold of a bottle and go and buy mustard oil from the market!" His son picked up the bottle and as he was about to leave, *Mullah* called him back. He said, "Just put that bottle aside." *Mullah* got up, walked across to his son and gave him four stinging slaps. His son started crying. His wife came rushing in and asked, "What happened all of a sudden?" The son complained through his tears, "I think my father has gone crazy. He has thrashed me without any rhyme or reason." His wife questioned *Mullah*, "Why did you beat our son?" *Mullah* said, "Look, our son was carrying this glass bottle to fetch oil. If he had dropped it on the way and broken it, all the oil would have spilt. Later it would not serve any purpose to reprimand him. That is why I decided to slap him well in advance. Now this slap will keep him on a tight leash. Now if he were to run into any of his friends or classmates, he will not pay much attention to them. Now this fool will go straight to the market and come back straight home." Do you understand what I am trying to say? I am *Mullah Nasruddin* and you are the son. Before I hand over this bottle of *gyana* to you, shouldn't I do something?

This *tattvagyana* is such a supreme form of knowledge that in order to know it, sometimes the disciple has to spend years and years together in the *ashram* of his *guru*. The disciple serves the *guru* with all his heart and soul and even offers his being to the *guru*. Service cleanses and purifies the mind. When he lives in close proximity to the *guru*, he does his *sadhana* everyday. This practice prepares him to light the lamp of knowledge in his heart.

Now understand that in *tattvagyana*, there is no provision for worshipping deities like *Rama, Krishna, Shiva* or *Durga*. All the scriptures of *tattvagyana* say that there is only one *Ishwar* for the disciple and that is his *guru*. That is it! It is in the *guru* that you instill the *brahmabhava*. It is in the *guru* that you discover the *Vishnubhava* and it is in the *guru* that you find the *Shankarbhava*. In other words, when the *guru* bequeaths the sutras of knowledge to us with affection, he is Brahma. When the *guru* corrects our mistakes and helps us understand them, he is *Vishnu*. When the *guru* is harsh on us and reprimands us over something, then he dons the *rudraroopa* of *Shiva*.

Here I am discussing *gyanamarga*. The *bhaktimarga* recommends the worship of *Shiva, Rama* or *Krishna*. But you must remember another thing. *Arjuna* was a devotee of *Krishna*, then how did he shake off his ignorance? Only when *Krishna* became his *guru* and *Arjuna* listened to the *tattvagyana* from him, that his attachment, his ignorance and his inner sorrow were dispelled.

Come to think of it, if the *guru* dies before you are able to ingest the *gyana* he is imparting, then your journey will be incomplete. That is what happened to *Shabri*. Her *guru* was on his deathbed when he said, "Do not worry! *Sri Rama* shall complete the work that I am leaving unfinished, *Rama* will guide you further." So *Shabri* kept waiting, and *Rama* finally came to her. Just see, she had no definite idea as to when or on which day or date he would come. So everyday she would sweep her house clean, gather flowers and arrange them in a basket for he may come today or he may come tomorrow. Patiently, she kept waiting.

That was the time when *rishis* and sages lived in *ashrams*. Renouncing the world, a disciple would sit at the feet of the *guru*, and that too with the *bhava* that as long as he does not step out of *dehoham* and step into *shivoham*, his ignorance would not dissolve. The disciple would pray, "*Gurudev*, I cannot rest until I have attained the state which will liberate me." The disciple would serve his master so that his mind attained purification.

Another question comes up. Someone has asked who we should meditate on? The *sadhaks* of the *gyanamarga* do not need to concentrate on any external image. The fact is that I am helping you rise above the form of your body too. What I am telling you is that you are not a body. Then what form would I recommend for your *dhyana*? You must have understood by now that when I initiate you into *dhyana*, the first stage is always that of prayer. While offering the prayer to the master, seek his or her blessings. In the initial stages you can focus on the guru's form, but once you enter into the process of *dhyana*, then you only have to concentrate on your breath or on the sound of your breath. As your mind calms down, the need to focus on the face or body of the *guru* will wane.

Come out of this body orientation. If your body is an illusion then isn't the body of an *avatar* or a *guru* also an illusion? Does consciousness have a form? None whatsoever. In the *Bhagavad Gita*, *Krishna* says, "Hey *Arjuna*! I am unmanifested." Unmanifested is something that we cannot see with our naked eyes. *Krishna* says, "I am the unmanifested one, but people around me think that I am no more than a body. But the truth of the matter is that whatever you see on the outside is not the real me."

In order to ingest this *gyana* you must observe three things. That it is not possible for you to understand this *gyana* easily. That the journey of rising from the state of *dehoham* to a state of *shivoham* is a long and arduous one. I can say this with a definite degree of certainty, because I know that if you are a very committed *sadhak*

you would have reached some place by now. And that you have to work very hard to snap off all the chains of the mind. Here your old chains are snapped off and there you go forging new ones!

The biggest rope that you have tied around your neck is that of attachment to the body and this sense of oneness with your mind. As long as you do not snap off this rope, you will not be able to enter the state of *shivoham*.

When *Krishna* left for Mathura, the *gopis* were crying. Sometimes the *gopis* would think of *Krishna* and say, "I am your *gopi* and you are my sweet *Krishna*." This *dhyana*, this memory continued in their minds all the time. While thinking of him, sometimes they would feel a oneness with *Krishna* to such an extent, that they would say, "I am *Krishna*." This is the highest form of love — it is the apotheosis of love — where the lover and the beloved become one, merging into one another.

When the pangs of love rose in the heart of *Radha*, even she cried her heart out. While crying, she suddenly rose above the limited mind and entered deep into love. As soon as *Radha* rose above *Jivabhava* and entered into *atmabhava*, she said, "I myself am *Krishna*. *Krishna* is not different from me. I am *Krishna*." Once this *gyana* dawned on her, *Radha* picked up Krishna's crown and placed it on her head. While going away, he had left his flute with her saying, "Now without you, I am never going to play it again." The moment *Radha* put the flute to her lips, all the *gopis* started looking at her with intense love and she seemed to be not *Radha* but *Krishna*. All of them worshipped her, not as *Radha* but as *Krishna*. It is the apotheosis of *bhaktimarga* that a *jiva* begins to regard himself as an inseparable part of his *Ishwar*.

But in *gyanamarga*, we first elevate ourselves from *Jivabhava*. We employ a method called 'neti neti', which means, 'not this, not this'. When we feel with conviction that 'I' am not the mind, 'I' am not the intellect, 'I' am not *chitta*, 'I' am not *ahankara*, then we are able to rise above the *Jivabhava* and enter the *shivabhava*. Once you look at the mind with *drashta bhava*, then you will start living in the state of: 'I' am not a body, 'I' am not the mind. Let us suppose your name is Santosh. Suppose someone says, "Santosh! Those relatives of yours were abusing you." Now if Santosh regards herself as a body, then she will immediately start fighting. But if somehow Santosh has realised that 'I' am not a body — the one that other people recognise — then they haven't really insulted me. In order to insult me, they first have to know who 'I' am. In order to know who 'I' am, they will have to know who they are themselves. And if they were to know themselves, they would discover that they are *Satyaswaroopa atman*. And that I too am *Satyaswaroopa atman*. Then who will criticise whom? Who will speak ill of whom? But the person who has overcome this dehobhava, this sense of being just mind-intellect and has entered the atmanbhava, proclaims:

Mado neiva me neiva maatsaryabhaavah

I neither have arrogance nor jealousy of any kind in me

**Na dharmo na chaartho na kaamo na mokshah
Chidaanandroopah shivoham shivoham**

Dharma, artha, *kama* and *moksha* are the desired goals of every human being. Everyone is seeking artha — wealth, and *dharma* — the fundamental rule of life. Everyone is looking for desire fulfillment and everyone should seek liberation i.e. *moksha*. But these goals defined by the sages are applicable to the mind. These rules do not apply to the self. It is the intellect that is afflicted with ignorance and it is the intellect again that experiences illumination. It is the intellect that slides into bondage and it is the intellect that liberates us from all bondage.

'I' the *atman* is forever, unattached, always free and eternal. 'I' neither enters into any bondage nor does it seek liberation from that bondage. This freedom is not accessible at the level of jivoham. I am repeating this again, there are three stages: *dehoham*, *jivoham* and *shivoham*. In this *Atmashatakam*, Shankaracharya is talking about the real self which is pure, virginal and an expansive existence. Time and again he nullifies the ignorance that 'I' am a body, senses, mind or ego.

Your pure 'I' is *anandaswaroopa*. Joy and sorrow happen in the mind and not in the self. Is it not amazing that you are *anandaroopa* and yet you do not even know it! This is what I am trying to tell you. That you do not have to go anywhere in the quest for happiness.

Once you go deep into yourself, descend into your own *swaroopa*, you will find endless joy (*ananda*) within you.

When you sit in meditation, you feel elated, peaceful and joyous. This *ananda* is your own, because in a state of meditation, your mind reaches a zero-point. When your mind is thoughtless, *ananda* begins to manifest itself. But if you have an insatiable longing for joy from the outer world, then it becomes a source of sorrow and suffering. My *swaroopa* is *ananda*. And if I live in memory of this, if I am conscious of what I am and how I act, then no sorrow can ever afflict my mind.

A lady wrote to me saying that she was very upset as she had lost her brother in an accident. Another lady who had come from Hyderabad was crying bitterly. Initially I did not quite understand what she was saying as she was talking through her tears. She was crying and all of a sudden she started banging her head on the floor. I said, "Stop her or else her head will split wide open!" People are really melodramatic! Once she had calmed down a bit, she told me, "I got a phone call yesterday. My mother has expired." Now that she had to leave for home she was crying. Only if she had understood the profound truth that all bodies are meant to die, then even in this state she would not have lost control over her mind.

Know this well, if 'I' am not a body, then who is your mother, who is your father, who is your brother and who is your sister? Reflect on this. It is only because you have wrapped yourself up in these false relationships that they tie you down — quite unnecessarily. If you shake off this *agyana*, then no bonds of affection or attachment shall disturb you.

When do the bonds of love and affection disturb you? Now I will tell you why we often feel sad. When you attach 'I' to the body and the mind, you will undoubtedly feel sad sometimes and happy at other times. Break this habit and be free of all emotional upheavals.

You are different from the garden of these five elements, you are the divine light and you are immortal, eternal and imperishable. Only the body perishes, only the body dissolves into nothingness; 'you' do not. Someone has sent a query to this effect. Did Ramakrishna Paramhans see *Kali* in the gross or in the subtle form? He saw *Kali* in the subtle form. It was his mind which was projecting the image. Have you ever heard that a Christian meditator saw *Kali* or that a *Muslim* saw *Krishna*? All visions are projections of the mind. For the person who is seeing the vision, the image is as true as your dream images are. Had he seen her in the gross form, then along with him others would also have seen her. He saw her only in the subtle form. It was his own mind which had created the image of *Kali*. This was the image lying latent in his mind, embedded in his manomaya *koshah*. The moment an optimum level of concentration is achieved, you begin to see what you want to see. It was Ramakrishna's mind which created the image of *Kali*.

If you keep reciting 'Shyam', and if Shyam were to appear in response to your recitations, then what will happen? Repeat '*Krishna-Krishna*' and at the most you will have a vision of *Krishna* — nothing more than that. Well, *Arjuna* could see him all the time and yet he was trapped in the vicious cycle of attachment. He shed his attachment only when *Krishna* gave him *tattvagyana*.

This *tattvagyana* is the same *gyana* that *Krishna* gave to *Arjuna*. If you wish to make a detour, do so by all means. If you wish to have visions and *darshans* of deities, please follow the path of *bhakti*. And sometime, whenever you are ready, your mind will project whichever image you wish to see. But how long will this image stay? Soon it will go! Our mind cannot remain still for very long. Then you will cry, "I want to see it again." And this will go on and on until one day the knowledge will dawn upon you that nothing seen is real — even if it is the image of *Krishna*, *Shiva*, *Durga* or anyone else.

It is quite possible that it takes you several lives to realise this *tattvagyana*. It took Dhruva one thousand lives to have a direct interface with *Vishnu* and when he did have that interface, *Vishnu* made him realise this very *tattvagyana*. After a long spiritual struggle, if you have a direct interface with *Krishna* or *Shiva*, the first thing they will do is tweak your ears and say, "You fool, whatever *gyana* Gurumaa imparted to you was the true knowledge, I will give you the same *gyana*!" Now, whether Gurumaa offers it or *Guru Nanak*, *Kabir* or Shankaracharya, it is the same *gyana*.

After all *tattvagyana* is not of different types — it is one and it will always remain the same.

The one who has experienced *tattvagyana* is called a *tattvagyani*. When a realised soul reveals the *tattvagyana*, then those who listen to it and understand it attain salvation that very moment. Of course the choice is yours. The greatest example of the *Bhagavad Gita* is before you. While listening to *Krishna*, *Arjuna* experienced this *gyana* and only then his sense of attachment and sorrow was dissolved. I have given you the essence of this very *tattvagyana*, which says that you have to rise above *dehoham* and beyond *jivoham* to attain *shivoham*.

Look, *jivoham* is actually charged with bhaktibhava. I had explained the *bhaktimarga* of *Narada* and sung many devotional songs too. Listening to these songs, we danced a great deal in *Vrindavan*. Narada's *bhaktisutra* is the product of *jivoham* — it is steeped in bhaktibhava. And yet it is replete with the sutras of *tattvagyana* and *shivoham*. Because *Brahma* initiated *Narada* into *tattvagyana*, he became a *paramgyani*. All these *granths* emphasise the same thing — that each person will understand this *tattvagyana* in direct proportion to his own ability and capacity. The one who does not have the necessary ability, returns from the field, after just a perfunctory playfulness. He is not quite able to fathom the depths of this profound *gyana*.

This knowledge is something you can gain only if you sit in the presence of a master and listen silently, almost in a state of meditation. It is more than enough if you are able to understand this while leading a disciplined life. This is something you must receive directly from the *guru* in his presence. You should consider yourself lucky, that you have got an opportunity to come all the way to this place to listen to this *gyana*, this interpretation of Shankaracharya's *Atmashatakam*.

CHAPTER 6

YOU AND I ARE THE SAME

All the living beings in this world are a manifestation of the one who is beyond imagination and classification. The entire manifest world emanates from one source. The eternal existence is the foundation of all life and of all sentient beings. What we see as the world is an inter-play of atoms. Forms are made because of the integration of atoms — they last for sometime and then disintegrate.

All things need a foundation to rest upon. My feet support my body, so the feet are the foundation of this body. The feet are a part of the body and the body is sitting on the stage — so the stage is the foundation for the body. And the stage in turn is resting on solid earth, which is its foundation. Man has been pondering over the question: what is the earth supported on? In the old times, people thought that it rests on the horns of a bull. Whenever the earth was hit by an earthquake, people were unable to explain the phenomenon. Innocently, they believed that when the bull gets tired he shifts the earth from one horn to the other. This shifting is what we call an earthquake!

In the ancient times, people based their conclusions on all kinds of conjectures. But then some logical person happened to ask a counter-question: If a bull is holding up the earth then what is holding up the bull? Now they get into a flux and start scratching their heads helplessly. Unable to find a convincing answer, they just silence the questioner saying, "Do not ask so many questions. It is a matter of faith after all and faith tells us that a bull is supporting this earth upon his horns."

But this does not help resolve the doubts. The question stands:

What is the earth supported on? What sustains life on earth? Then scientists did some research and found that the earth is living, that it is the gravitational pull that supports the earth and that it revolves around its own axis. The earth is not supported by anyone or anything. The life you see on this earth is the result of the sun's energy. In other words, the earth will stay alive as long as the sun is alive. If the sun were to turn cold, all life on this earth too would disappear.

But the question still remains: What makes life on earth possible? If you want to understand this, let us look at the elements of which the earth is made up. This earth is composed of five elements. All the sources of water that we see on this earth — rivers, lakes or oceans — are supported by the earth. We often say that there is nothing but water in the oceans — this is not true. Beneath the surface of the ocean is the earth; this is fascinating. The ocean has its own plant and animal life which is very different from terrestrial life. If you measure the depth of an ocean, you will be astonished to learn that it is several miles deep. At such depths, it is so dark that sunlight cannot reach there. The ocean is several miles deep, and deep inside it is an amazing sea life — various kinds of plants, fish and marine life.

If one goes into a mine one has to wear a special hat that has a torch fitted on it. When divers went deep into the sea, they were amazed to see that many of the fish had lights on their heads. God has given all these sea creatures a kind of a torch with the help of which they can see in the deepest areas of the ocean and float around freely without banging into rocks and mountains. The first time the divers plumbed the depths of the ocean, they were surprised to see all this. In their effort to unravel the secrets of the seas, they had to turn back after a short distance as they did not have enough oxygen to facilitate their descent. The oxygen cylinders were exhausted half-way through. After years of research they were able to invent a twin-system of cylinders which lasted much longer. They could then dive to the lowest depths of the ocean, where they again found that it is the earth that supports the ocean.

So the question still remains — who supports the earth? Who is responsible for keeping it in position? Who is at the base, at the foundation of it all? What is the foundation of these *pranas*? After all, there cannot be anything without a foundation. What is the foundation of the sky? Or of fire for that matter? The answer is: ParamBrahman — the one who is truth, super-conscious and bliss — is the foundation of this entire world. Only when you know what truth is, do you discover the real nature of *maya* — the illusory world. Whatever you see or experience does not exist in reality. It is an interplay of atoms and the centre of the atom is the nucleus. Within the nucleus a constant dance is going on. This world is nothing but an ongoing dance of electrons, protons and neutrons. When Shankracharya said that the world is an illusion he did not mean that there is no matter, but was pointing towards the fact that nothing is static or still. The matter that we see is nothing but energy waves and we project ideas and see what we want to see. Quantum physics has changed the entire thinking and everyday scientists are coming closer to mystics.

Everything is changing. The molecules of your body and the atoms in everything are changing. Nothing is the same; every moment this drama is happening. The body looks the same as it did yesterday, but is it really the same? Are the clothes you are wearing the same, or the body which is wearing them the same? Well, nothing is the same. The cloth is visible, but it is not the same cloth that it was before it was washed. Before it became a piece of cloth it was cotton. Let us go a little further back. Before it became cloth it was thread and before it became thread it was a cotton plant. And before it bloomed into a cotton plant it was a mere seed. And much before it became a seed it was just a part of the earth. This is the history of the cloth in reverse gear! It was just a seed which was a part of the soil. In other words, the earth is the origin of this piece of cotton cloth.

Now let us think ahead. The cloth gets worn out and you throw it away or burn it. So what does it become now? It turns into ash and the ash mingles with the soil. So it came from the earth and went back to the earth. Now this cloth has several names. Once it was soil, then a seed, then a plant, then a thread, then on being woven on a handloom it became a piece of cloth, and then it was dyed. When we wove one thread with many others, it became a cloth or a piece of silk.

In the beginning it was dust and finally it again became dust. In between these two stages, the cloth assumed several different names — thread, cotton, and sometimes plant. The names kept changing, the shapes kept changing, but one thing did not change. You know what? It was its state of 'is-ness'. First we kept saying, "It is a seed, it is a plant, it is cotton, it is thread." Then the thread was woven into a piece of cloth and once the cloth was tattered and torn it disintegrated and was turned to ashes which mingled with the soil. Now it is soil.

This 'is-ness' is the essence of all existence. In *Sanskrit*, this 'is-ness' is called *sthir* — one which is immovable. Existence is of sat-chitta-ananda. Pure consciousness is the foundation of this world. So in a manner of speaking, this mike is 'I' and 'I' is in this sofa too. This sofa is the same as the sky. What is present in this earth is in the plants and the rocks as well. It is the same 'is-ness' that permeates every living and non-living being. Man is, tree is, earth is, ether is, temperature is, heat is and the cloud is.

You have seen how this 'is' is being used everywhere. You cannot utter a word or a sentence which does not make use of 'is'. You must understand this 'is-ness'. This 'is-ness' belongs to *Brahman*. If *Brahman* is not there, nothing is. In Guru Nanak's *Bani*, it is beautifully conveyed:

Hai too hai too hovanhara, kate naa bhayo dorahi

You are, yes you are everywhere, never ever can you be away.

Wherever there is something, O God! You are there; except that you hide behind a screen of name and form. When I break the screen of name and form, I find you are there already. There is this *bhajan* I often sing:

In every particle I see you
But only the one who has wisdom will know
Namdev cooked bread and a dog ran away with it
And Namdev ran after him with butter in his hands
Let me put some butter on the bread
And why are you hiding your real form from me
You and I are one in essence

Your form is of dog and me a human
So why be shy, come and eat with me!

This world is his caravan, but only those who have wisdom are able to recognise him. Once *Namdev*, a devotee of *Krishna* was making bread when a dog came barging in and ran off with the bread. *Namdev* ran after him with a pot of butter in his hand saying, "O God! At least let me put a little butter on it and then you take it. The dry bread will get stuck in your throat." But the dog simply refused to listen and ran away. So *Namdev* again pleaded, "O *Vithal*! What kind of a game is this? What kind of an animal form have you chosen? Just remember that your form may be that of an animal, but I know who you really are. You are *Satchidananda*."

Let me add another thing here. *Namdev* was a devotee, a *bhakta*. He was a Vashnavite — a devotee of *Vishnu*. The devotee is able to idolise *Bhagwan* and he says, "I am your servant." It is his feeling that the God permeates everything but is living in the idol. *Namdev* says, "Though you are *Bhagwan* you have assumed the shape of a dog." Now this is not something that a *bhakta* would ever be able to voice. These words explode from within the *tattvagyani* who may not be able to suppress this truth for long. He ends up saying, "You are disguised as a dog and me as a human being." In other words it means that you and I are one — *shivoham*.

The journey of a devotee starts from the outside world. He has a feeling of godliness for everything outside of himself — the trees, birds, plants etc. But not for himself. He thinks he is impure and at best can only be a devotee. The only difference between the *bhaktimarga* and the *gyanamarga* is that a *bhakta* starts from the outside world and reaches inwards, worshipping his chosen deity as someone different from himself, only to merge with it. A *gyani* renounces the outside forms, focuses on his self and discovers that he is *Brahman* — one who is beyond time and space. This is the only difference between the two *margs* and the difference is not much.

Namdev says, "Your form is that of a dog and mine is that of a human being. Though our names are different, our essence is the same." It is the same '**is-ness**' in both. Here the distinction ends. *Namdev* is sat-chitta-ananda and so is everyone. But because of your attachment to the body, mind and *chitta*, because of your ignorance and indifference to your real *swaroopa*, you are not able to understand your inner reality.

In this very world lived *Krishna, Rama, Guru Nanak, Kabir, Namdev, Surdas*, Meera, Sahajo, and Dadu — all of them. But they lived on a different plane of consciousness. The mystics were intoxicated with bliss whereas you continue to howl and wallow in self-pity. You are as much *Brahman* as they are. The only difference is that they remain fixated in their *Brahman* consciousness whereas you live in your body consciousness. That is the only difference.

Sometimes people wish to touch my feet and I invariably restrain them from doing so. Why do I stop them? Let me explain. You are as much of a *Brahman* as I am. If you are not lower in stature than I am, then how can I allow you to touch my feet! I see that it is alright from your standpoint, respecting me as a *guru* and offering greetings in a particular way, but from my point of view it is not required.

Krishna's life is called *leela*. It is said that *Krishna* created as many images of himself as there were *gopis*. Each felt that *Krishna* was with her. There is a profound meaning hidden in this story of raas-leela. With each *Gopi* — atman, *Krishna* — *Brahman*, is eternally present. Once *avidya* is eradicated, the seriousness of life is removed. Your life gets filled with laughter and joy. There is no room for fear, no room for tears. The *Hindu* religion is the only religion that describes the world as *leela* and not as a creation. Islam and Christianity refer to this world as a creation, but *Vedanta* does not refer to it as a creation. *Vedanta* does not look at the world as separate from the creator — this world is the *leela* of existence.

Your real *swaroopa* is *Satchidananda*, but your vision is obstructed by these veils of ignorance to such an extent that you consider these veils to be your real *swaroopa*.

Na cha praansangyo na vai panchvayuh
Na vaa saptadhaaturna vaa panchkoshah
Na vaakpaanipaadou na chopasthpaayuu
Chidaanandroopah shivoham shivoham

Na cha praansangyo na vai panchvayuh means that 'I' am not *prana*. There are seven types of minerals — the basic elements from which our body is constituted. Medical science talks about minerals but it mentions only phosphorous, zinc, manganese, iodine, fluoride, magnesium, sodium, iron, potassium, hydrogen and carbon. Yesterday I was talking to someone who said, "When I was preparing for the medical entrance exam, my teacher told me that when the human body is burnt, phosphorous is released from the body and this can be seen in the form of a thick white layer floating above the burning pyre. He was of the view that this was the basis of man's belief in the existence of ghosts. When people see this white layer they think it is the ghost of the dead person." It is nearly impossible to extract these minerals from the human body either in its living or non-living form, yet Shankaracharya is talking about all these. Just look at the way he expands the scope of this discussion on 'I' am not a body by postulating: 'I' am not minerals either.

Na vaa saptadhaaturna vaa panchkoshah

In order to understand *panchkoshah* you will have to be extra attentive and vigilant. The first of these *panchkoshahs* is 'annamaya koshah,' second, 'pranamaya *koshah*,' third, 'manomaya *koshah*,' fourth, 'vigyanamaya *koshah*' and the fifth is 'anandamaya *koshah*'. I would like to remind all those people who believe that *dharma* is nothing but a form of blind faith, a superstition, to see how a deep and analytical study of the body, nerves, organs, mind and brain was done by the sages and that too almost five thousand years ago, when the word science — *vigyana* was nowhere in the wildest imagination of the West. Indian sages had already introduced this concept of *vigyana*.

So if the word '*koshah*' means container, you could say that our *atman* lives inside these five containers. You must have seen a toy called the 'magic box'. You open a big box and find a smaller one inside. Then, as you open each box, you find a still smaller box inside. And in the last box you do not find anything. This world is a *leela* and you are hidden within these five sheaths.

Annamaya *koshah* refers to our body. The *koshah* that is born of the *anna* (grain), is nurtured by the *anna*, is sustained by the *anna* and finally merges with the *anna*, is called the annamaya *koshah*. I have already said that the way cotton is made out of the soil, in the same way this body of ours is made of our father's sperm and mother's ovum. How are the ovum and the sperm produced? They say that whatever food grains you eat contribute to the making of the sperm and the ovum. Where does grain grow? In the soil. And when the grain reaches the body it is assimilated and sperm and ova are produced. When the sperm and the ovum come together, a baby is conceived in the womb of the mother.

So this body is made of food grains. The food — milk, vegetables etc, that the mother eats, nurtures the baby's body. The *prana* of the mother is the *prana* of the baby and the breath of the mother is the breath of the baby. The baby grows in eight or nine months and is then born. Now it has to be fed. If it is not fed from time to time the body becomes weak and finally perishes, because it is just food and water that sustain it. It is not just the water we drink, as fruits and vegetables too contain a large quantity of water. The best examples of this are watermelon, pumpkin and cucumber etc. There is eighty percent water in all the vegetables we eat.

So it is the food grains that create our body and nurture it as well. If you do not get food then after some time your mind will stop functioning. The way car needs petrol, in the same way our body needs food to sustain itself. This body is born of food, and once it is cremated or buried it is reduced to a handful of ashes which return to the soil once again. So this body is a toy made of dust and is sustained by food that grows out of dust. That is why it is called annamaya *koshah*.

After the annamaya *koshah* is pranamaya *koshah*. I have already elaborated upon the nature of *prana* and *prana shakti*. Our annamaya *koshah* can work only if the pranamaya *koshah* is there to support it. Without the *prana* this body is a mere corpse. Without the *prana* these eyes and ears are simply dead. Remember the devotional song of *Kabir*? When the body dies, both the eyeballs turn upwards. The reason is that the *pranas* have left the body. It is only because of the prana *shakti* present in the body that the eyes are able to see, the ears hear and the feet walk. If there is *prana shakti* you can work with your hands. Without *prana shakti* this body is no better than a corpse. What is it that a dead man lacks? He has everything — eyes, ears, nose, mouth, hands and feet — the only thing he lacks is *prana*. Only because of the pranamaya *koshah* does the body or the annamaya *koshah* function. All this has to be understood in finer detail. The *pranas* do not keep our body just alive, but also fit and healthy. People who know the secrets of the *prana shakti* harness this energy to earn substantial spiritual and physical gains.

It is said that once a blind man came to meet Jesus. He ran his hand over the man and the man was cured. Now he could see everything. At this point, let me share something with you. In almost eighty of hundred cases, such things are only a fraudulent enactment of a cure. Some *mahatmas* are so keen to impress others that they depute two or three disciples to plant such stories from time to time. Look at their audacity! They claim to possess powers they do not have! And the lesser mortals are of course waiting to walk into such a trap!

A couple of times I too happened to meet some people who claimed that they could cure others or make others healthy. When one such person came to meet me I said, "Now that I am here, why don't you restore the health of one or two people in front of me." Though he wrestled and struggled with his self-professed abilities, he could not really do anything. But this does not mean that such a power does not exist at all. *Prana shakti* is a very mysterious thing. It is on the basis of *prana shakti* that we can step outside this body and see it from without. With meditation one can have an out-of-body experience and also see one's *prana* body.

In deep meditation, some people feel that the body is far away from you and you are watching it from outside. Because of a deep rooted fear of death, many aspirants get nervous and are scared. As a result, you deny yourself the joy and knowledge of fascinating experiences which you could otherwise have had.

A *sadhak* engaged in deep meditation will experience this sooner or later. This alone will give an experiential glimpse of the fact that you are not the body. Unless you experience this, you will not be able to know the truth of your self. The intellectualisation

of *gyana* does not work — you have to experience it. You do not have to become a parrot and verbalise this knowledge. Knowledge does not work — experience holds the key.

At the instance of *Jehangir*, the fifth *guru Arjan Dev* was arrested on charges of speaking against and vilifying Islam. After putting him behind bars, they made him an offer, "We can let you go, provided you agree to become a *Muslim*. And if you refuse to convert, then you will have to accept whatever punishment is ordained for this crime." *Guru Arjan Dev* said, "You do what you want to. You cannot force me to accept your orders. I will not convert." In order to torture him, they got a special bathtub and made him sit in it. Boiling water was poured on his head. Seeing their dear *satguru* in this condition, all his disciples began to cry. How could the disciples bear the sight of their gentle-as-a-flower *satguru* in such a state? They were heart-broken. But faced with the cruel might of the state they were helpless. One of his disciples said, "*Gurudev*! You always tell us that someone says '*Rama-Rama*' and someone *Khuda*, so how does it matter whether you recite '*Rama-Rama*' or '*Khuda*'? Why don't you become a *Muslim*? We will not be able to tolerate this. How will you go through so much physical suffering?"

Gurudev said, "Just as you see the bodily suffering of others, in the same way I am able to see my body as different from myself. So whatever pain or torture they inflict on this body — I will witness it. I would like to live my life according to the principles I believe in. And if I am not able to live in accordance with my convictions, then death is preferable to me. But under no circumstance shall I compromise my conviction and principles!"

Now, how did he reach this state? It was possible only because he had a fine understanding of pranamaya *koshah*; he knew the art of using his *prana shakti* too. It is not that the body did not feel the pain, but on the basis of his *prana shakti* and his convictions, he was able to see his body as separate from himself.

Pranic healing is also an integral part of the pranamaya *koshah*. The pranic healer sits in front of the ailing person and transfers his pranic energy to the ailing body, thus healing the patient. Though today the number of such pranic healers has really grown, it is difficult to say how many of them actually understand this technique.

Manomaya *koshah* is the third sheath. To put it crudely, the mind is the manomaya *koshah*. Shankaracharya says, "'I' am not manomaya *koshah*." *Atman* is different from manomaya *koshah*. It is compiled of the thoughts and feelings that ripple through the mind. In a manner of speaking, the first body is of *anna*, the second of *prana* and the third of the mind. Mind is subtle, so you are unable to see it with the physical eyes. The pranamaya body can be seen but not the manomaya *koshah*, which is felt but cannot be seen. All thoughts too have a body and these thoughts change into images and forms in dreams.

Just try to peep into your mind. From the time you were born, how many thoughts have floated in and out of your mind? If it does not make sense to you, then sit down with a copy one day and keep jotting down all the thoughts — good or bad — that surface in your mind. At the end of the day read whatever you have recorded.

You will get the feeling that these are the outpourings of a crazy mind. You may be sitting here but your thoughts flit in and out of this country, go darting to your relatives, your shop, your childhood, this that and the other. I wish scientists would invent some gadget like a car's speedometer, which could measure the speed of our mind. There is a machine which creates a graph of alpha, beta and theta waves. But this gadget does not help you sift the thoughts flashing on the mind's screen. The first time this machine was attached to the brain of a patient, the patient and the scientists were surprised to see so many thoughts crowded in. Thought has its own body. Always remember that the manomaya *koshah* does leave its impact upon your *prana* and annamaya *koshah*. Sub-conscious, conscious and unconscious are the three major levels of the mind in the manomaya *koshah*. In the waking state, the conscious mind is working. In dreams the sub-conscious mind rules and in deep sleep the unconscious mind works. Mind and body are deeply inter-related and whatever happens in the mind, affects the body and whatever goes on in the body affects the mind.

When your mind is racked with anger, then its impact can be

seen on your body too. Pain, anxiety, desire, stress, tension, worry, resentment — all forms of fear — are caused by living unconsciously and are a part of the manomaya *koshah*. When we expect too much, do not wish to share, hold on to things and people, we give rise to resentment, jealousy, sadness and bitterness. All kinds of negativities are the result of being attached to the past and by being future oriented. If you live in a constant state of desire, then you invite all sorts of turmoil and anguish. Most people think that a state of total consciousness minus all negativities is not possible. But the truth is, it is possible for the mind to be silent and for the present moment to be quiescent, simultaneously. It all depends on us. Do we allow our mind to take over? In a situation where the mind is handed over the reins of power, it will manipulate and subjugate you. The mind can work like the devil and can make you suffer. The mind has two parts — one which obsesses with the past and another which is fixated on the future. What if this happens? What if that happens? When we lay down conditions for being happy, we actually assure punishment for ourselves. What you need to learn is a new style of living, where you cultivate compassion, dispassion and sharing; all this will happen easily if you begin to accept your present. Situations may not be comfortable but fighting with them is also not a solution. We can resolve a situation without resenting it.

How you look at the world around you depends on you alone! Someone abused Bulleh Shah, "You filthy dog!" *Bullah* immediately fell at the feet of that person saying, "Thank you! Thank you! You called me a dog. A dog is a really great animal."

One of his poems says:

Never does he leave the threshold of his owner
Though you may beat him with a hundred shoes
What is more, he stays awake through the night

The dog stays awake through the night. That is why his owner is able to sleep in peace. Sometimes he barks so much through the night that his owner gets angry and starts beating him. Even when he is beaten to a pulp, he keeps licking the feet of his owner. He never leaves the threshold of his owner's house, regardless of whether he is beaten or offered food.

Bullah wrote: O mind, you should do whatever you can to propitiate your master, or else the dogs might beat you at this game too. What kind of useless fellow are you, that you are not doing anything to please your master. When a person of Bulleh Shah's stature is abused, he interprets it as a compliment. You should never lose patience! Regardless of what you hear, good or bad, if you listen to it with patience, beautiful meanings will emerge.

CHAPTER 7

LIBERATION FROM I

The one who is able to establish himself is able to go beyond all dualities. The one who is able to experience this wonderful state is able to go beyond the cycle of joy and sorrow, birth and death. As long as you remain seated on the throne of attachment to your body, mind and senses, you will experience all kinds of fleeting emotions of love-hate and pain-pleasure.

You just have to do one thing to come out of these dualities; you have to snap out of this excessive attachment to the body. The day you are able to do so, even the Gods and Goddesses will descend from their high pedestal and touch your feet. Just release yourself from this attachment to your body. Neither am 'I' this body nor is this body mine. Neither am 'I' this corporeality nor is this corporeality mine. You only have to take the first plunge and the rest is taken care of by God. The minute the attachment goes, you get established in your atmanswaroopa. Once that happens, self-realisation is not far behind.

Have you ever thought about how strong this attachment to the body is? The one who is attached to the body has no qualms selling himself for the small pleasures of this world. But once you have secured your release from attachment, you taste eternal and true freedom. It is *maya* (illusion), which has blinded you and tied you down. And this creates a delusional state of mind, of which duality is born. There is me and you — from this a new relationship game begins. You, me and others — and the interactions between us — is the whole *samsara*.

Other delusions are 'mine' and 'thine'. They will either

become friends or end up as enemies. If they become 'friends', then your attachment and affection for them will grow and if they are 'enemies', then your pain will increase manifold. We all seek *ananda*. Whosoever gives me *ananda*, seems to be a friend. Those who are a hindrance or an obstacle, seem like enemies. These roles are not permanent and the one who is an enemy today, can become a friend and a friend can become an enemy anytime. Our love attachments are basically self-oriented. We love ourselves so much, that whoever gives us love, attention, care and respect, seems to be our own. And those who do not, seem to be villains. Love and hate relationships are formed and these relationships set you on the road to turmoil, pleasure, sadness, depression etc.

Once a journalist asked a habitual defector, "You have been a party loyalist for more than twenty years. What happened overnight that you decided to change your party?" The leader said, "Do not ask me what went wrong. I thought of changing my party and so I did!" The journalist said, "It is alright if you have changed your party, but how long will you stay with it?" "Even if I stay till evening, it is more than enough. If someone else gives me a better opportunity, I will join them."

Unnecessarily you accuse politicians of switching loyalties. Whatever applies to the politician, applies to you as well. One minute you call someone your friend, but if he refuses to go along with you, he becomes your enemy. And if your worst enemy helps you through a crisis, he will become your best friend.

So who gives happiness? Your friends? And who inflicts misery on you? Your enemies? No! No one gives you pain or pleasure. It is all in your mind. First you believe that 'I' am this body and then you make friends and enemies. You have to fight a pitched battle to win over friends and defeat enemies. Of course it is not easy to retain friends. You fulfill their demands and indulge their whims. The day you do not, they get angry. Sometimes an old friendship breaks over a trivial issue; old friendships snap over petty things.

So your mind is not really to be trusted. Due to changes in external circumstances, your mind keeps changing. Because of the ever-changing responses of your mind and the changing colours of your relationships, your mind is unable to find peace, stability

or equilibrium. All the time you are consumed by the worry of whom to trust and whom not to. No one ever thinks of making a stranger his own. Deep inside you is a nagging worry, that those who are your own should not become estranged.

It is always 'me' and 'my' house, 'me' and 'my' car, 'me' and 'my' shop, 'me' and 'my' bank balance, 'me' and 'my' wife,' 'me' and 'my' children. Never mind how useless and stupid your children are! If you develop such an excessive attachment with this structure of flesh and bones, why won't you get attached to all material things too? How will you snap out of this network of external ties? The mind has a habit of forging new relationships every now and then. You break out of one set of relationships and walk into another. And this process goes on endlessly.

You never ever tire of forging new relationships. Even here you keep playing your worldly games — this is good and that is bad. Why don't you ever give up the bad habit of justifying your behaviour to others? All the time you are worried about what others may think. Will the day ever come when you stop worrying about what others think and start thinking about yourself? Actually you do not think about others but about yourself. As you need friends, you wish to displease no one. When will the day come when you stop worrying about others and start worrying about yourself? Remember that the pursuit of happiness in the outer world is futile. A great deal of unhappiness comes from the mind when it is not programmed well. We seek happiness in money, fame, status, alcohol, and in so many things that give us transitory pleasure. What is the result of such behaviour? We become exploiters and use people for our selfish ends. In turn we are used by others. We use people as long as they serve our purpose and if they are not of any use then we sideline them and look for others. This results in jealousy, hatred, anxiety, tension and so on. Our continued search for happiness actually produces the opposite effect and we become tense and unhappy.

Much unhappiness arises due to identification with the body, mind, job or family. Instead of identifying with the unchangeable and the permanent — like the core of our being — we identify with transitory things. If we can disassociate our self from the mind and

129

see things as they truly are — that is, impermanent — detachment occurs, and this will instill a degree of peace and calm in the mind. But the habit of identification is so deep, that on the conscious level, even if you wish to break this pattern, you fail. It is such a habit that you cannot really break free from it, even if you want to. If you liberate yourself from this attachment to your body, then you will get freedom from mental and worldly ties.

Fear, anxiety and tension exist because of our selfish motives. A mind which is free of this nonsense saves itself from all problems. We need to remove emotional and mental problems, so that we can prevent a crisis in our lives.

One day Mrs. Jhunjhunwala said to her husband, "I have heard that you have got yourself insured." Jhunjhunwala said, "Yes, but how did you know?" She said, "Your secretary told me." "Yes I have bought an insurance policy. It is worth ten lakhs. But you have to pay a hefty premium too." So his wife said, "Let that be! Tell me when will you get the money?" "The day I die they will pay you ten lakhs," he said. Then the wife asked, "Will they pay up the full amount?" He said, "Of course." Now Mrs. Jhunjhunwala said, "So when are you going to die?" Others may not gain much while you are alive, but once you are dead they definitely stand to gain a great deal!

In other words, the insurance agent sells you the idea of death and you buy it. Well, it just takes care of a sense of security that man is always hankering after. Some people feel that as long as they are around, everything is right with the world. In Europe and America, a person who buys an insurance policy never makes the mistake of disclosing it to the partner. To inform your partner is a sure way of inviting death. The hefty amount they get after the partner's death is enough to make many people lose their integrity!

All is mine, all is mine! Repeating this you reach a stage where to think of religion or God becomes as arduous a task as climbing Mount Everest. With your feet tied with ropes and the weight of mountains on your chest, you cannot possibly climb Mount Everest. Those who climb Mount Everest carry a very light load. In fact the further they climb, the lesser the burden they tend to carry. They

also discard some of the things they otherwise need, because beyond a point it becomes impossible to climb with a heavy load.

In the same way, those who wish to scale the heights of *gyanamarga* will have to unburden their chest of all the weight and be much lighter than they are now. You are holding on to so many worries in your mind. You have tied so many ropes. It takes just one rope to turn into a noose round your neck. And you have so many ropes around your neck. One worry tugs at you from here and another from there. In such a situation, how can you ever know happiness? All this occurs in the mind. And this conscious mind, along with the unconscious and sub-conscious mind is a part of the manomaya *koshah*.

This mind too has a body. The mind is not a small thing. As a matter of fact, this whole network of annamaya and pranamaya *koshah* functions only though manomaya *koshah*. Our unconscious mind registers everything that the eyes see, the ears hear, the nose smells, the tongue tastes and the hands touch. A huge bank of *samskaras* — impressions are created and these affect our mind — the sub-conscious mind directly and the conscious mind, indirectly. Our habits, moods, emotions and thoughts are all designed by these *samskaras*. Our senses are the doors through which the mind functions and gains new information. All motor and sensory activities such as seeing, talking, smelling, walking and sex happen through the mind.

Let me give you an example. What do I have in my hand? I have a watch. Now the eyes recognise the colour and identify a particular shape. The eyes first saw the shape and then recognised the object. The dial is black, the hands white and there are numbers on it. The eyes just saw the shape and the colour but who told you that it is a watch? Your mind said that this is a watch.

Whenever we look at something, our eyes see only its colour. But it is our mind that gives us an understanding of what it actually is. Whatever you think about it, is all conditioned by society and family. They instilled the idea in your mind that you are a human being — a man or a woman. Even the idea of your name has been planted in your mind. All your day-to-day transactions and operations depend upon the mind.

How did you study? With your eyes you saw the book. Initially you saw the colour, but the name of that colour was not known. A child is taught everything — colours, names, shapes, the alphabet, food, language, manners and personal hygiene etc. Each and everything has been fed into your mind. All this information is imprinted and stored in the manomaya *koshah*. The entire information is stored in this treasure house of the subconscious mind.

Everything from the Hindi alphabet to the Hindi language, from *Sanskrit* to mathematics, from history to geography — all the knowledge that you have gained is registered in your manomaya *koshah*. Earlier I told you how the knowledge of colour and form is instilled in your mind. A child is told that his name is Tom. Family members repeat his name until he begins to respond to it. Each and every word and sentence you have learnt, knowingly or unknowingly, goes into the manomaya *koshah*. I am sure you do not remember the days when your mother would make you lie down next to her on the bed and point out; that is a fan, a cycle, your father, your grandfather, bread, water etc. And the child's mind learns everything, absorbs everything — whether good or bad. A child is unable to speak. This does not mean that it does not understand what you say; it is able to understand everything.

A child's mind is so impressionable that it absorbs like a sponge and internalises everything. Everything a child sees, tastes, touches; all information is imprinted in its manomaya *koshah*. And once it begins to speak, the mother knows that it recognises a fan, a sparrow, a glass, a plate and her too.

Once a child is told what his religion is, his mind accepts that, and slowly he gets conditioned to believing: 'I am a *Hindu*', 'I am a *Sikh*', 'I am a *Muslim*', 'I am a Christian'. You make that religion a hallmark of your identity. But this is not your true identity. If the hospital makes the mistake of giving a *Muslim* boy to a Christian family, or a *Hindu* baby to a *Muslim* household, their whole upbringing will differ. A child growing up in a particular household will learn whatever he is taught there. Whatever ideas are planted in a child's mind becomes the truth for that child.

If with the help of a magic wand your manomaya *koshah*

could be deleted, you would lose all signs and sense of identity, recognition of the self and of others too. You will not even be able to deal with your day-to-day business of living.

Suppose a new born child is brought before you and you are asked whether he is a *Hindu* or a *Muslim*, a *Sikh* or a *Parsi*, a *Buddhist* or a Jain? What is he — a communist or a socialist? Can you answer? All these labels are the products of social conditioning. I wish all people in this world could live without labels — it would be wonderful! It would ensure perfect peace and harmony in the world. Right now, because of this labelling, one label hates the other. *Hindus* and *Muslims* are fighting, *Muslims* and Christians are fighting, *Muslims* and Jews are fighting and *Jains* are fighting with *Hindus* and so on and so forth. The turmoil in the world is growing everyday as everyone believes that he is better than the other. A country believes that it is superior to another country. If I could, I would abolish all labels! We are all one, made from the same elements, live on the same earth, breathe the same air, share the same sky, moon and stars. Nothing belongs to us and yet every thing is made for us. Why fight to own when we can share and live in harmony?

This manomaya *koshah* is an old companion of ours. The physical body or annamaya *koshah* changes in every birth, but manomaya and pranamaya *koshah* continue to be the same. It is in this manomaya *koshah*, that the information of your previous births is stored. Your entire history is recorded here.

For instance, if I ask you where your home is, you can answer almost instantly. If I ask you how old your house is, you will probably be able to answer it with effortless ease. Many people are in the habit of turning the pages of history. "In 1935 our grandfather bought the land and in 1946 our father laid the foundation stone of this building and then in 1955 I was born in this very house." Sometimes when I go to people's homes, they start reeling off their personal history. It is good to be aware, but if only this awareness had been total! If I ask you where you were before birth would you be able to answer? You know the history of the house you live in, the country you live in, but you do not know your own history.

The master gives you your identity. Master helps you find your truth. This is the magic. You go to the *satguru* with dehobhava, knowing that 'I' am no more than a body, rooted in the ignorance that this mass of flesh and bones is what constitutes my 'self'. But listening to the guru's *gyana*, an arrow of true knowledge pierces your heart and though you come repeating '*dehoham*', you return singing '*shivoham*'. The disciple says, "I had gone to the *guru* burning in a cauldron of desire, love, affection, possessiveness, suffering and *raag-dvesha*, repeating, "I' am a body', but once I understood the *gyana* given by the *guru*, the consciousness of *dehoham* was shattered to smithereens and then *Shiva* and only *Shiva* was left. Now *aham* — the self, has merged with *Shiva*, and I know that 'I' am *shivoham*."

Now the *atman* knows that 'I' am not annamaya *koshah*, 'I' am not pranamaya *koshah* and 'I' am not manomaya *koshah* either. The manomaya *koshah* — meaning thereby the body of the mind — is also not mine. Let me explain the manomaya *koshah* in somewhat greater detail.

Jiva and *jagat* — world and *Ishwar* — God, are encoded in this very mind of ours. It is because of your mind that you accept a particular religion and a particular caste. The way the conviction develops in the mind is the same way in which the conviction that 'I' am a *jiva* builds up. 'This is *jagat*' and 'This is *Ishwar*'. The thought of *Ishwar* is also embedded in your manomaya *koshah*. It is on the basis of your mind that you develop faith in God. The one, who believes in the existence of God, does it on the basis of his personal beliefs and convictions. And the one who does not believe also does it on the basis of his belief system and convictions. So the caste, religion or nation we often accept as our own, are also based on the convictions encoded in our mind. The difference between the theist and the atheist is that of the mind. Belief is a part of the mind. Thus *jiva*, *jagat* and *Ishwar* are also the products of the mind. Well, the God you believe in is not the one you do not know about, but a product of the mind, and the world which you see is not really the world which exists. Your mind lives in a world created by itself.

Of course, the world has now undergone a sea-change. But some fifty-sixty years ago, when TV and internet had not entered our lives, had some German, Dutch, European or Russian been shown Krishna's picture without being told who he is, it is unlikely that he would have said, "This is a an incarnation, a God." He would probably say that this child's photograph is attractive — wonderful clothes, holding a flute in his hand and a bewitching smile. He would not know that this is a picture of *Sri Krishna*.

In Switzerland, I visited a place where there are caves made of ice. Everything is carved out of ice — roofs, walls and the floor too. There was one huge cave spread over more than five hundred square yards. Inside it were courtyards, rooms and big halls as well. The cave is at a great height and the trolley carries you some six-seven thousand feet above sea level. There is a huge difference between the temperature below and the temperature above. Even the oxygen is in short supply. In those caves there are beautiful idols of human beings, fish, bears, dolphins and seals. They have carved in ice, all the creatures found in that particular region.

Now, let us assume that we decide to put Shiva's idol there. The onlooker will not know that he is a God. He would probably think that he belongs to some tribe that encourages love of reptiles! That is why he has snakes all over his body! Seeing Shiva's dry, matted hair, he would think that he needs a good shampoo! Who will recognise this image as that of *Shiva*? Only the one whose mind has the information.

There have been incidents where the entire family is wiped out in a storm and only a baby survives on an island. Wolves have brought up such children. Rather than eating up the child, female wolves have been known to nurse such babies. In one of such incidents, on growing up, the child started walking like a wolf. When other human beings saw such a child, they got him back with a view to educate and civilise him. But that never happened! In less than six months, the child died. How could he live? If animals have nursed him, he will behave like animals, walk like animals, dig his long nails into your skin, sink his teeth into raw meat and eat like an animal. He would not know how to speak like humans; he would know no language, no religion and no social or moral code. He would not have any awareness of what is right and wrong, what is moral and immoral.

All this information is in your manomaya *koshah*. *Adi Shankaracharya* says that 'I' am beyond these *koshah*s. 'I' am distinct from all of these. From here we come to vigyanamaya *koshah*. *Gyana* means wisdom and knowledge. 'I' is used as a prefix for *atman*, to reaffirm the intensity of the knowledge which is derived from the experiences and memories gained in past and present lives. There is a storehouse of knowledge in each one of us, but we are not educated enough to experience that inner wisdom. Now in order to understand the vigyanamaya *koshah*, you need to reflect more deeply on it. Your mind may recognise a particular object, but how and when that object is to be used, is something you understand only on the basis of this *gyana*. Vigyanamaya *koshah* has the aspects of *chitta* and *ahankara* associated with it. *Chitta* means the ability to know, to become the observer of what is actually happening and to be able to live a reality without speculating or fantasizing. *Ahankara* is the ego aspect in the real and not in the gross sense. *Ahankara* is the knowledge of 'I', of becoming aware of the identity of the self. This understanding comes when we work with the vigyanamaya *koshah*.

Once we have worked with and understood the identity of 'I' — the identity of the 'self' which is manifest in the world in the third dimension, and which experiences pleasure and comfort, pain and suffering — then we move into the experience of anandamaya *koshah* — the dimension of bliss, happiness, wholeness and contentment.

An animal's vigyanamaya *koshah* is not fully developed and remains hopelessly shrunk. Only man has the ability to develop and expand his vigyanamaya *koshah*. Man is not superior to animals because he walks on two feet, stands erect or has a straight spine — not for any of these reasons — man is superior because he has the ability to develop his vigyanamaya *koshah* in the course of a single life. I would prefer the word intellect to vigyanamaya *koshah*. We are not able to use our intellect in an optimum manner. We just do not know how to do it.

The only difference between a scientist and an ordinary person is that one has a highly developed vigyanamaya *koshah*, while the other has a less developed one. This vigyanamaya *koshah* has infinite possibilities. It is this vigyanamaya *koshah* that makes a scientist a scientist. A musician is a musician because of his manomaya *koshah*. If someone's manomaya *koshah* is highly developed then his sensitivity is sharpened. Painters, singers, poets, dancers and sculptors, usually have a highly developed manomaya *koshah*.

CHAPTER 8

BOUNDLESS JOY

Once, on his way back from a ritualistic bath in the *Ganga*, Shankaracharya was passing through a narrow street in *Kashi* with his disciples. Walking ahead of him, his disciples were shouting for people to move aside and clear the way. It was a narrow congested street in *Benares*. They saw a big, burly, broad-shouldered man standing right in the middle of the street, with a couple of stray dogs in tow. His clothes were full of dirt and filth. He was a low-caste man — a *chandaal*. He was standing right in the middle of their path. Though Shankaracharya's disciples were saying, "Step aside! Step aside!," he just stood his ground, barring the way.

The *chandaal* was broad and the street narrow. They couldn't possibly squeeze through the side even if they wanted to. As they neared him, Shankaracharya also said, "Just step aside. Let me go!" Then the *chandaal* spoke in a loud voice, roaring like a lion, "What do I step aside from? From the body or from *maya* (illusion)? From the mind or from the *panchkoshah*? What do I step aside from?"

On hearing an ordinary *chandaal* mouth the *Vedanta* in this manner, they were all stunned. He asked once again, "What do I withdraw from?" It is said that Shankaracharya was flummoxed on hearing his loud, sonorous, booming voice. It was as though someone had rudely woken him up from a deep slumber. Deep inside, he was shaken up. His intuition told him that this booming voice was not that of an ordinary person. He meditated, and discovered that the *chandaal* was none other than *Shiva* himself! He threw himself at Mahadev's feet. His disciples were surprised

to see their *acharya* bending down and offering obeisance at the feet of a *chandaal*.

They wondered how their *acharya* could fall at the feet of a *chandaal*, because Shankaracharya was a high-caste *Brahmin*. Their *acharya* was known to be amongst the best *sanyasis*, one who had been on a triumphant march across the length and breadth of the country. So impressive were his thoughts, his style of oratory and so awesome and beautiful his personality that all the great scholars and saints he had defeated in scholastic debates would fall at his feet. And here he was bowing at the feet of a *chandaal*. Shankaracharya had disciples like *Mandana Mishra* who was known to be the greatest living scholar of the *karmakanda* theory. Shankaracharya initiated *Mandana Mishra* into *sanyas*, but history is not very clear as to what happened to his wife.

As Shankaracharya was paying obeisance at the feet of *Shiva*, he started singing verses in his praise. Then he sought forgiveness from *Shiva*. Disguised as the *chandaal*, *Shiva* spoke, "You say, 'Step aside! Step aside!' Now tell me, what do I step aside from? If you have experienced the truth and are established in *Shiva Tattva*, then why is someone untouchable for you? The one who is detached from the body, makes no distinction of caste and creed. You think that you have gone beyond the consciousness of the body. Then tell me, who is standing in front of you — a *chandaal*, a low caste or *Satchidananda*? Is there some special *Satchidananda atman* inside you that is not in other beings? Are there different types, different categories of *atman*, too?"

I have told you that when you look into a pitcher of water the reflection of the moon is seen in it. One moon is in the sky and the other inside the pitcher. Suppose we place ten thousand pitchers, then how many reflections will there be? Well! As many as ten thousand. But will that affect the moon in the sky at all? Will it diminish the moon somewhat? Now, whether it is a small vessel, a big one or a river, it is the same moon that is reflected everywhere. The moon does not say that just because you are a pitcher with a small mouth I cannot enter you. There too it is the same reflection. *Jiva* — the individual soul, is a reflection of *Brahman* in *avidya* (micro-unconsciousness), and *Ishwar* is the reflection of *Brahman* in *maya* (macro-unconsciousness).

Sometimes due to ignorance, you think that God and *Brahman* are one, but it is not true. God is the presiding deity of *maya* and *Brahman* is beyond *maya*. Incarnations or *avatars* are considered to be *Ishwar*, meaning one who never loses his inner state, one who has descended from a higher consciousness to the body. The word *avatar* comes from the word *avataran* which means to come down. *Buddha, Krishna, Shiva* and *Durga* belong to the category of Gods — a consciousness which is the highest — and they never forget their reality. But the intelligence is limited and forever remains oblivious of its real *swaroopa*. As long as the *satguru* does not initiate *jiva* into *gyana*, it does not realise the truth.

Rama and *Krishna* are in the physical body for sometime and then they leave the mortal frame. Whether or not they are in the physical body, they are in a higher consciousness. But *jiva* has to evolve and grow spiritually, as its capacity as *jiva* is too limited. Here the affect of the unconscious is more and the conscious is at a lower level. With the grace of the *guru* and with his spiritual *sadhana*, the *jiva* can tear down the wall of *avidya*.

Now whether it is *Rama, Krishna* or someone else, all of them did this little charade of going to a *guru* and seeking initiation. But they enact this little drama only because they have appeared on the earth as human beings and they play their role well. The scriptures say that an enlightened master too is an *avatar*. This means that every *jiva* has the opportunity to evolve and become *Ishwar*. The one, who has broken the sheaths of ignorance and has awakened his or her super-consciousness, is similar to *Ishwar*.

Being compassionate, such evolved saints choose to be born again and again, so that they can help fellow beings awaken. *Ashtavakra* was a *rishi* even when he was in his mother's womb. His father was busy studying the *Vedas* and their grammar. Now in the *Sanskrit* language, enunciation is considered to be extremely important. To learn *Sanskrit* grammar, one has to work for almost twelve years. *Ashtavakra* was still in his mother's womb when his father was busy enunciating the *Vedas*. Once his father happened to falter over the pronunciation of a particular word and the child spoke from the womb itself, "Father, you have mispronounced the word." Now tell me why would such a person need a *guru*?

Apparently there is no mention of whether *Ashtavakra* ever had a *guru*.

The father was enraged and said, "You are so insolent. From the womb itself you are pointing out my mistake. I curse you! May your body be twisted and be out of shape." It is said that *Ashtavakra* was born with eight different contortions to his body. The father was a scholar, but not a *tattvagyani* — one who knows the quintessential truth, while the son was a *tattvagyani* from birth. So, *rishis* like *Ashtavakra* do not really have to go through the rigors of meditation.

Ishwar is *gyani*, but *jiva* — the individual soul is not. The difference is only of degree. Now whether the river is big or small, the reflection of the moon remains unchanged. The moon makes no distinction whatsoever. Once when *Krishna* was a baby, he was playing in the courtyard. His eyes fell on the moon and he insisted on getting it. Now it was well beyond the ken of *Yashodha*, his mother. Had it been some earthly object, she would have got it for him. But how could she get the moon? *Krishna* went on crying, kept stamping his feet and screaming. When Nand returned home he asked, "Why is he crying so much?" *Yashodha* said, "Well, your son wants me to get the moon for him." A woman's head is governed by her feelings; Nand used his intelligence. He got a huge vessel, filled it with water, kept it in the courtyard outside and the moon came right into their house. When they showed it to little *Krishna*, he was pleased. Crawling, he went closer to the vessel and tried to catch the moon, but its reflection dispersed. He started crying all over again, "Get me the moon. Where is the moon?"

Jiva has no freedom. *Jiva* is essentially in a state of bondage. It has to reap the rewards of all its actions. If it does evil it suffers evil; if it does good deeds then it reaps rich rewards. Who is ultimately responsible for rewarding or punishing *jiva* for its deeds? Some people believe that *Ishwar* is responsible for it. But *Ishwar* is completely detached from *jiva*. All he says is, "Child! As you sow, so shall you reap! Now what can I do in all this!"

You need to reflect on the self, but before you do this you need to understand that to know the self, you have first to target what is not the self. You need to recognise that the self is beyond

141

the body; beyond the mind; beyond the intellect and beyond the *panchkoshah*.

An onion is just one layer upon another — you peel off the outer layer and there is another one inside. You peel it off again and find yet another one. This goes on until you reach a point where there is nothing left to call a layer or an onion. *Panchkoshah* are like the five outer layers of the *atman*. Or we can understand it like this: the *atman* is behind five veils — the outer veil is the annamaya *koshah* followed by the pranamaya *koshah*, manomaya *koshah*, vigyanamaya *koshah* and the anandamaya *koshah*.

Now, in the case of an onion, we know that if you go on peeling the outer layers, ultimately you are left with nothing at all. Similarly, as you keep moving away from all the *koshah*, you ultimately discover your true self. For this, you need to constantly develop a heightened awareness and a discriminating intelligence, which is called pragya in *Sanskrit*. As of now, your identification is with the body and more than the body it is with the feelings, emotions, thoughts, unseen thoughts and the modifications of thoughts. It is really a subtle exercise to peel off these layers, as they seem to be an integral part of you. A highly refined mind can perform such an operation, where you develop heightened levels of concentration which mature in meditation. And matured meditation is *samadhi*. Stage by stage you have to progress, but is this possible for a mind which is disturbed, oscillating, scattered and a slave of the senses? The answer is a definite no! You need to understand that as long as you are attached to temporal and transient things and beings, this evolvement is not possible.

To some the word *atman* implies a wandering ghost! Too much of cinema and this is the *gyana*, the knowledge you have about *atman*. The impressions of people and cinema have affected you deeply. So much so, that you think that *atman* is the one that goes around in a white *sari*; the one whose feet are twisted; the one who visits you at midnight with a lighted candle in one hand. Even the time is fixed; it is twelve at night. You think that *atman* is the one with big teeth, a grotesque face and dishevelled hair. What the movie people are showing is the subtle body, a ghost, but they call it *atman*.

Yes, there is one more thing. Whenever anyone talks about the *atman* — in movies or in general — they invariably use the female gender to refer to it. Is it that men don't ever appear in the guise of a ghost? As if the whole idea of ghosts comes naturally to women alone? If man is *Magneto* (villainous), so can a woman be! If a woman can be petty-minded, so can a man be. We should not discriminate on the basis of gender. As it is, all these distinctions pertain only to the body.

What is a ghost? It is a subtle body. The truth of the matter is that after the physical body is dead, until another one is found, everyone is a ghost. The only difference is that some are 'holy ghosts', while the others are only 'ghosts'. In Christianity, they believe in the concept of the 'Holy Ghost'. They refer to *Ishwar* — God, as the 'Holy Ghost'. So, many times death came, but you simply refused to die and it could not touch you. Many times death has visited you and yet you have remained unscathed, beyond its reach.

In the *Jataka tales*, *Buddha* has talked about his ten thousand births. He mentions how in the course of his ten thousand births, he was born as a human being, a bird, an animal and a tree. He was born and then his body died. He was born again, and again his body died. Even after dying so many times, you do not die, because your real *swaroopa* — essence, is eternal, immortal and indestructible. Read the *Bhagavad Gita* and you will enjoy it immensely. The *Gita* says:

Na Jayate Mriyate va Kadachin Nayam
Bhutva Bhavita va na Bhuyah
Ajo Nityah Shaswatoyam Purano
Na Hanyate Hanyamane sharire

When the body dies *atman* does not die. *Atman* never died in the past and will not be extinct in the future either. By killing the body, the soul cannot be killed. You are beyond death. Death dies in front of you — it is an illusion that someone or something has died. The manifestation of form occurs and after a period the manifested goes back to the state of the unmanifested. From emptiness everything rises and to emptiness everything returns.

The notion that you are merely a body is the root cause of all sin and of all human misery too. As you move from *dehoham* to *jivoham*, you will realize how carefree you become. Why? Because *jiva* says, "My relationship is only with *Ishwar*. Regardless of the condition *Ishwar* keeps me in, I am happy. *Ishwar* has granted me life and birth and he may keep me in any condition he deems fit. Every condition is acceptable to me. This body belongs to *Ishwar*, this world belongs to *Ishwar*, we are his and he is ours. So let him decide!" The devotee simply surrenders to the almighty and then his heart and mind resonate with peace.

There is a great sense of liberation and relief in this *jivoham* bhava. And blessed are those who reach up to *atmabhava*. The one who does his *sadhana* and reaches this stage, experiences immense joy and *ananda*. Look, now it is for you to choose whether you wish to remain in a particular stage, or scale greater heights. Whether you want to remain associated with the body, or to expand your vision and evolve to *shivoham*.

It is the joy of the *satguru* to give *gyana*. To follow or not to follow his teachings is something that the disciple or the listener has to decide. One gentleman has sent a letter saying, "Almost thirteen hundred years ago, when Shankaracharya wrote this, the people who heard him were overwhelmed by a sense of gratitude. Now when we are listening to this discourse on 'Atmashatakam', after a gap of thirteen hundred years, we are again experiencing a sense of rare joy and fulfillment."

This is your story. It is neither of *Rama* nor of *Krishna*; *Vishnu* nor *Shiva*. This *katha* is essentially your own and it is dedicated to you. I am sitting here and singing your praises. This is your real *swaroopa*, which you have become oblivious of and which I am trying to remind you of. Why have you become oblivious of it? Well that is the very nature of *jiva* — to forget. You forget because it is in your nature to forget. In the state of '*jiva*', ignorance is inescapable and in the state of *Ishwar*, the play of *maya* is inescapable. *Ishwar* is always *gyana* and jiva's nature is of ignorance. That is why *jiva* has to work hard, has to travel the distance from *dehoham* to *shivoham*. But *Ishwar* does not have to work at all.

You should always live in the *bhava* that you are Satchidanandaroopa. Do not identify yourself with the body. Some letters say,

"We try our best to stay wide awake but slip back into a state of forgetfulness. We try to retain the consciousness that we are not the body and this consciousness does stay for a while, but is then forgotten. What should we do?" The answer is that as long as the awareness of forgetfulness is present, you should count yourself blessed. The moment this consciousness turns into amnesia, you pinch yourself and again pull yourself out of it. This is an ongoing job. When you are forgetful and fall asleep or slip into a state of amnesia, do not worry. Try to pick up the threads of consciousness as and when you remember. Do not regret remaining oblivious for such a long time. Do not think that you should never forget, or that you ought to be aware at all times. Do not think that you are a fool if you forget once again. There is no point in repenting. Some people think that repentance does help a great deal. I am of the view that it does not help at all. In fact repentance is a way of making excuses, so that we go on making more mistakes. It is no big deal; first we make mistakes and then we repent.

If someone says, "Please forgive me this time, I will not do it again," you should never trust him, because he is insuring himself against another mistake and another apology. If you forgive him once, he will feel that you could forgive him twice, thrice and four times as well. So in my opinion, there cannot be a sillier sentence than, "I am sorry." You would probably feel that people often say that it is a good thing to seek forgiveness or to do penance. Now, they say what they think is right and I say what I think is right — to each his own, according to his standards.

If you have made a mistake, then rather than doing penance you should try to understand the reason for it and draw the right lesson from it. Grasp the significance of being wakeful. And whenever you wake up, it is morning for you! You must wake up!

Does it ever happen to you that it is morning and you are still in bed humming the song — "Wake up, O dear one, it is a sweet morning"? You refuse to pull your face out of the quilt. Or it is summer and the air conditioner is running; you are enjoying the early morning sleep. All the alarms are buzzing. All your family members are up and about, but you are still sleeping. Everyone is shouting at you, "Get up, now! Get up! It is morning already!" You say, "I am awake", though you continue to loll around in bed!

When a mother wakes up her child he says, "I have woken up mummy!" But the moment the mother goes out, the child goes off to sleep again. Turning around, the mother walks right back saying, "You have not woken up so far? You will be late for school!" Again he says, "I will be up in a minute", but goes on rubbing his eyes. She drags him to the bathroom and when she returns after ten minutes, she finds that he is still not out of the bathroom. He would most probably be sleeping on the toilet seat. The western toilet seat is becoming very popular these days. You know why? Because you can sit comfortably on the seat and sleep.

It is very difficult to step out of your sleepiness. If you cannot give up the sleep of this body, how will you shed the sleep of your mind? You can well imagine what all you will have to do to awaken your mind. You see how difficult it is for a mother to wake up a child? The *satguru* is also like a mother who is constantly trying to pull you out of your sleep. He says, "Wake up! Recognise the true value of life! Do not forget!" That is why the *satguru* is both a mother and a father to you. Like a mother he treats you with love and compassion and like a father, the *guru* sometimes acts tough to discipline you.

The *guru* must have both these qualities, only then is he successful. The *guru* has to be a mother, a father, a companion and a friend. The *guru* is your friend as well. So, in this critical hour of ignorance, who could be a better friend to you than your *guru*? Who else but he shall release you from the clutches of ignorance, from the attachment to the body? Tell me, who can help you regain and claim your release? Not your biological parents, your brothers or sisters, your family or friends. No one can, except your *guru*. Only the satguru's *gyana* can help you rise above *dehoham* and enter the state of *shivoham*.

The *bhava* that 'I' am a body, 'I' am the mind, is so deeply ingrained that you see people as ugly or low-born. But once you realise that in every pitcher is the reflection of the same moon, in every mind is the same *atman* and it is the reflection of the very same consciousness, you finally enter into the realisation of the

self. We are all connected to each other. And if we are connected, then where is the room for undercutting each other or fighting and harbouring hatred for each other. You sit together and try to look into each other's eyes. What will you see? You will see yourself in the other's eyes and he will see himself in yours.

Perhaps that is why people do not look into each other's eyes; they just avoid gazing at each other. If they were to do so they would see their own reflection in the eyes of the person sitting in front of them. Then how will you fight with him or nurse hatred for him? All *raag-dvesha* (attachment-hatred) is born of the belief that 'I' am the body or the mind. The very moment you see the 'self' as separate, you cut through greed, affection, pride, possessiveness, jealousy, attachment and suffering.

When do you experience pain and suffering? When you forget your 'self' and the mind takes over the controls. The mind divides and distorts and sees things from its biased point of view. Only when you step down from the *atmabhava*, do you slip into the dehobhava. All distinctions such as, I am elder, he is younger; I am good, he is bad, result from your attachment to the body. Your mind always remains trapped in such mean thoughts — everyone must respect me and no one should disrespect me. Just once you need to rise above the tidal waves of this mind and see who you are. And the moment you are aware, the mind stops playing its games. You must have travelled by an aeroplane. Once the plane is air-borne, all the earthly distinctions begin to appear meaningless. From a height things seem different. All distinctions of rich and poor, good and bad melt away.

There are so many divisions created by man — of position, social respectability, wealth, job, status. The moment you are up in the air, what do you see below? Everything is reduced to a mere blur. In the same way, as long as you remain trapped in *dehoham*, you continue to draw boundaries of me, you, they, ours, theirs — and fight for your territory. It is so animalistic — animals mark their territory with their urine. Well, you do not mark it in exactly the same manner, but still you have created boundaries. Everyone is fighting with everyone else to claim what they think is theirs. Once you transcend this body-consciousness and enter into the state of chidanandaroopa, all distinctions cease to exist. Then there is no hatred for another and no jealousy either. As there is no one left who can be called the other, it is you who is reflected in everyone — or, one *Brahman* reflects in every one.

Dharma, artha, *kama* and *moksha* occur in the vigyanamaya *koshah*. The distinctions of *dharma* and adharma (ethics and non-righteousness), occur in the manomaya and vigyanamaya *koshah*. Your intellect and mind are holding and defining these facts due to their deep seated *samskaras*. A child has no understanding of artha (economics), *kama* (sex), *dharma* (ethics) or *moksha* (liberation).

Once a father offered his young son a choice, "You can either take a hundred rupee note or the loose change which I am holding in my hand. Tell me, what do you want? You can pick only one of the two." The child picked up the currency note and also the change. The father said, "Why did you pick up both?" The child said, "I will wrap this change in the paper." For a child, a hundred rupee note is worth no more than a piece of paper!

Moksha will be sought only by those who feel the pain and anguish of bondage. The world may be a burden to someone — full of conflicts and troubles, but to another it might be heaven. If jail is enjoyable, why would one want to come out of it? The one, who is fighting for freedom, knows the desperation to attain it. *Moksha* is meant for those who know the pain of slavery. This is all experienced by the mind and it is the mind which seeks, whether bondage or freedom. The world is as you want to see it, or as your vision is.

The vigyanamaya *koshah* deals with your higher intellect and the knowledge that one receives from intuition or from unexplained sources. There are three levels of the mind — higher, middle and lower. The lower mind is the unconscious mind, which runs the body systems; the middle mind propels us towards the sensual world which holds all the impressions of the millions of experiences we have had, and the higher mind is the one which experiences knowledge and wisdom.

Anandamaya *koshah* is transcendental in nature. It is here that the influences of the mind are not present and great experiences are received. The awakening of the *kundalini*, states of bliss etc, are experiences which happen in the anandamaya *koshah*.

For now, know that these *koshah* are nothing more than a theory for you, but with persistent efforts in *sadhana* you will be able to understand and experience them. Man does not even know his lower and middle mind, what to say about the higher mind! One after another, the layers of *koshah* have to be peeled away to know the *sakshi* — the witness. The knower, knowledge and the known — this trinity is *maya*. And you are beyond these too! Mind-intellect is the knower, the perception you receive from the senses is knowledge and the sensory world is known through this process. You are not the knower but the witness of all this. When the mind knows, then you are a witness to it and when the mind does not know, then too you remain a witness. This whole drama is happening in front of you.

CHAPTER 9

I AM ETERNAL

Nothing is possible in life without the grace of *Sri Gurudev*. Of course in matters of spirituality, along with the guru's grace, your dedicated efforts are also needed. But the truth is that even in ordinary life, only those people progress who are blessed by a *guru*. *Guru* is the *tattva* that helps you transcend the barriers of the body. And once you outgrow this attachment to the body, you get established in your real *swaroopa*. All the attachments that prevent you from crossing this worldly ocean, can easily be eradicated by the grace of the *guru* and by pure knowledge. The external *guru* helps us find the inner *guru* and this is the *guru* who will give you everything — knowledge, wisdom, enlightenment, joy..... ask and you will have it! What can the human mind possibly ask for? Well! Whatever you ask for can never satisfy you for eternity. Thus the only thing that can really satisfy you and give you true contentment is — emptiness. Once emptiness is found, then this desire too will get eradicated on its own.

If you wish to uproot a tree, you cannot do so just by pulling out its leaves, twigs or branches. You have to strike at its roots. As long as man is not able to fathom his real *swaroopa*, as long as he does not experientially know, 'Who I am', all his efforts toward freeing himself from worldly attachments, dispelling ignorance and attaining *moksha* come to naught. Those who claim that they can attain the highest state of perfection only through the observance of rituals are simply fooling themselves. All these tools — prayer, pilgrimage etc, are just ways of purging your mind of impurities. This is necessary for the purification of your mind, because only

a person with a clean and pure mind has the right to imbibe *tattvagyana*.

Do you have a pure heart and mind? Be honest in your assessment. Do not the objects of desire delude your senses? Only the person who is a detached soul has the right to receive *gyana*. The question is: Are you a person with a detached mind?

Your mind is full of all kinds of worldly attachments. You are attached to your mother, father, husband, wife, brother, sister, property and wealth. Are you not attached to each one of them? On the one hand, you are interested in this worldly game and on the other you pretend to be interested in *satsang*. But the question arises — who deserves to receive *tattvagyana*? Only those who are detached from *samsara*, fulfill the prerequisites of being a true receiver. The mind should remain undisturbed, regardless of whether anyone is attached to you or hostile toward you. A sense of equipoise means that you refuse to react even when a person insults you either behind your back or directly to you.

The great sages have said that a person who is not always aware is a captive of his senses and of his mind. The mind that is filled with attachment has no right to be a recipient of *gyana*; one has to work on the level of the mind first. No wonder then, that the sages have repeatedly emphasised the importance of following the *bhaktimarga* and doing selfless service. If you do not have purity of mind, then just by listening to the words of *gyana* you will attain nothing but ego.

I am always in touch with people who are incharge of meditation centres in different cities. They tell me about those who attend the Sunday meditation sessions regularly. Sometimes, I make surprise visits to these centres, because almost everyone pretends to be a good disciple in front of the *guru*. People are great actors and can carry off the deception with great élan. But deception has a short life and falls on its own.

I am not pretentious and have nothing to do with people who are. When it is announced that Gurumaa is coming, the entire town shows up. All those who turn up on such occasions are no better than just a crowd for me. And I have nothing to do with crowds; I prefer to deal with genuine disciples.

Some people turn around and tell me, "We have great love and affection for you. But we are someone else's disciples." In a way it is good that you are not my responsibility! After all, one can take responsibility only for one's own disciples, not of the listeners. How can I take responsibility for the listeners? Today, through the medium of T.V., millions of people are listening to me, so how can I take responsibility for all of them? But I can definitely be a catalyst for all who are trying to mould their lives in accordance with the sutras of meditation and those who are determined to take their lives in the right direction.

Adi Shankaracharya expounded wondrous sutras, sitting on the highest peak of consciousness and you are listening to them, sitting on the plains below — it is quite possible that you will not be able to understand what he is saying. If someone is sitting on a high mountain peak, he will say, "How beautiful the clouds are! How wonderful the sky is! How chilly the air, it is snowing!" Sitting in the plains, you will probably say, "Here there are no clouds, no snow, no cold winds. Here it is sweltering hot. Which place is this fellow talking about?" The experience of those who are on the highest peak is very different from those who are in the plains.

The person who has cut the roots of ignorance is an enlightened person — an *atmavit*. A person who has realised the 'self' is called *atmagyani*. A realised person is at the highest pinnacle, he has cut off the roots of ignorance. The one who is able to see himself as separate from the body, mind, *buddhi* and *chitta*, gets established in his 'self'. Those who are attached to the body remain rooted in pleasure pursuits and sensual gratification alone and they are the ones who are living in the plains. The difference between both is great — where the ignorant are stuck and tied to the earth and earthly pleasures, the realised person is at great heights, soaring high in the inner skies. There is a big gap; hence a worldly person finds it difficult to understand the words of the master and that is why it is not easy to understand pure *Vedanta*.

Walking on the path of knowledge is like walking on the razor's edge. In the *Guru Granth Sahib* it is said: It is like walking on a path smaller than a hair and sharper than the edge of a sword. A single hair is so delicate and your weight so much, how can a hair

support your body weight? If someone asks you to walk on the edge of a sword, how will you do it? This is how it is on the path of knowledge and of *Vedanta* too.

Only the courageous and the wise can tread this path. The first step is listening to the words of the master with great love and surrender; the second is cultivating awareness; the third is realisation. There are no short cuts, so do not make the mistake of thinking that just by listening you can achieve something. The information that the Eiffel Tower is in Paris, is not enough for you to enjoy the feeling of being on the topmost floor of the Eiffel Tower. For that you need to get a visa for France, buy a ticket, sit in a plane and actually go there. Then you have to buy another ticket for the tower, sit in the lift and go to the top floor.

Whatever I have discussed so far, is just my way of giving you an analogy, a comparison, a hymn in praise of what *tattvagyana* is. All of you should understand this *tattvagyana* with the *bhavna* that you still have a long way to go. You should know that you are trapped by attachments. By describing the conditions that exist on the peak of the mountain, maybe I can lure you to move towards the peak. Amongst other suggestions, I would like to say that if you really want to reach this goal, you must listen with total concentration. Your concentration should be so complete that your attention should not drift away even for a split second.

I have heard that *Guru Amardas* would be very tired after the day's work at his guru's home, yet when he sat down to meditate he would take off his turban and tie his hair to a peg. At any point in time that he felt drowsy or sleepy, his head would move and his hair would be pulled causing him physical pain. But this pain would wake him up and he could continue with his practice. This level of dedication is required for something to fructify.

So be alert and vigilant. The other suggestion is that you should observe silence whenever it is possible. I believe speaking less works wonderfully. When you observe silence, you are able to stay away from useless and trivial talk. This saves you from unnecessary entanglements of the mind. For the fulfillment of a specific goal, you need to conserve all your energies. Your goal is the awakening of the consciousness. So if it requires you to do something, you should never hesitate to do whatever is needed.

You should always be active and alert. And as far as food is concerned, I suggest you eat in balance — neither too much nor too little. The more you eat the more sluggish you tend to be. I am not saying that you should starve yourself. If you eat in the right proportion, it will help you tread the path of *dhyana*. When people do not have a regulated lifestyle, it shows up in the form of disease and lack of concentration. When you eat a balanced diet and do your *asana*, your body remains fit and your sleep will also be balanced. In order to gain inner balance and alertness, this is absolutely necessary.

Purity of mind and body is the most important thing that we cannot ignore. The body is an extension of the mind, so both have to be in harmony. Doing yogic *asanas* is not just for the sake of good health, but also for the integration of the mind and the body.

If I speak about pure *Vedanta*, you will find it very hard to digest. Music brings in some kind of relief. It is exactly like a pill of *Neem* being easier to swallow if you sugarcoat it. I know a seer who is a Vedantist. Once he was my guest and was so pleased with me that he said, "You do a good job of explaining the *Vedanta*." Now, he is quite senior to me in age. I have been visiting him ever since I was a child. I have been in touch with a good number of seers and beyond doubt; all of them have had a lot of affection for me. A true seer will spread nothing but love amongst people. There are some *sadhus* who are habitually quarrelsome. They always fought with me and still do. But true seers have always had immense love for me. They have always blessed me; their love has never been found wanting.

This Vedantist and I were sitting alone. He said, "Sometimes I feel I lack something that you have. I can explain the *Vedanta* threadbare, but I do not know how to sing. But when you speak you weave such magic with the medium of music, that difficult things are also coated with sweetness and delicacy." He said, "Your singing and your music sweep people away from their minds and this makes deeply philosophical things easy to imbibe. I wish I could sing like you."

I said, "All right, let us assume for a minute that what you have just said is right. You said that you cannot sing but you can

talk on *Vedanta*. You also said that I can sing just as well as I can expound on the matters of *Vedanta*. Now, I have no illusions about how I sing. Though you have praised my singing, I know very well where I stand in relation to it. Coming to you, you are here but mentally you are somewhere else." Listening to music attentively soothes the nerves and makes the mind concentrate. Concentration brings a sense of equipoise which makes you a deserving candidate for receiving *gyana*.

In a sutra, Shankaracharya talks of how 'I' is separate from the five elements. Now, this external garment that I am wearing is not Gurumaa. Let me give you a much simpler example. Would you say that this piece of garment I am wearing is Gurumaa? Suppose after I have removed it or discarded it, you ask me if you may take it. I say, "Yes, please go ahead! Take it." Would you say, "I have got Gurumaa," or would you say, "I have got Gurumaa's garment?" A garment is a garment after all. It will get dirty and I will put it away for washing or it will wear out and I will discard it. How can 'I' be a piece of garment?

Sometimes out of love, people begin to believe that there is no difference between the two. Once one of my disciples presented my photograph to a judge. As soon as he opened the cover and saw the picture, holding it close to his forehead and heart he said, "Gurumaa has come into my house." He is not calling it a photograph, but Gurumaa. If you say it out of affection or reverence then it is fine, but 'I' am not my picture. Just as my picture or my clothes are not 'I', in the same way, your body is a garment for you. How can you be a garment? If your garment is torn or dirty, you just take it off and throw it away. In the same way, when this body starts ageing and is worn out, it becomes dispensable. Death comes and takes it off, carries it away.

Sometimes little children get attached to their new clothes. If you ask them to remove their favourite clothes they start fighting. Even if the clothes get dirty, they are not ready to take them off. It is very difficult to make them understand. Adults behave the same way. In your ignorance, you begin to believe that this body is 'I,' you have convinced yourself: "This body is mine". And when death appears at your door, you are not ready to let go of your body. But neither are you a 'body' nor is this body 'yours'. This body does not even belong to 'you'.

This body is made up of five elements and has been handed over to you by virtue of the karmic cycle; it is the creation of nature. This body is like a toy and it will work as long as the *prana* will survive, for as much time as God wants us to have it. And he takes this toy away from you whenever he wants to. What right do I have over it? Just as I am separate from this 'body', I am different from this mind too.

The way you wear an undershirt beneath a long robe, in the same way your gross body is the external garment and the subtle one is the inner garment. Our subtle body consists of mind, *buddhi*, *chitta*, *ahankara* — the five senses of motor and sensory skills, and the five *pranas*. There is a third body too — the causal body.

'I' am different from all these three veils, these three types of body: gross, subtle and causal. You have to look beyond these three veils to discover who 'I' am. You are chidananda, you are *chittaroopa*, and you are *anandaroopa*. You are a form of truth itself. I am not saying that *buddhi* is a form of truth. I am not saying that *ahankara* is a form of truth. 'You' are the truth. In the classical language this 'you' is called *atman*. *Atman* is truth.

Often when this word *atman* is mentioned, people begin to think that it does not really exist and is more of an illusion. They wonder if it really exists. *Atman* simply means 'I' and it has no meaning other than this. The *guru* says, 'I' am the truth and the disciple experiences that 'I' am the truth.

If I have to experience that 'I' am the truth, then first my *buddhi* has to understand how it is so. How am 'I' the truth? How am 'I' consciousness? How am 'I' *ananda*? How am 'I' chidananda? Everything cannot be understood in a single instance. That is why you must constantly reflect on what you have understood. Only then will the inner secret reveal itself to you.

In order to understand how 'I' am the truth, you first need to know the distinction between truth and non-truth. What is truth? That which is present in all the three phases of time is truth. And what is not present in all the three phases of time is non-truth. And these three phases are: past, present and future. The one that exists

in all these three phases is called truth. And the one that does not exist in all the three phases is called non-truth. Time as such is a fragmentation of the mind and the mind is an illusion.

That which changes, can change, is changing is untrue. Your body is present now. But was it there earlier? Suppose your body is 52 years old now. So 52 years ago this body was not there. Once, in a home, family members were sitting and leafing through the family album. They were talking in this vein, "We had gone to see the Taj Mahal, visited Agra and Delhi." A small child was watching all this. Suddenly he said, "Mummy, why am I not there?" His mother said, "Son, you were not even born then." And the child asked, "If I was not born, then where was I?" His mother tried to explain, "You are not in this album because you had not come into our family then." The child asked, "What do you mean by saying that I had not come into this family?" The mother said, "Because you were not with us in this family?" Again the child asked, "If I was not in this family, then where was I?"

Who is your mother and who is your father? You keep screaming 'mummy' all the time. The word 'mummy' means a corpse. In Egypt, they had a practice of embalming the dead bodies of kings, queens and princes and then burying them, constructing a pyramid on top. Remember that the structure of a pyramid is not like a grave. The shape of a pyramid is such that it generates a great deal of energy; as a result the bodies buried inside do not decay for a very long time. When these pyramids in Egypt were dug up for the first time, the corpses buried thousands of years ago were found to be well preserved. But for the skin that had disintegrated in places, the rest of the body was in fairly good shape. The structure of a pyramid does help a great deal in meditation, as it helps conserve energy. It does not allow any leakage of energy. When the British historians dug up the bodies buried under the pyramids, they called them mummified bodies or mummies.

Now, I do not know since when the English word 'mummy' came into circulation. As long as we do not understand it, it is all right. I am in no way trying to build a case against the English language. The word 'mummy' does refer to a corpse. The only difference is that it means an Egyptian corpse. All right, let us say not an Indian but an Egyptian corpse. Does it make any difference whether it is an Indian or an Egyptian corpse? It is much the same thing. So rather than call mother mummy, you should call her a corpse. "Namaste corpse! I offer my salutations to you corpse!" And if you are gender conscious, then you must call your father 'he-corpse' and your mother 'she-corpse,' the way you make a distinction between a cock and a hen, or a horse and a mare.

The question that the child asked was, "When I was not in this family, where was I?" Now I ask, where were you before you acquired this body? If you do not know the answer and I am sure you do not, does it mean that you were not there at all? It is not possible that you were not there at all. Where was 'I', I do not know but 'I' was there. Only if 'I' was there earlier could I incarnate into this birth. In this body, in this birth, the 'I' has come only because 'I' was there much before this body was created.

In the same way, when this body returns to the five elements, 'I' will still remain. You will say, "How do I know whether or not 'I' will survive?" Look, the way you now claim that 'you' are there, either you know it or you have to be told that 'you' are there! 'I' exist, is something that I alone have the consciousness of. For example, suppose you are sleeping and someone comes and wakes you up and says, "Come on get up, we have to go and do this." Now, if you are pretending to sleep, if you are not really sleeping, only then do you know that 'I' am not sleeping. In the same way, it is the 'I' that knows of its own existence. When the body dies, whether or not 'I' will survive is something 'I' alone knows.

Often people ask questions like: Who knows whether or not we will survive after death? The way you know about your existence now, in the same way, after death too you will know about 'your' existence. Before this body, you acquired so many other bodies. Shankaracharya says:

Punarapi jananam punarapi maranam,
Punarapi janani jathare shayanam

Born again and again
Dying over and over again
Residing in the mother's womb, again and again

So sometimes this body is there and sometimes it is not. Now this body is here and before birth it was not here. After death again it will not be there. But before this body, 'I' was there. And the fact that 'I' am there is something 'I' alone knows.

I had told you that something that is present in all the three phases of time — past, present and future, is truth. 'I' am not a mere body and 'I' am present in all the three phases. So by this logic, the real *swaroopa* of 'I' is also truth. 'I' am a form of truth.

The first step towards *gyana* is: 'I' am not a body; this body is not mine.

The second step towards *gyana* is: 'I' am not the mind; this mind is not mine.

The third step towards *gyana* is: 'I' am not *buddhi*, this *buddhi* is not mine.

Between the mind and the *buddhi* are the *gyanindriyan*, they help you create a bridge between you and the world. You see with your eyes, hear with your ears, smell with your nose, taste with your tongue and feel with your hands. All these sense organs are not 'I'. 'I' am separate from all of these — 'I' am a form of truth.

'I' am truth and 'I' am consciousness. Consciousness is that which has the power to know or that which knows. Now, what is it that knows that: This is my body? What is it that knows when the eyes cannot see properly? It is the 'I' that knows all this through the mind. A person goes to an eye doctor for a check up. The doctor sets the frame on the tip of the nose and puts the lens inside and says, "Now read what is in front of you. Try to read the first line." The person reads it and the doctor asks him to read the middle one and then the last two lines. If the person cannot, then the doctor keeps on changing the lens until the right number is identified.

Now, there is no other way for a doctor to know which lens will help you see clearly. The doctor has only lenses in his possession and he asks you to test them and only you know which lens helps you see clearly. Who is it that knows whether the ears have the power to hear or have lost it? You may say, "It is your mind that knows." But the intellect cannot know anything on its own. As long as there is no 'I' behind this mind, how can it know anything? Mind is the instrument of 'I'!

The 'knower' is different from the 'known'. All right, I will explain it with the help of an example. I am holding this small box in my hand and I can see it even from a distance of six inches or a foot. But if I were to hold it right next to my eyes, will I be able to see it? Suppose your child comes home and sticks his report card right in your face and says, "Mummy look, I stood first in my class." You will say, "Oh, you silly fool, just take it off my eyes. How will I be able to see how many marks you have got?"

You need distance to see things clearly. If you hold something too close to your eyes how will you see it? Indian women put collyrium in their eyes. If they do not use a mirror, how will they be able to see whether they have applied it properly or not? Sometimes the woman does not even get to know about it because she cannot see her own face? You need distance to see your own face. The mirror maintains that distance and so we are able to see ourselves.

The 'knower' is different from the thing that is to be 'known'. The one who 'knows' is separate from the object he wants to 'know'. 'I' know that this body is mine — so 'I' am separate from this body. Who knows the sense organs? 'I' knows the sense organs and that which knows is called *chaitanya*.

All right, remember one thing, your body is not conscious. The body is non-sentient. The body does not even know who resides in it. Now let me take a leaf out of Shankaracharya's life. *Adi Shankaracharya* renounced the world at the age of eight. Since the age of seven he had started harping to his widowed mother: "I want to be a *sanyasi*." Sometimes his mother would scold him, sometimes laugh it away and sometimes just ignore it. Once he went out for a dip in the river where a crocodile suddenly grabbed his foot. He quickly asked his mother that since he was going to die, why does she not give him permission to become a *sanyasi*? The moment his mother said, "All right, go ahead and become a *sanyasi*," God alone knows what miracle happened. Whether it was Shankaracharya who managed to pull his foot out of the crocodile's jaws or whether it was the crocodile that let go on its own, he just swam across to the shore. Touching his mother's feet he said, "All right mother! Now that I have your permission, let me go."

accident in life. You too must have been through some sad and tragic experience. In India, it was a sad tradition that intelligent people retired from worldly affairs so that they could focus on their mind and *sadhana*. Sages were never escapists; they were strugglers and hard working people. But with time, things have changed a lot; as deterioration creeps into every sphere, so it has happened with religion too. Now, people are becoming *sadhus* for all the wrong reasons — if someone's wife dies, he goes to *Haridwar*, gets his head tonsured and becomes a *sadhu*. Someone's husband dies and she comes to the *ashram* and starts reciting '*Rama-Rama*'.

While I was still in college and even till many years later, people said things like, "She was in love with someone and he deserted her that is why she has become a *sadhu*." The people who concoct these stories go so far as to suggest that I was once married. I even had a son, they say. Then there was a fight because I was more into *bhakti*. My husband did not approve of it so we separated and he took the son away to America!

I do not know about others. I do not even know about these *mahatmas* sitting here — as to why they renounced the world. I can only talk for myself. I have not renounced anything. To renounce you have to own something and I know this well that I do not own anything.

A person who has lost all attachment; a person who understands that 'I' alone am the source of eternal bliss, may either live in his house or in a forest, it really does not affect him. Marriage or celibacy neither can make you great. If you think you can become great just by abstaining from sex, then you are mistaken!

If *Shukdev*, *Narada* and *Ashtavakra* did not marry, it was not because they had something against marriage, but for the simple reason that they did not want to! *Rishi Vashishta* was married to *Arundhati*. *Hazrat Jalaluddin*, *Farid*, *Guru Nanak* were married. But in a way, it is difficult for me to describe *Guru Nanak Sahib* as a householder. On the insistence of his parents and his sister he agreed to marry, but after sometime he said goodbye to them and went off to propagate the truth. Who can tie down a free spirited *fakir*? When I used to frequent *gurudwaras*, I often ran into the so called wise people there. They would tell me, "Look, if *Guru Nanak Sahib* could be a householder, why can you not be one? Why have you not married?" And every time I would tell them the same thing, "I cannot be the kind of householder *Guru Nanak* was. He was not really a householder in the true sense of the word." When they first heard me say that, they were furious and protested, "How can you say that?" I said, "I will tell you! If you do not remember his life story, I will remind you of it."

A few years after his marriage, *Guru Nanak* announced, "I am going to travel the world to teach." When his sister got to know of it she came running. His wife was crying; his mother was crying; his father was scolding him; but he was busy packing his bags. The sister tried her best to plead with him, saying "What sort of a pilgrimage are you going on? Where will you go? Just sit at home."

Guru Nanak said, "No, I must go. I listened to you and got married. Now you will have to listen to me. Do not create any obstacles." When nothing else worked, Nanak's sister told his two sons, "Go and grab your father's legs and do not allow him to leave." They started crying so bitterly that on listening to their pleas, even a stone-hearted father would have melted. Holding on to their father's legs, both the children were crying. Their aunt had tutored them rather well and had also told them that this was probably the only way out. *Nanak* kept listening to their cries for sometime and then disengaging their arms from his legs, very gently he said, "Now I give your responsibility to those who have sent you to me." So Nanak's sister Nanaki was caught in the trap of her own making. She had to take on the responsibility of the children!

Not once, but many times over he left his house. He went as far as Iran, Nepal, Sri Lanka and Afghanistan. Now, those who say that I too should become a householder like *Guru Nanak* do not really understand his life very well. *Guru Nanak* kept wandering for several years and travelled far and wide. Despite being a married man, he was a detached soul and remained an unattached *fakir*. His children were taken care of by their aunt. *Nanak* was never home to serve his parents.

He lived his life in great freedom; he married knowing what he wanted to do and never allowed marriage to overpower him. Why do you compare me with him? He was an awakened man. He

belonged to the category of *Ishwar*, a *gyani* right from his birth. And you say that I should do what he did! I am me; the best example of me is me; how can I follow or imitate anyone? It was Nanak's choice to get married and it is mine not to.

Wife or no wife, *Nanak* was great; wife or no wife, *Kabir* was great. I am reminded of an incident in Kabir's life. *Brahmins of Benares* had tutored a woman and sent her to *Kabir* to discredit him. The *pandits* were really annoyed for they were not being respected in *Benares*. They were not too happy with the fact that the king of *Benares* showed unusual respect toward an ordinary weaver like *Kabir*. Though a *Muslim*, the king would come and prostrate himself at the feet of *Kabir*. So in order to defame him, they hired the services of a woman who was pregnant. They instructed her to go and catch hold of Kabir's hand in full public view and say, "Why are you leaving me in the lurch now? Why not keep the promise you made?"

When the woman repeated these words in full public view, Kabir's own disciples ran away. When the entire society started maligning him, *Kabir Sahib* just stood there, listening to all the accusations. He said to the woman, "If you say you have nowhere to go, then come with me. I will take care of you." The woman had thought that this drama would start in the public place and end there itself, but she had not bargained for this! Not even once did *Kabir* say, "This woman is lying." Amidst so much of commotion, who would have listened to *Kabir* anyway?

She got nervous and scared. This was not part of her script at all and she was afraid of people's reaction if they came to know about the truth. She felt ashamed. Night was about to descend and she was going through pangs of remorse. She wondered why she had agreed to enact such a drama to discredit a *sadhu*. She thought to herself, "I humiliated him so much, yet not even once did he scold me or beat me or threaten me." At midnight she fell at Kabir's feet and started crying, "Please forgive me. I have committed the most heinous of sins. But I have one question, why did you not oppose me?" *Kabir* said, "You are a woman after all. You must have had your own compulsions. I respect womankind. Seeing your tears and wails I kept quiet. But I know what your reality is. Do not worry, you can stay here. But this interchange shall remain a secret between the two of us. Now if you wish to go, you may go." She said, "No, I will not go like this! Now I will stay here till morning. And in the morning when the bazaar opens, I will go to the same roundabout where I had falsely accused you; I will proclaim your innocence in public. I will tell everyone that this was a conspiracy hatched by the *pandits* who were bent on maligning you."

Celibacy has been unnecessarily endorsed as a great virtue; sex is neither ugly nor a sin. Sexuality is a sickness — a disease, but sex is a natural phenomenon. Celibacy is not a sure shot way of attaining *moksha*. A *sadhu* is no greater than a house-holder.

If a person becomes a *sadhu* because he has been through some tragic accident or incident in his life, he is an escapist. I am of the view that a real *sadhu* is neither forced by unfortunate circumstances, nor by financial bankruptcy to renounce the world. A person becomes a *sadhu* only when he understands that the real source of happiness lies inside and he has to explore this hidden source. He does not seek the gratification of worldly desires because he has tasted the nectar of desirelessness. Now, whether or not he stays in the house, a real seer is a person who knows that 'I' am *Satchidananda*.

This stotra of Shankaracharya says:

**Na punyam na paapam na soukhyam na duhkham
Na mantro na teertham na vedaa na yagyaah
Aham bhojanam neiva bhojyam na bhoktaa
Chidaanandroopah shivoham shivoham**

He says, "There is no sin or piety in me. There is no joy or misery in me, neither *yagna* nor *Veda* in me. The notion of sin and piety is lodged in our minds. The custodians of religion have set up such a trap of sin and virtue — paap and *punya* — that an ordinary man is unable to extricate himself from it. Scriptures and priests lay down rules: if you do this, then it is a pious action, if you do that it is a sinful action. They have even settled this question: What is a pious action and what is sinful? They have also made out a regular list of what is recommended and what is not.

They also claim that who performs pious actions will go to heaven and who indulges in sinful deeds shall go to hell. In some religious places, you actually get maps of heaven and hell. The sinful, they say, will have to cross a river of fire on their way to hell. Once the river of fire has been crossed, one has to go along a path paved with iron nails. And these nails are such that they hurt and bleed the soles, but never go deep inside nor do they remain fully outside — you have to walk on them. Then there are huge cauldrons full of boiling oil and sinful creatures are fried in these cauldrons! Just look at the flight of imagination! They claim you have to cross a river of fire in order to reach heaven as well. All those who are sinful fall into this river; they burn but do not die. But the pious and the pure-hearted are able to go across the ocean and never come to any harm.

Once I read a story. A religious-minded person died and went to *yamloka* (the land of death). He did all kinds of good deeds, yet after death he found himself surrounded by the messengers of Yamraj. The messengers said, "Come on, Sir! Since you have come from earth, you will have to cross the river of fire. But you should be careful. If you entertain even a single sinful thought in your mind, you will fall into the river. And if your thoughts are pious, you will sail through without any trouble. Now we have discontinued the practice of maintaining a register of your good and bad deeds. Now we have this new system in place, so you will have to cross this river."

He was still taking stock of that man's actions when a beautiful woman landed there. The messenger said, "Now that you are here, you too shall have to cross the river. And if you entertain any sinful thoughts, you will go hurtling down into the river. If you do not, then you will enter heaven."

The woman said, "All right." She was an extremely attractive woman. So the messenger of *Yama* opened the gates for both of them. They saw a river of fire raging in front. The woman started walking ahead, followed by the religious person and the messenger followed too. As they walked, they could hear the other person's footsteps. Then after a while, the woman turned around to see why there was no sound behind her. She saw that both had fallen into the river and had been burnt. Both of them were entertaining sinful thoughts!

So there are maps showing the geography of heaven and hell. And they have different categories too. They decide whether you deserve to go to 'A', 'B' or 'C' category. There are categories in heaven as well. This whole business of heaven and hell is the brainchild of the *pandits* — the custodians and propagators of religious dogma — who want ordinary people to be caught up in the vicious cycle of sin and piety, so that they can make money out of it.

These selfish and dishonest people also teach that no matter how hungry you are, you must never refrain from giving alms to others. Once I went to participate in the *Kumbh Mela* at Allahabad. In the evenings, I used to do *satsang*. Hundreds of people, dressed in rags and tatters, carrying their possessions in dilapidated trunks, come to the *Kumbh Mela* wishing to do some donation. One such group came to me and a woman said, "We want to give you seedha." Now I did not really understand their language. I asked what they meant by 'seedha' and was told it meant that they wished to donate food grains. If you looked at her, she was the picture of hunger — no more than a mere skeleton. I asked her, "Why do you want to give it to me?" She said, "Because we have been told that if you give charity on this occasion, you go to heaven." And who would she have offered all her charity to? Obviously to the *pandits, mahatmas, swamis,* and *mandaleshwars,* who are already affluent and well fed.

I said to that woman, "I cannot accept it from you." She said, "What sin have I committed?" Now what do I say? Perhaps she thought that I had refused because she was from a lower caste. So she said to me, "We belong to a high caste, we are *Saraswat Brahmins.*" I said, "Ma! My problem is not your caste or which family you belong to, but I cannot accept because it is you who need to eat and not me. I have enough. If you offer me rice and wheat, I will cook it and offer it to you."

But these *pandits* keep insisting that you must give something for charity. There is a story of Munshi Prem Chand in which a son raises a loan to perform the last rites of his father; to pay the *pandits* for the cremation; to offer food to the community; to give

gifts for the rituals performed. By the time everything was over, the loan had piled up into a huge amount. Whatever he earned, he would pay off as the interest, but the principal just stood where it was. The loan kept piling up and he died, weighed down by the burden of his debt.

Then his son went to the same money-lender and asked for more money to perform the last rites of his father. The money-lender said, "Why do you not mortgage the house? And if the house is gone, then your land." Whatever money he thus raised was spent on performing the last rites of his father. Again the loan kept piling up and so did the interest. The house was lost; the land was lost — in order to ensure that the *shradh* (last rites) could be performed properly.

The custodians of religion have set up their own shop. Do pious actions, not sinful ones. Pious actions are no longer pious when you have a selfish motive. A meditative person can never commit an evil act. Because he knows that whatever he does, ultimately he has to suffer its consequences. Such a person does not need the authority of religious injunction to prevent him from committing an evil action, as his own inner consciousness always shows the right way.

As a matter of fact, *punya-paap* should be discussed only in this context — if you do evil, then someone else will come and punish you? No, no! If you commit a sin, it is your own conscience that will inflict a punishment on you. It is your mind that punishes you in the guise of *Dharamraj*. But the mind that is caught up in the vicious cycle of *punya-paap* lives in burden and guilt.

A dip in the *Ganga* is not a passport to heaven; the water of the *Ganga* is cool, clean, inviting and for several centuries countless sages and seers, mendicants and *mahatmas* have been meditating on its banks. To take a dip in this river is akin to embracing *Mahadev Shiva*, as this river flows out of his matted hair. But do religious people — scores of *Hindus* — take a bath in the *Ganga* for this reason?

They go for a dip in the *Ganga* so that it may wash off all the impurities they have accumulated. Do you think a mere dip can

183

help you gain the *punya* of a lifetime? Or will it make you more arrogant with the thought that you are now free of all sin?

I have heard this satire from an extraordinary seer, who used to live on the banks of the *Ganga* at *Haridwar*. He would often say, "People come here thinking that they will take a dip, leave behind all their sins and carry back only piety with them. But now the sins have smartened up! The *Ganga* once prayed, 'How long will the sinners keep washing off their sins in my waters? How long will I accumulate all the filth? O God! Do something about it.' So God created another system and explained a couple of things to sin. When the man preparing for a dip is busy taking off his clothes, the sin slips away and stands on the bank and says, 'Go ahead and take a dip my dear, I am secure on the bank and waiting for you to come out'!"

As soon as the man steps out of the water, his sins re-attach themselves to him. But there is a great meaning hidden behind this sarcasm. The *Ganga* refuses to wash off the sins of the dishonest. The truth is that if someone takes a dip with pure conviction, then his conviction itself shall purify him completely.

An ordinary person is always caught up in this vicious cycle of fear of sin and need for piety. If he goes to serve someone, it is not because he genuinely enjoys the idea of serving but because he wants to add to his list of good deeds.

Once a teacher in a missionary school told her pupils, "Everyday, you must do at least one good deed. You may help the old, feed the hungry, or tend to the sick. But one good deed must be done every day." The next day the teacher asked, "Did you do a good deed yesterday?" Some children raised their hands. One of them said, "I found an old and helpless woman standing by the roadside. I helped her cross the road." She asked the second, "What did you do?" He said, "I helped an old lady cross the road." The third said, "I too helped an old woman cross the road." The fourth one said, "I too helped her cross the road." The fifth said, "Helped her cross the road."

The teacher was taken aback. "How come everyone met an old woman? How many old women had set off from their homes yesterday, that all of you could help each one of them cross the road?" They said, "No, not at different places. As soon as we stepped out of the school, we saw an old woman outside." The teacher said, "All right, you made her cross the road. This does make sense. That you did it once is understandable. But how did five of you help her cross the road? After all, a person would cross the road only once. Not so many times over!" All the children spoke in unison, "Teacher, this was the problem! She just did not want to cross the road. So we forced her to. In the process, we dragged her as we were determined to do at least one good deed yesterday." So one of them dragged her to the other side and the other dragged her back! Because one good deed had to be done everyday! Now what is it really, sin or piety?

In another story, a *mahatma* was basking in the sun. A lady came with a glass of cold lassi and said, "Please have it!" The *mahatma* said, "I can understand if you offer tea, but cold lassi in this cold weather!" She said, "Only yesterday I heard in the Bhagavad, that by offering cold lassi to a *mahatma* you can please *Krishna* and he sends you straight to heaven. So please have it!" The *mahatma* said, "What if this cold lassi makes me sick?" The lady said, "Well, that is your problem."

In the name of piety and good deeds, often people end up doing foolish things. Even if they engage in good deeds, they tend to get arrogant and claim credit for whatever they have done.

It is just an ego trip and nothing else. If you do a good deed with the intention of telling others, for making it known to others, then you have not done anything pious. When *Rama* met *Shabri*, did she tell him that she had waited for him for so many years, months, weeks or days; that she had kept sweeping the road he had to come by? She did not say, "I have offered you fruits and flowers all these years, now give me my reward, now grant me heaven."

When do you commit a sin? You commit a sin only when you sleep-walk through life. Now, whether the deed is pious or sinful, you have to reap the harvest of your actions. No one can escape the fruit of his action.

If sin binds, does piety liberate? No! Piety also binds! It binds us because of our arrogance. If you see the arrogance of people

185

who perform rituals, you will be shocked. The sinful ones might still turn penitent, but the pious never do.

What is a pious action? The one that adds to your humility or enhances your *satvik* disposition is essentially a pious action. The one that adds to the *rajoguna* in you constitutes sinful actions. If a particular action puts your heart under strain and you are scared of being found out, then that act is sinful. And what is a pious act? If a particular action makes us feel light and joyous and if it enhances the 'purity of heart', it is a pious action.

Once you transcend the mind, you reach a state called 'na punyam na paapam' — neither a pious action gladdens your heart nor a sinful one fills it with sorrow. Once you go beyond the realm of paap-*punya*, then you experience neither joy nor sorrow.

Once someone asked a seer, "Do seers always remain happy?" The seer said, "No." Then he asked, "If not happy, then do they always remain sad?" The seer said, "No." Now this is a very strange answer, the seer should either be sad or happy. We have heard that the way worldly people are full of misery, in the same way seers live in a state of perpetual bliss. The seer said, "The seers are neither miserable nor happy, because they do not live in the mind, a seer lives outside the mind."

A *Sufi* wrote:

Joys come and so do sorrows
In the midst of it all, we remain in a trance
Sometimes it is respect all the way and sometimes it is
humiliation all the way
In the midst of this respect and humiliation,
we just remain in a trance
Singing in this way, the fakir says,
Someone is born and someone dies
In the midst of these ever-changing scenes,
we remain in a trance

A seer is neither happy nor sad. Sadness and happiness complement each other. Good deeds bring happiness and bad deeds bring misery. But *gyana* helps you transcend this vicious cycle. Once you are established as a 'non-doer', — you claim no

credit for deeds done by you — then there is neither sin nor piety; then 'I' does not get any rewards for piety and 'I' does not get any punishment for sin. In this state of *atmabhava*, there is no duality of sin or piety and there is no happiness or misery.

Is it not somewhat strange and also somewhat dangerous? Someone might think that Shankaracharya is saying that 'I' the *atman* is beyond the realm of sin and piety. Then you will not have to go to either heaven or hell and are therefore free to do whatever you choose to. If your mind is thinking along these lines, then beware! You are misinterpreting the whole thing.

I have said no such thing, nor has Shankaracharya. All he is saying is that the norm is that piety shall bring joy and sin misery. But all this joy and sorrow is experienced within the mind and 'I' am not mind, 'I' am *Satchidananda* — the one that witnesses the processes of the mind. This *punya-paap* is not of the witness.

Shankaracharya is not saying that you are free to do whatever *punya-paap* you wish to, or that *punya-paap* do not exist at all, or that regardless of what you do there will be no consequences whatsoever. Why will the consequences not be there? There will be consequences; if you are a doer then you have to be a reaper.

The actions of a *gyani* are always motivated by *viveka* (discerning intelligence). The enlightened one's behaviour is not dictated by the mind but by his awareness. When the situation demanded, *Krishna* lied and made strategies to kill opponents in war. When the *Kauravas* conspired against the *Pandavas*, he instructed *Arjuna*, "You do whatever is necessary, for their destruction is inevitable. This is the only goal we have." But *Yudhishtira* dug in his heels saying, "No, I will not tell lies." He told *Yudhishtira*, "You just spread the word that *Ashwathama* has been killed, and the moment *Dronacharya* hears this, he will instantly break his vow." *Dronacharya* had taken a vow that he would participate in the war only as long as his son was alive. It was the affection of his son that had prompted him to enslave himself to the *Kauravas*. Even when *Krishna* tried to reason with *Dronacharya*, he refused to listen. He was really fond of his son *Ashwathama*. He wanted that just as he was living amongst the princes, his son too should lead a princely life.

Then one day *Duryodhana* rebuked *Dronacharya*, saying, "You think of yourself as an *acharya*? We have lost so many heroes in this battle, but you have not killed even a single Pandava so far. Only when you kill one of them will we be convinced that you are on our side. Otherwise *Gurudev*, we will think that you are deceiving us. Though you may be on our side, yet you are working for the *Pandavas*."

Dronacharya felt hurt. Then he took a vow that the next day he would kill at least one of the *Pandavas*. The secret agents of the *Pandavas* immediately informed them about this vow. *Draupadi* felt very insecure, and she said to *Krishna*, "What will happen tomorrow? Even if one of my five husbands is killed, what is the point of your being there?" *Krishna* said, "You don't worry!"

An emergency meeting was called and *Yudhishtira* was instructed, "Tomorrow you make the announcement and we will manage the rest. Around noon you should proclaim that '*Ashwathama* has been killed', and then blow your conch shell. On hearing this, when *Dronacharya* is thrown off balance and starts wailing, then as per his vow, he will give up arms and *Arjuna* will attack and kill him." *Yudhishtira* said, "But I refuse to tell a lie — I am *Dharamraj*. I will not say that *Ashwathama* is dead." *Dharamraj Yudhishtira* was greedy for *punya*. And because telling a lie is a sin, *Yudhishtira* refused.

People who insist on doing good deeds are often very stubborn by nature. This is also a kind of foolishness. *Krishna* is trying to explain, but this fool is simply not willing to understand. He is trying to show off his commitment to *dharma*. When in full public view he had decided to stake the lives of his brothers and his wife in gambling, had he not lost his head then? Why did he not use his intelligence then? Now he is trying to prove to *Krishna* that he is very intelligent.

Again *Krishna* said, "All right, there is an elephant in the army of the *Kauravas* who is also called *Ashwathama*. Bhima, you kill that elephant and then *Yudhishtira* can announce, '*Ashwathama* is dead.'" Adamant *Yudhishtira* replied, "No, I will say *Ashwathama* the elephant and not *Ashwathama* the man is dead."

Crazy fool! Now, all the four brothers wanted to do what *Krishna* had suggested. They had to exercise immense self-control

to fight the impulse to oppose their elder brother, as they were all bound by ethics, idealism and the principles of respect. I somehow feel that if they could, they would have given him a sound thrashing — it would have been much better. He was such a foolish man. Sometimes, I find it surprising that despite all the mistakes he made, he is still referred to as *Dharamraj* — king of *Dharma*.

Often religious minded people are stubborn and inflexible. As they follow just the letter of dharam and not its spirit. Finally *Krishna* said, "All right, at least he has agreed to proclaim that *Ashwathama* the elephant and not the man is dead." The next day, in the battlefield, when the elephant *Ashwathama* was killed, he urged *Yudhishtira* to make the announcement. The moment he said, "*Ashwathama* is dead," *Krishna* had prepared every one to sound the bugle in unison. All of them started blowing the bugle with all their might. The rest of Yudhishtira's sentence was drowned in the din of the bugles.

Krishna is called a God only because he has *viveka* — awareness and practicality. He is not called a God just because the *shastras* have declared so. He is called a God because he has godliness in him. What is godliness? In other words, he possesses the awareness and greatness of *gyana*; he maintains his sense of balance and equipoise; he remains calm and aloof in the face of all provocation. Whatever he does, he does with spontaneity and a great deal of *viveka*.

So a *gyani* neither insists upon *punya* nor upon paap. He transcends the dualities of *punya-paap*. I will tell you what is the greatest *punya* — to know your self is the biggest *punya*. And what is the biggest sin? I would say it is to believe that 'I' am this body.

All sins emerge from mind and body identification. Greed, lust, arrogance and vanity come out of this false identification with the mind and the body. Once you cut through the sheath of ignorance that says 'I' am body, mind, *buddhi*, *chitta*, *ahankara*, then all the dualities of the mind drop. Your entire being begins to glow with this knowledge.

Rise above body obsessiveness and then you will be able to fully understand this *gyana*. But your problem is that you rarely ever stay in *atmabhava*. This is the root of the problem. You always live in dehobhava. There is no dearth of people who can expound on the *Vedanta*. But if you just utter the word or catch the word, how does it help? Real gain is not possible unless you catch the meaning and essence, 'the *tattva*' behind the words. And you can catch the meaning only if you inculcate the qualities of love, devotion and service in yourself.

Be loving and respectful toward others. Really, if you know how to give love, then you can win over your worst enemies. How will anyone fight with you if you are full of love? Innocence and purity will give you clarity of mind and also the capacity to understand this higher knowledge.

You are the pure one, this is your intrinsic nature. Nothing can change this, but your mind cannot enjoy this until it is pure, still and calm. *Dhyana* gives this knowledge and selfless service gives purity to heart and mind.

CHAPTER 11

WITNESSING IS REAL MEDITATION

Tattvagyana changes your perception of the world completely. For those who are deprived of *tattvagyana*, this world has one meaning and for those who perceive it from the perspective of *gyana*, it assumes another. For the worldly person this world is true. Such a person believes that the world is real. But this is as false as the dream you see at night; which seems real when it is happening.

In my view a seeker should meditate upon his dreams. I am not saying that you reflect on the story of your dreams, but reflect on the dream, as to why and how it happens. These days you get many books in the market which interpret your dreams. They tell you what your dreams mean. People who are looking for a meaning in their dreams are confused people. To focus on dreams, you have to raise your awareness in the waking stage and only then can you remain aware in the dream state. At the time of retiring to bed, you must resolve to remember the dreams you have. It is very important to meditate silently before you go to sleep. I suggest 'Yog Nidra' before going to sleep for it will induce a deep sleep and also greater meditativeness — which is what is needed in any case.

Meditation means awareness. To be aware, to be fully in the moment, that is meditation. The method or the procedure is not *dhyana*. Your mind is in such a bad state that it is always trapped in a net of desires. To achieve its goal, the mind thinks obsessively, always in a worldly rat race. And this monologue of the mind does not allow you to sit still. That is why I have to involve you in these procedures. To follow a method, you have to be fully awake and when you are fully awake you are able to meditate. And then, as long as you are in meditation, every rat race is put on hold.

All the masters narrate wonderful stories. They know how to tell stories, but since they do not publish them and do not participate in any contest, they do not get any awards. Have you ever heard of a seer getting an award for the best storyteller? There is this great *Sufi* story. Once a man bought an empty bottle from a junk dealer. When he opened the cork of the bottle, a naughty *jinn* sprang out of it. When he saw the *jinn*, he was so scared that he started running, calling out "Allah, Allah!" As he ran, the *jinn* also ran after him, shouting, "O my master! Where are you going? I am your servant. Why are you scared of your servant? I am your servant after all."

The man took some time to come to terms with the situation. Once he did, he turned around and saw a giant-sized shape in front of him. The *jinn* said, "You took me out of the bottle in which a *khwaja* (mystic) had imprisoned me. You liberated me. I had decided that I would serve the one who sets me free." The man said, "I am not even sure of my own boarding and lodging, how can I look after a slave? Besides, I am not in a position to reward you for your efforts, nor can I pay any salary. Please go! Get off my back!"

The *jinn* said, "I do not want any salary, nor do I want food or clothing. You just have to order and I will do your bidding. I have no special needs. A *jinn* does not need any food. But let me warn you, I am not in the habit of sitting idle; our contract shall be valid only for a period of six months — then if you do not give me work, I will swallow you alive!" So the man ordered the *jinn*, "Build a house for me. Get me horses, camels, food, loads of money!" Whatever he was asked to do, the *jinn* did happily. It was almost as if he was creating everything with a magic wand.

The man was happy. People around were surprised, wondering where he got so many things from! How did he become so rich? But how could he tell the story of the *jinn*? As the period of six months was about to end, he began to worry. He thought that if the *jinn* stayed idle then it will gobble him up. He would finish any task in a jiffy. Now the man was getting scared, so he went to

a *Sufi* and narrated the entire story about how he found the *jinn*, how he had been running errands for the past few months and how the period of his contract was coming to an end. The old *Sufi* suggested a way out. He said, "You go and buy a long pole and fix it in the ground. And when you have no work for him, just ask him to climb up and down the pole! Say to him, 'Now this is your work. Until I find another job for you, this is what you have to do!'"

He did as he was told. Now the *jinn* was thinking that soon he would get to swallow this man alive. But a man is a man after all and is definitely wiser than a *jinn*. Six months went by. On the very next day, he said, "Go and get a pole and dig it in the ground. I order you to climb up and down this pole, until I give you another instruction."

The *jinn* got really worried. Within a few hours, he fell at the man's feet and said, "I liberate you from the second clause. I will not eat you up. But this climbing up and down is just not possible for me. I just can't keep doing that without getting anywhere. Set me free. I take back the threat I had held out to you earlier, I will always do as you order!"

Our mind is also like this *jinn*. It has to do something all the time. It keeps thinking of something or the other. It always wants something to chew on. It will think of yesterday, today or tomorrow — but think it must — friends, relatives, family, good things, bad things, politics, weather! Who knows what all? Not even for a split second does our mind stay empty.

It is true that the main function of the mind is to reflect; it is to think in terms of possibilities and choices. But this mind should be your slave and the moment you order the mind to be still, it should obey you. But you keep saying, "O mind! Stay quiet," and it just refuses to do so.

So in other words, your mind is in the habit of thinking nonsense and that too endlessly. Besides, your mind is trapped by so many ties and bonds. With so many attachments and ties of affection tightening around your neck, how can you meditate — it is impossible.

People are scared of *dhyana*. When you are living a normal

life, you are not aware of your mind and you do not listen to the commotion inside your mind. The moment all the external activities — speaking, seeing, listening or doing something are halted; when all the external activities cease, the noise and commotion inside our mind becomes audible and this disturbs the mind a lot.

For instance, right now I am speaking and my voice is reaching across to you. All other sounds in the atmosphere have faded; my voice has masked the other voices and sounds. If I stop speaking now, then you will be able to hear so many sounds which you cannot hear right now. There is the whirring sound of the fan; there are sounds of insects and flies, and the sound of the nightingale. As long as I am speaking, you will not be able to hear any of these sounds. But the moment I stop talking, all these sounds will become audible.

That is why people find it so hard to do *dhyana*; the moment you are silent, the noise of the mind is blaring. People talk and talk and the mind thinks continuously. When there is no one to talk to, you feel bored and desperate. The mind is so obsessed with talking that even when there is no one to talk to, you talk to yourself! You ask a question and you answer it too. And your mind does not supply just one answer but multiple ones. Talking is such a waste, what will you talk about? Individuals, people, events — the whole focus remains on others and you miss yourself.

Excessive talking is a disease just like fever or tuberculosis. Talking is a waste of time; nothing creative will come out of it. Learn the art of being silent. In the ground of silence, meditation grows. But you waste your time and go on chattering — you talk as if there is no tomorrow. Even after coming to the *ashram*, you have not been able to fight your impulse to talk and chatter. You can imagine what must be the case at home where there is no check on you. You must be getting on the nerves of so many people! The one who is given to excessive talking does not qualify as a *sadhak*; the one who is given to excessive eating does not qualify as a *sadhak*; the one who is given to excessive sleeping also does not qualify as a *sadhak*. An aspirant should conserve his energies.

Wake up from this state of drowsiness and slumber. My only selfish motive is that you find your way out of the morass

of ignorance and move forward into light. My only interest is to somehow prevent you from getting sucked into a vortex of misery, to help you out of it and to set you on the path where you realise that your true self is *anandaswaroopa*.

The person who weighs his words before he speaks is never in trouble. The person who has a habit of talking excessively invites all kinds of problems, because every time he opens his mouth he ends up saying something that will annoy or hurt the listener. And then such a person offers all kinds of explanations, saying, "I meant this," or "I meant that." You live your lives in such a state of unconsciousness that often you do not reflect on things of such importance.

In the *Mahabharata*, much of the bitterness was caused because of irresponsible speech. It is not as though there was no bitterness between the *Pandavas* and the *Kauravas*, but irresponsible speech added fuel to fire. For instance, *Draupadi* said to *Duryodhana*, "You are the blind son of a blind man." Was she justified in saying this? If someone has a handicap, is it right to ridicule him? These words hit *Duryodhana* like an arrow. When *Yudhishtira* lost everything in the game of dice, *Duryodhana* ordered *Draupadi* to be dragged into court and said, "Disrobe her! Because all of us are blind and cannot see anything."

So, in a way *Draupadi* was responsible for her own disrobing. She may have been responsible only partially, but she was responsible, she certainly was! When this was communicated to *Krishna*, he reprimanded *Draupadi* and said, "Why did you have to use such words?" *Draupadi* said, "I am ashamed. I will seek forgiveness from *Duryodhana*." Then *Krishna* said, "Now there is no point in seeking forgiveness. The arrow has already pierced his heart!"

Right now a *mahatma* is sitting with me. He has taken a vow to observe total silence for four years. He has no worldly responsibilities and is free, so if he wants to observe this vow, he can. It is a matter of joy for him, a kind of bliss. But if a householder wants to observe a similar vow, it will not be possible to do so, and it is certainly not practical at all. But we can always be conscious of speaking less. We should speak as much as is necessary. We should eat as much as is necessary. We should sleep as much as is necessary. I have seen so many people who just go off to sleep if they have nothing to do. In other words, if there is no work then all they want to do is sleep. Too much sleep is a sign of *tamas*, it is an expression of tamoguna. When we speak less we save our energy. We can utilise this energy to stay alert and awake. When you remain silent, you will be able to hear the noise of your mind. If you go on speaking endlessly, then how will you hear all the commotion inside your mind?

Many people say, "If your mind is not stable, you should go for *satsang*. Our mind is already quite stable." It is not that their mind is stable, but somehow they have immersed themselves in such a rat race, that they have virtually no time to reflect on the state of their mind.

I have seen so many people who work eight to ten hours a day. All they can think of is work and more work. They will not sleep or eat; all they can think of is office and that is it. Now, if you tell such a person to meditate he will probably say, "Oh dear! I am enjoying my life and meditation is such a waste of time." Do they really know what life is or what true joy is? Have they ever peeped inside their mind? Running after wealth, status and relationships, you have forgotten that all you wish to own is transient and mortal.

Sit quietly and watch the flow of your mind and the different colours of your mind will begin to unfold before your eyes. It is important to listen to the noise of the mind. The truth of the matter is that when you begin to watch the noise in your mind, you will see that slowly the thoughts will wear off. Your mind is like a child — as long as you do not pay much attention to it, it will keep making a noise. But the moment you start observing it, it stops playing pranks.

The mind is in a flux; it reflects on events from childhood and speculates on current incidents; it is forever agitated. Observing the thoughts will disassociate one from the mind and the mind will begin to behave. Whatever thought is rising, whichever way it is rising, you just have to witness it without being judgmental. All meditation techniques are just tricks to achieve this.

Now I will take up a question: We know that 'I' is not the mind but we do not realise it within us. How do we discover that this 'I' has gained consciousness of the self?

This is something very subtle. You have heard the *gyana*, but the question is — Have you really understood and has it become your experience? Your intellect has understood the fact that 'I' am not body, mind, *buddhi* or senses. But this is not enough; this is just the beginning. First the *buddhi* has to know, then you have to take a quantum leap out of the mind. When an iron vessel is heated, the heat and the vessel become one. The fire heats up the vessel and the fire also becomes part of the vessel. When the fire is put out, the vessel cools down on its own.

If you try to lift a vessel which is hot without the help of a cloth, it can burn your hand. The heat in the vessel is not its own but of the fire, yet the vessel has acquired from the fire, the capacity to burn. So the heat of the fire is in the vessel, but it does not remain there permanently. After sometime it gets discharged on its own. In the same way, *buddhi* is connected with 'I' and it is through *buddhi* that 'I' am able to understand myself. From this understanding, *buddhi* moves on to a deeper reflection and a stage comes when *buddhi* is left behind and the veil is lifted — the job of the intellect is done.

'I' is separate from this *buddhi*. Now the question arises how 'I' the *atman* will be known through *buddhi*. Now 'I' is not *buddhi* and it is through *buddhi* that we understand everything. The one which you have cannot understand! Therefore, it is said that *guru* gives you the gift of a new *buddhi* — divine intellect, and it is through this new *buddhi* that you are able to know who 'I' am.

Krishna Bhagwan says:

Dadami *buddhi* yogam tam

Arjuna! I give you those eyes which shall enable you to see my real *swaroopa*.

Guru gives you that vision, those eyes with the help of which you are able to look at yourself. And it is in the form of *gyana* that *guru* offers you that divine intellect.

There is a beautiful word for divine intellect — pragya; it is through pragya that we are able to understand ourselves. So the relationship between *buddhi* and 'I' is such, that both are one and yet not completely one. *Buddhi* cannot function without 'I' even though 'I' can function very well without *buddhi*.

'I' am not body and this body is not mine. Does it mean that when someone cuts, lacerates or hurts you, you do not feel pain? You definitely will. Because this body is connected with the mind and the mind is connected with the *buddhi* and the *buddhi* is connected with 'I'.

Sometimes I am asked, "All right, 'I' is not body, but if someone beats it or kills this body, will it not feel the pain?" It is your mind that experiences pain, not your body. Whenever a surgery is to be done, the doctor administers local or general anesthesia. Once you lose consciousness, you do not feel any pain the way you would if you were fully conscious. As the anesthesia is administered, the nerves that carry the message of pain to the brain are drugged and desensitized, and temporarily the connection with the brain is cut off. When the connection of the nerves which send the message to the brain is suspended for a limited time, there is no sensation and there is no message being delivered to the brain and so the brain too is at rest.

Pain has nothing to do with *gyana* or *agyana*. Pain is felt by the mind and mind is associated with 'I'. When body, mind and *buddhi* are not functioning, even then the existence of 'I' is as bright as ever. Right now, *buddhi* is unable to understand these reflections. But in order to convert these reflections into experience, one has to work on witnessing.

Listening alone will not help matters. Listening is only ten percent of the total job. It should be followed by eighty percent of contemplation and the rest of the ten percent is that experience which we call *atmasakshatkar* in Hindi and 'realisation' in English.

Na mantro na teertham na vedaa na yagyaah

'I' am neither *mantras* nor the words of the *mantra*. So you cannot attain *atmadev* by merely chanting *mantras*. *Mantra* chants cannot ever fathom the depths of 'I'. Words are just like sign-

posts, they point towards a direction, they are not a destination in themselves.

The real meaning of the word *mantra* is: that which brings the mind inward. When the mind turns inwards, you get to take a dip in a vast ocean. And when the mind is immersed in the deep ocean, it ceases to be. So who will repeat the *mantra*? All the *mantras*, whether they are of *Hindus* or *Sikhs, Jains* or *Buddhists, Sufis* or Christians are recited in the mind by the mind. How far can a *mantra* reach? Only as far as the mind can.

First you learn the *mantra* with a deep devotion of the mind and then recite it with devotion. What do you gain by reciting *mantras*? Well, if you recite *mantras* with love and devotion, then you do gain concentration. Now, many people do not know what the mechanism of a *mantra* is. All they have been told is, "You just rattle off the *mantra*!" So they catch hold of a rosary and start parroting, "*Rama, Rama, Rama, Rama, Rama.*"

Remember that *mantras* are not meant to be recited forever. *Mantra* is only the means — the way shoes are meant for walking. If you do not have to go anywhere, you just take off your shoes and feel relaxed. *Mantra* is used for a purpose and the purpose is to gain concentration and equipoise, and once this happens, it matures into meditation.

Mullah Nasruddin was abusing his shoes saying things like, "These shoes are useless. They keep pinching me all the time. They are so useless. The fellow who made them must be an ass and the one who sold them a bigger ass. Even I am an ass to have bought them." Someone said, "*Mullah*, why do you keep abusing your shoes all the time? If they are so bad, why do you wear them at all?" *Mullah* said, "I wear them because all day long I remain miserable on account of these shoes, but when I remove them in the evening, the relief I experience is beyond words. This is the only joy in my life. When I liberate my feet from these shoes, I feel tremendous relief, perhaps the only solace in my life. That is why I wear these tight shoes. Of course I know they are tight!"

The logic people use is rather strange. Everyone has his own argument, his own way of seeking happiness in life. Shoes are the means to walk comfortably and *mantra* is the means to gain concentration and consolidation of the mind, as only a concentrated mind is eligible for gaining higher knowledge.

No matter which *mantra* it is, you must recite it with love, devotion and concentration. Allow it to enter your mind. If you are reciting it the right way, then a stage will come when the mind will become silent and then the *mantra* will drop off. The peace that is experienced then, is the only true reward of its recitation. *Mantra* chanting is a wonderful, method to cool down the mind.

Usually people think that the more you chant the *mantra*, the more *punya* you will earn and the more pleased god will be. So they have created a *mantra* bank. Somehow people find it difficult to outgrow the culture of bank accounts. At first you had a bank account to manage your business affairs. Now that you have entered the sphere of religion, you have opened a *mantra* bank account. You keep recording it in your copy and then you deposit the copies in the bank. People are writing *mantras* in their copies — ten thousand *mantras* in ten copies, one lakh *mantras* in a hundred copies. So the calculations go on all the time. There are even *ashrams* that have *mantra* banks! And they do boast that they have the highest number of *mantras* deposited with them!

I have never been able to understand the rationale behind it. Why calculate? If you love *Rama* then recite his name. Why write it down? And what are you hoping for? That *Rama* will send you a letter of thanks and say, "Oh, I am so grateful that you repeated my name so many times over!" *Rama naam* is not meant for continuous repetition. *Rama naam* is meant for total immersion. Perhaps these custodians of religion do not want others to develop their minds, so they keep telling them to just recite *naam*. They organise programmes where people assemble with *dholak* and *manjire* and the *kirtan* of '*Rama Naam*' continues uninterruptedly. The *kirtan* continues for a few hours. At some places you find that an uninterrupted *kirtan* is performed for a good twenty-four or thirty-six hours! When after repeated recitations, the voice tires, then they start writing it out in a copy. This is what they call *Naam Yagna*.

Some people are smarter. They say, "Why write it down? Why turn the beads of a rosary? They just write '*Rama Rama*' on a sheet

and wrap it around themselves. If you go to *Benares*, you will find a sheet with 'Om Namah Shivaya' printed on it. You will get a sheet with the *mahamantra*, 'Hare *Rama* Hare *Krishna*' printed on it. People think it is good enough to wrap it around their shoulders. This means, they neither have to recite it nor do anything else. Whom are you trying to deceive? Yourself? I told you earlier that some people are given to the habit of talking excessively. I would like to give such people a suggestion: they should utilise their power of speech for reciting *mantras*.

Na mantro na teertham na vedaa na yagyaah

Teertham means pilgrimage. Ordinarily, visiting religious places is called *teertham*. Every religion has places which are known as pilgrimage centres. Each religion has its own set. For *Hindus* it is *Benares, Haridwar, Ganga, Gangotri* etc; for *Muslims* it is *Mecca* and *Medina*; for *Sikhs* it is *Harmandir Sahib* etc. According to their own belief systems, people have set up pilgrimage centres. But which is the real one? *Vedanta* says: The real pilgrimage is the master, the *satguru*. Pilgrimage is the place where you become a *sadhak*, where you listen to *satsang*, where you reflect over it and learn to lead a pious, pure and unattached life. It is a place where you perform pious deeds. The pilgrim who wanders in pilgrimage centres is just losing precious time, but those who are greedy for *punya* are always travelling and amassing virtues which just make them more and more egoistic. *Atman* cannot be known by travelling outwards.

Shankaracharya says:

Na mantro na teertham na vedaa na yagyaah

He says that neither *mantra* nor pilgrimage, neither *Vedas* nor *yagna* can help us gain access to *atmadev*. The *Vedas* can definitely comment on the significance of *atmadev*, but are not immanent in *atmadev*. The word *Veda* means *gyana*.

Though *gyana* helps me understand my real *swaroopa*, yet this *gyana* is not immanent in this *atmadev*. Of course I have understood myself only through *gyana*. The real function of *gyana* is to illumine the intelligence or *buddhi*. Once the intelligence has been illumined, once self-realisation has taken place, then *gyana* also outlives its function. That is why sages have suggested that once self-realisation takes place, even *gyana* has to be renounced.

Mantra helps you attain a degree of concentration. By undertaking a pilgrimage, you purify your mind and this enhances your capacity for absorbing *gyana*. Both *Vedas* and *gyana* illumine your intelligence.

Aham bhojanam neiva bhojyam na bhoktaa
Chidanandaroopa shivoham shivoham

Just look at the beauty of the sequence of these words written by Shankaracharya: 'Bhojanam, Bhojayam, Bhokta.' He says, "'I' is neither the food, nor the man who eats the food and not even the man who boasts of the fact that he has eaten." When you eat your food, you say, "I have had food." But *gyana* says it is not true. 'You' have not eaten. 'You' cannot eat food at all. How far can the food go? First it enters your mouth and your mind feels the taste. When it is swallowed it reaches the stomach and is mixed with the juices and broken down. The nutrients are absorbed by the body and the waste matter is eliminated. So the food constitutes only the body and not 'I'. 'I' am not the body, not the mind, not the *buddhi*. 'I' am not food, not tongue, not stomach. 'I' has never eaten food, nor can 'I' ever consume any food.

Let me remind you of the story of sage *Durvasa*. *Gopis* wished to meet Sage *Durvasa* but discovered that the *Yamuna* was in spate. They turned to *Krishna* for help. *Krishna* said, "Go to the *Yamuna* and beg her with folded hands and say, 'If *Krishna* is a *brahmachari* (celibate), then kindly allow us to go across.' The *Yamuna* will make a path for you to cross." The *gopis* started laughing, "You, a celibate?" *Krishna* said, "Well, this is what you have to do." So standing on the banks of the *Yamuna*, they repeated these words. Though they did not trust him, they just repeated what they were told. The section of the Bhagavad which describes the *Maharaas* of *Krishna* and the *gopis* is full of *shringar rasa*. Many people believe that when the *Maharaas* was performed *Krishna* was still a child. A child does not have *kama bhava* (lust).

When the *gopis* repeated what *Krishna* had asked them to,

202

the *Yamuna* allowed them to go across. The *gopis* were shocked and perplexed. On reaching the other side of the bank they paid obeisance to sage *Durvasa* and offered him food. As there were many *gopis*, they had brought a large quantity of food, butter and curd. Very affectionately, the *gopis* put everything in front of him and then prayed, "Lord! Please accept this!" *Durvasa* just ate up everything that had been offered! The *gopis* were happy to see that he ate all the food, but were amazed at how a man could eat such a large quantity.

When it was time to leave they asked sage *Durvasa*, "How do we go back, the *Yamuna* is flooded?" "If the *Yamuna* is in spate, how did you come in the first place?" asked *Durvasa*. When the *gopis* told him the entire story, *Durvasa* said, "Use the same method for going back that you used for coming here. Go to the banks of the *Yamuna* and say, "If *Durvasa* lives off only fresh air, then allow us to go." The *gopis* found this very strange, after all he had just finished off all the food! They kept quiet as *Durvasa* was known for his fiery temper. This is a beautiful story, suggestive and meaningful. So they went to the *Yamuna* and as instructed, requested with folded hands, "If *Durvasa* lives off fresh air and has never had any food, then allow us to go." Again the *Yamuna* made a path, the water receded and they waded through.

Now the *gopis* went to *Krishna* and asked, "*Madhav*, please tell us what this is all about?" *Krishna* replied, "You look at me as a body, which I am not. I am *Chidanandaswaroopa*. And *Durvasa* is also a *brahmaveta*, a *Brahmangyani*, who has gone far beyond the arrogance of being a body, senses, mind and *buddhi*. *Atman* neither eats food nor has the pride of eating food. In other words, the actions of the body are not the actions of *atman*."

Indriyani Indiriyarthesu Vartanta Iti Dharyan

In other words, the senses play upon your desires, but an agyani (ignorant), begins to believe: '*Kartahmiti manyate*' or 'I' am the doer.

The *gopis* said, "We still have not understood. Even if we do accept for a while that both of you are detached and pure as far as your *atmabhava* goes, what do you say to the fact that *Durvasa* ate

203

up everything we offered? And even after eating everything he said, 'I live off fresh air'. This is something we do not really understand. Also tell us how can any living being eat so much food?"

Krishna explained, "*Durvasa* did not eat that food with *Jivabhava*. He ate everything with '*Aham Vaishvanaro*' *bhava*. Though you saw the food going into his mouth, it was not really going into his stomach. With the help of his *prana shakti*, he sent that food to the whole world, wherever it was needed. *Durvasa* is a *yogi*, so anything is possible for him."

Once a seer was asked his age. He answered, "Infinitum! Endless!" The body has its limits. The body was born a few years ago and will die after a couple of years. But 'I' is not a body. The age of 'I' is endless. You do understand that there is a drop in the ocean and an ocean in the drop as well? Now, who would know this or try to understand this? Drop means the *jiva* and the ocean means the *Brahman*. And *Brahman* is in this very *jiva*, the one who reflects over it! It is *gyana* that has the power to liberate.

Na me mrityushanka na me jatibhedah

Death cannot touch me and there is no distinction in the self. 'I' can never die, only this body can die. The body dies and the *pranas* are released. *Kabir* says:

Kaun kaho Sri *Guru* Maryo hai?

"Who says *guru* ever dies?" *Kabir* issued this statement: "What are you crying for? For the body? It was made of dust and has now returned to dust." The flames convert your body to dust and ash. When fire consumes the human body, the water inside evaporates. A body weighing nearly seventy to eighty kilograms is kept on the pyre and burnt; what is left — a bagful of ashes!

In another verse *Kabir* says, "O you, the grieving one! Who are you crying for? Just look at it, what kind of delusion is leading you astray? Who are you crying for? Try to understand the fact that only the body dies. 'I' the *atmadev*, never ever dies."

Na me Mrityushanka

There is not the slightest doubt that 'I' never dies

'**Na me jatibhedah**' means that 'I' is casteless. If we want peace in the world, there is only one way of getting it. People should drop their family name, caste name and political boundaries. No Hindustani, no Pakistani; you should say we are neither. We are only human beings. Now you tell me, can there be a fight between one human being and another? Drop these religious denominations. You should say, "We are all the children of God." The higher castes fight with the lower ones. They dominate, oppress and torture them as well. Then the lower castes rise and seek revenge from the higher castes. This violence will not stop until we rise above the pride of belonging to a particular caste.

Some *mahatmas* say that though it is right that we are all Hari's children, for practical reasons people should be kept in their place — high in a high seat and low in a low seat, the way a *guru* is made to sit on a high pedestal and a disciple on a low platform. If a disciple were to say, "We are all God's children, so why can't I sit on my guru's shoulders," will it not create confusion? Similarly, if you say that a lower caste person should not be given unnecessary importance, then what is the point in my saying all this?

A person lost in the pride of his caste can never become a *sadhak*. Shankaracharya says, "Arise! And go beyond these distinctions of caste and creed!" Someone could turn around and say, "How could he say that? He was a *brahmin* after all!" It is true that he was from a family of *Brahmins*, but you must remember the story that I narrated to you earlier. It is a favourite of mine and I narrate it often — it carries such a beautiful message!

Once Shankaracharya was passing through a narrow lane in *Benares*. His disciples were shouting, "Get aside, make way for the master." It is said that to teach Shankaracharya a lesson, *Shiva* took the guise of a *chandaal* — a keeper of the cremation ground, and blocked his way. Now, bang in the middle of the street stood the *chandaal* barring the path and looking into Shankaracharya's eyes he said, "From what should 'I' get aside? Tell me, should I get aside from the body, the delusion or the evil knowledge? You tell me, I will get aside immediately. But first you will have to tell me from what I should get aside? Speak up now!"

CHAPTER 12

THE GURU POSES A RIDDLE

Na me mrityushankaa na me jaatibhedaha
Pita neiva me neiva maataa na janm
Na bandhurna mitram gururnaiva shishyah
Chidaanandroopah shivoham shivoham

The relationships that start with the body also end with the body. In a way, everyone knows and understands this, but this knowledge is no more than mere information. It is as though this is just one of the several things we know. We tend to retain information about things that are in no way directly connected with us. We keep piling up useless information, thinking that one day we might need it. Some people do not even think about whether or not they are ever going to use it. They just keep stacking information in their mind's store. So many little bits of information! Even the newspapers are full of such useless information and the readers lap it all up rather religiously, almost as if they are reading a scripture.

Not that I do not read a newspaper, of course I do. I am not criticizing the habit of reading newspapers, but only of collecting useless information. And what do I mean by useless information? The people who have leisure read everything published in a newspaper — so much so that they even read the obituary columns. "Whose *shradh* is it and when? Who is to be cremated and when? The address, the time!" Every small piece of news and information is read carefully, even though it may have nothing to do with you!

Newspapers should not be called newspapers, but information

papers instead. Some newspapers publish vulgar and obscene photographs, which are not in any way connected with the lives of ordinary people. For example, you may see a woman in a bikini bathing in the sea somewhere in Europe. They just click her somehow and insert her photograph in the newspapers. If she is bathing, let her. It is not that that woman has a problem. No, none whatsoever! The fact that she is bathing hardly makes for news, but because they are interested in her half-naked body and so are their readers, her picture will be carried. Now this is no news!

In India, only those people learn to swim who happen to be living on the banks of a river. Or the very affluent go for a swim to a hotel or a swimming pool, or a pool in a farmhouse. These days the trend is changing somewhat. In big cities even small children are being taught to swim. Swimming is an excellent exercise — it exercises our limbs, heart, lungs, back and stomach.

My *Gurudev* was very fond of swimming. I haven't really seen him from very close quarters, nor have I ever stayed close to him. I had told you earlier as well, that I just met him six or seven times. All this information has trickled down to me through his disciples. His old disciples, who have stayed with him, tell me that *Maharaj* would always walk across whenever he wanted to go somewhere. He used to live out in the fields because he never liked living under a concrete roof. There in the fields, someone or the other would set up a small hutment for him. This is the way he used to live when not many people knew about him.

He loved living out in the open under the shade of trees. When he had to go from one place to another, he often walked along the embankment of the river. One or two disciples would accompany him. All of a sudden, he would hand over his *kamandal* (pot for holding drinking water) to one of his disciples, open the knot of his *dhoti* and jump straight into the water. Then he would tell his disciples, "You walk along the embankment. I will swim across." He had a very healthy body. He would observe the vow of silence most of the time, and not many people had seen his eyes wide open, for he would be in meditation. Meditation without procedures! Only the middle level *sadhaks* need to take recourse to different procedures. A high level seer or *sadhak* does not need

207

any such procedures. When the mind does not vacillate, then why make an effort to stabilise it? He would play football for a while and then stop playing it. If he found himself on the banks of a river, he would jump into the water and start swimming, he was an excellent swimmer after all! Now you tell me, can one ever swim while wearing clothes? If you were to swim wearing your clothes, they would become heavy as the water will fill up inside, and then you would drown.

The first time I went to America I had a desire to see the Pacific Ocean. My host was somewhat reluctant. He said, "You will find young girls and women in bikinis there. You may not like it. How can we take you there?" I said, "Neither am I *Vishwamitra* nor are they *Menakas*. Besides, I do not need your protection for my security." He said, "No Gurumaa, you do not understand, people here have an open lifestyle. They just hold each other's hand and roll down into the sand there and then. I said, "You don't worry. I can very well understand, but please know that I am going there to see the ocean and not the people. And it should not be your worry how people behave there. On the contrary, we may offend them as we will go there fully dressed! If we go fully dressed to the beach where everyone else is in swimsuits, then they might wonder what kind of people we are! They might even point out that we are not suitably dressed for the occasion. They may think that this is no way to come to a beach!"

Why is nakedness an issue? Should it be? All animals wander around naked; they don't even wear underclothes! Do you ever feel ashamed that a dog is naked? The animals are not even conscious of going about naked. Men have started imposing their consciousness about clothes upon the animals too. It happened in London; some members of high society raised the issue that people who walk their dogs in the park should dress them up properly.

They should not bring their dogs absolutely naked to the park — the dogs should wear something. Later other people raised this issue in other public parks as well.

Well, if that is the logic, then the legs of tables and chairs should also be covered. Now legs are legs, whether these are of people or of tables and so must be covered. In the Victorian period, English people used to say that we must cover the legs of chairs and tables, that a piece of cloth must be tied around them. Or the entire table should be so covered that its legs are not visible at all. What shame can a chair feel just because its legs are uncovered? But man is such a fool that he starts dressing up tables and chairs!

I used to love going to the Lodhi Gardens in Delhi for a walk — it is such a wonderful garden with beautiful old trees. There I once saw a dog wearing a sweater in winter. Such dogs look rather strange. I say if you make a dog wear a sweater, why not make him wear an underwear too? You have not made any effort to cover his private parts which need to be covered!

We people think about such things, but if you go and see the tribals, you will find that they do not have any issues over clothing. Their women do not cover the upper half of their bodies. In certain parts of Orissa which are poverty-ridden, you come across fair populations of tribals. Their women just wrap a loose saree around their waist. It is just the lower part of the body that they cover. They have no tradition of wearing a blouse. No man ever stares at a woman. Everything is so simple and so natural. So if the obscenity is in your mind, if the vulgarity is in your eyes, then even on seeing a fully dressed woman your mind will have lustful thoughts.

What you must understand is that unless your disease is brought out into the open, you will not make any effort to find a cure for it. There is hardly any difference between the newspapers and the magazines here. Even if it is a health magazine, they will put a provocative picture on the cover. Only because of such things their magazines sell. The disease that afflicts your mind prompts you to lead unnatural lives. And taking advantage of your vulnerability, the print media makes a profit — just because you choose to lead unnatural lives.

A thousand and one useless little bits of information we store in our minds. Among other things, we also read in the papers about the scriptures — that we are not going to live forever, that this body will die one day. Among a thousand other little thoughts, we read this as well, but it has no meaning for us – none whatsoever.

Everyone keeps saying that we have to die one day and this

body shall be burnt one day. Who doesn't know it? Everyone does. In spite of this knowledge, detachment is rarely ever awakened in the mind. So many times it happens that a parent dies and while the body is still lying in the house, the children start fighting over the property. The dead body is still there and the children say, "Doesn't matter. We will burn it later."

If one has eyes, then it must occur to one that just as mother or father has died, so will I. Who knows how long I am going to live, so why should I fight? Most people think that as we are still around we should gain from all that belonged to the deceased.

When *Guru Ravidas* says, "*Pruni* kya tera kya mera," he is not saying anything novel. There is nothing new about it, everyone knows it.

Jaise taruvar pankh basera

The way birds come and perch themselves on the branch of a tree, sing their song and then fly away, in the same way we human beings also come into this world, do our duty and go away. The birds hardly ever settle anywhere permanently. Their nests are temporary. When a bird is to lay eggs, she collects little pieces of straw and builds a nest, lays eggs and then protects them. Then the little ones break out of the eggshells and step out; soon they learn to fly and one day they are gone. Thereafter the parent birds do not return to the same nest. Their nest is not their permanent address.

For some years I was travelling, never staying in one place for long. I remember I was in an *ashram* at *Vrindavan* when the *sadhu* who presided over it called me at eight o'clock in the evening and asked, "So where are you going next?" After this conversation, it became impossible for me to spend even a single night there. I left that *ashram* the very next day. At that point of time, I had no idea where I was going next. In some of the *ashrams* they did welcome me. But the moment they learnt that I was a good speaker they would say, "At least you could do *satsang* in the mornings." It was mainly to get away from the crowds who would throng me that I had come here. Again here they wanted me to do *satsang*. In a way these people were also justified. Who can feed another mouth

free of cost? They felt that if I was eating food at the *ashram*, then I must do something to help them as well. So this is how I would end up doing *satsang* wherever I went. And every fifteen days or so, I would be off. It was as though every other day I was preparing to leave.

Then after two-three years of wandering, I felt that it was much better to have a small hutment of my own. Had I been a man, I would possibly have compromised and done exactly what pleased other people. The first thing is that because I had a woman's body, people always felt slightly uneasy in my presence. The second is that I was of a very independent frame of mind. The third is that I am and will remain free.

A sage says: "This body is like a pillar of water; this body is like a pillar of air." You live in this body; if you have no attachment with this body into which you are born, then how can you be attached to anything else? Tell me, what kind of an attachment can you have with others? Your *gurus* and *sadhus* say, "Give up attachment. Do not be attached to your wife, your son, your house!" But how is it possible not to be attached to others. Because as long as the root cause of attachment abides: 'I' am body, this body is mine, attachment will not go away. As long as you do not strike at the root of attachment, how can you give up attachment with external things and people?

Sufis call *atman* — *rooh*. *Rooh* is separate from the body. *Rooh* has nothing to do with the body. *Rooh* is present in the cage of this body, but the way a bird is separate from the cage, in the same way, *jivatman* or *rooh* is separate from the body. If it has any connection, it is with paramatman. It cannot be with anything else! It really does not matter how many relationships you go on developing, ultimately you are alone and will remain alone. Can anyone accompany you in your deep sleep which is your most peaceful state?

Husband and wife love each other so dearly. But the moment one of them dies, it is all over. Then the body which they had kissed and loved has to be given a send off. There is a method of meditation called *Mrityudhyana*. This *dhyana* is to be done in the corpse pose. After following the esoteric method of breathing you are guided into visualisation. You see your body as dead and you see your funeral procession and your family members grieving over you. You are also able to imagine your own body burning on a pyre. If your visualisation is good and if you are able to imagine properly, then you will feel your entire body is burning and is finally swallowed up by the engulfing flames. This experience can be so real, that often for those who are not ready for it, it can be very painful. So this meditation is done only in the presence of a master and also when the master sees that you are ready for it.

Normally when someone dies and is cremated, once the body is consigned to the flames, the family feels that their job is over. That is the end of the story in a way. They begin to think that cremation too is an onerous task. This shows a total lack of feelings and stone-heartedness!

The story of the *Buddha* says that when he — Siddhartha, saw a burning pyre, it disturbed him immensely, and it was only then that his desires and attachments were burnt to ashes. Not only that, he also held the ash from the pyre in his hands and felt it. His charioteer Channa asked, "O Prince, what are you doing? You should not touch this ash with your hands. Let his family members attend to it. Why are you touching it? It is impure!" But Prince Siddhartha started crying at the thought that one day even his body would be reduced to ashes in the same manner. Holding the ashes in his hand, he said, "Channa, will my ashes also fly off like this? Will my ashes also be immersed in the water? Will my fate be no different from this? If this is the end of all life, then what does life mean? Then what is the purpose of life? And death appears to be something that could strike any time and no one really knows when it will come? Is this body the limit of my existence? This body shall ultimately be reduced to a heap of ashes. No one is mine, father or mother. I am related to none and my relationship is with the omniscient one alone."

Pita neiva me neiva maataa na janm

I have no father and no mother and neither have I taken birth. I am *atman*. All these physical bonds are of this body alone. When it comes to reflection, then your body is not yours, your parents

are not yours, your brothers and sisters are not yours. You have nothing to do with any of them. No worldly relationship has the power to touch me, the *atmadev*. All relationships cease to have meaning in the context of *atman*. Who is the mother and who the father?

There is one thing you must understand. We often repeat, "Twameva mata cha pita twameva….", meaning thereby that God is my father and mother. Why do we say this in relation to God? Then why do you say that we have no father? What we need to understand is that at the level of *jivatman*, this relationship with paramatman shall have to be recognised. A *jiva* is a *jiva* as long as the *antehkaran* — mind, *chitta, ahankara, buddhi* is there. If *chaitanya* is seen in its pure form then what we are left with is pure *Brahman*. Then what kind of father-son relationship can you envisage? Relationship is possible with *Brahman* as long as *jivatman* is in *Jivabhava*.

Dehobhava, *Jivabhava* and *atmabhava* are the three *bhava*s. Dehobhava is where this body alone appears to be 'I'. Most people are born in this *bhava* and die in this *bhava* too. The second *bhava* is *Jivabhava*. If you rise a little beyond the dehobhava, then you enter the *Jivabhava*. *Jivabhava* means that 'I' is not this body alone; it is much more than that. It is essentially the reflection of *atman* in the *prana*, five senses, mind, *buddhi, chitta ahankara*; all these put together are called *jivatman*. There is another name given to it in the *shastras: chidabhaas*. It means that you remove mind, *buddhi*, and *prana* from the *Jivabhava* and then look at the pure state of your *swaroopa*. As soon as you enter that state, then as Shankaracharya says, "I am *shivoham*. I am not body, senses, doer or receiver. I am neither son to anyone nor have I a mother or a father."

Aham nirvikalpo niraakaarroopo
Vibhurvyapya sarvatra sarvendriyaanaam
Sadaa me samatvam na muktirna bandhah
Chidaanandroopah shivoham shivoham

There are two forms of 'I', one impure and the other pure. Shankaracharya is using the word *shivoham* for the pure 'I' and not for the impure 'I'. Now, what is an impure 'I'? It is the same one

213

that you are familiar with right now. 'I' had come, 'I' had gone, 'I' was sitting, 'I' am very rich, 'I' am very educated — all such foolish thoughts are caused by the impure 'I'.

Now, what is the pure 'I'? If you purge the impurities of the impure 'I', then the pure 'I' manifests itself on its own. Now what does an impure 'I' have in it? I will give you an example. Although it is not something that can be verbalized, yet you need to understand what I am going to say. You say, "I had gone there." Now if you were to examine this statement closely, you will be able to understand what I am saying. Who had gone — the body. In fact, what is it that you should say? This body had gone there. Why are you using 'I' unnecessarily? The impure 'I' says: "I had food." If you were to look at it in a discerning manner, you would know that it is the body that has had food. It is the *pranas* that feel the pangs of hunger, and we say it is the body that is hungry. The body feels hungry and once you have food, the hunger of your body is satiated. Now from where does 'I' get into all this?

Aham nirvikalpo niraakaarroopo

'I' am neither the food nor the one who eats, nor even the one who feels satiated on eating. This is the discerning intelligence and this is the pure 'I'. Of course all of us are familiar with the impure 'I'. When you say 'I' am very educated, the question arises: Who is intelligent and educated? It is the *buddhi*.

Once a shastri (scholar) was talking to a young man. He said, "I have been educated in Gurukul. I have read grammar for twelve years. I am an *acharya*." He started reciting *Sanskrit shlokas*. The young man kept listening to him for some time. Then he said, "You have told me what you know. Now it is your turn to listen. The whole world is a drama! You do not know when your part is going to finish." He started reciting Shakespeare, showing off his knowledge of English. The young man said, "If you claim to be a *gyani* of *Sanskrit*, then I am a *gyani* of English. Switching languages does not make a difference? You are a master of that language and I of this. Why be arrogant?"

The academic knowledge that you gain with your *buddhi* comes to naught if your *buddhi* does not function properly. So why be proud of academic knowledge? One moment you were busy flaunting your knowledge, wanting others to recognise you as a great academician, and the next moment a disease may strike you causing you to lose your memory altogether. All the *gyana* stored in your brain goes to seed if the blood pressure increases, or the nerve centres of the brain are affected. So how can you ever be proud of the *gyana* stored in this *buddhi*? 'I' am very educated, 'I' am very wise — it is the *buddhi* that is both wise and foolish. 'You' are neither wise nor foolish.

Due to ignorance, when you associate the self with the *antehkaran*, then it is the impure 'I', and when you move beyond the mind, intellect, body and senses, then it is the pure 'I'. This pure 'I' is Chidanandaroopa; this is *shivoham*. Now it might occur to some that this statement is dangerous, for *shivoham* means 'I' am God. Well! It might be part of the *Vedas* and the *Vedanta*, but it cannot be a part of a living being's speech. The devout do not really think in this manner. How can God and I be one?

Namdev says, "*Hindus* worship in the temple and *Muslims* in the mosque, but if you ask a *Brahmangyani*, he will tell you that his God lives far beyond the walls of temples and mosques. He is not to be found in these confined spaces. Beyond dehobhava and *Jivabhava*, there is another state called *atmabhava*. There is no difference between paramatman and me. While still in *Jivabhava*, if you were to claim that there is no difference between *guru* and 'I', then there are problems, for you have not really understood this very well.

This is the riddle: you do not know that you are the 'truth'. Under the sheaths of the physical, subtle and causal body you are hidden, and you have to find yourself. Look within and see. But to look within you need to divert your mind inwards and only then, with the sharp edged sword of true knowledge — brahmagyana — will you be able to cut through the veil of *maya* (ignorance). Those who have solved this riddle are called liberated; those who have not, remain bonded with imaginary bondages. A life which could be a celebration has become a dreary drudge. Wake up and see the truth, you and only you can break this barrier of ignorance. Arise, awake and see the truth — Now!

CHAPTER 13

SURRENDER THY EGO

**Na bandhurna mitram gururnaiva shishyah
Chidaanandroopah shivoham shivoham**

A *guru-shishya* (master-disciple) relationship is one of the most important of all relationships in the world. When the *guru* is a true *guru* and the *shishya* is a true *shishya*, then much of what happens between them is beyond the grasp of even God. God feels small, even dwarfed in the presence of the *guru* and shishya's mutual affection and love. It will be no exaggeration to say that this relationship between *guru* and *shishya* is a special chemistry that destroys all sins. The word '*gurudev*' points toward man becoming a God and then God becoming a living embodiment of *Brahman* itself.

To find *satguru* or *gurudev* is as difficult as extracting a flowing river of ambrosia from loose sand grains. It just will not flow! How can it? Where is the water in this vast arid soil of the desert? But if someone claims, "I will squeeze water or oil out of the sand grains," he is mistaken, because there is no oil or water in the sand. Sand grains are not the seeds of *sarson* (mustard) that if you grind them, oil will start flowing. Now whether you purify the sand or put it through any other process, it will not yield oil. Sand can only kick up dust, not give oil.

In the same way, if someone were to claim, "I have discovered the real essence of life, and that too without the help of a *satguru* or in spite of a *satguru*", it is equally impossible. *Brahman* itself constitutes the essence of *guru*. Or you could say that when the

nirguna (attribute less), *nirakaar* (formless) decided to show his shape and form to the world, he re-created himself in the image of the *guru*. Had he not shown his form, had he not asserted 'I am also here', how would this gross, ignorance-ridden world have learnt of the kingdom of *Brahman*? How would we have known that *Brahman* or God exists?

My feeling is that man learnt about God only when God incarnated as *guru* and appeared among men. It is somewhat like the divine glow of the sun. The sun is a body of fire, but in its *nirguna* form fire as such is everywhere. The entire world is composed of five elements. Of these five elements, the third one is fire. Of earth, water, fire, ether and air, the third element is fire. In a manner of speaking, fire is present in everyone, in everything and every object. But in its formless form, fire cannot dispel the darkness of our home. Fire is dormant even in wood. It is there in the house in which you live. And it is there in your body too. The moment you put a thermometer in your mouth, you know the temperature of your body. The thermometer tells you what the temperature of your body is — whether it is rising or falling.

So there is fire inside our body. Now if at night, everything is suddenly plunged into darkness, the fire inside your body shall not be able to light your room. Fire is in the house too. Fire is there in the house and furniture too, but that does not produce light. For light we need a special form of fire — that is a flame. The flame has the power to light up your entire house.

If at night a firefly were to enter your room, there will be a sudden light. A firefly is such a small insect but its tail is always lit. People who remain imprisoned within the four walls of their houses spend their entire life counting currency notes or playing with their sons and grandsons. Always busy inside buildings of their offices or homes, never ever breathing fresh air. The person who has not spent time in the company of nature has not really lived, only existed. Have you ever spent a night under a canopy of stars, watching them; bathed in moonlight? Have you ever wandered through a forest aimlessly? Just walk through a forest without any specific purpose and try to befriend the plants and trees, the wild fruits and the wild flowers. The wild flowers bloom on their own and need no one's intervention.

In Uttarakhand, we have the world's most spectacular place called 'Valley of Flowers', where thousands of varieties of flowers can be seen. It is almost as if a huge multi-coloured carpet is spread out. Every year these flowers bloom only in the month of September. This 'Valley of Flowers' is much more beautiful than the Gardens of Holland or Butcher's Garden in Vancouver, Canada. Both these gardens are beautiful, but still they are man made creations. There they do not allow the plants to grow beyond a certain point, they keep pruning them. And they also give them any shape they wish to. Untouched by human hands, the beauty of jungle flowers is awesome.

Did you ever get an opportunity to see the trees and plants that have been grown and nurtured by nature? Now what should I say! How do I teach you *gyana* when you do not even know the art of living? If you laugh, it is only with your family members; it is conditional. Even if you love, it is confined to eight or ten people. Other human beings do not matter to you.

The real man always tries to push the limits of his mind and the frontiers of his being. A child is a child after all, whether it is yours or someone else's. Every child is beautiful, but you do not find it so unless it is yours! You only love your own children and not those of others. You get to see such memorable scenes of nature's beauty. I remember, once I was travelling through Himachal Pradesh and decided to stay on the banks of a lake. After a long time, I had got an opportunity to be with myself as there was no one with me. No friends, no disciples — no one. Disciples are useless; they just get after your life. They are all dishonest and hypocritical. I am yet to come across those who are prepared to die for the sake of their *guru*; I know you are certainly not one of those who would. I have no such expectation from you either. I talk to you hoping to polish your rough exterior in order to see the real beautiful You come out. So for now I sing my own tune, because I love to do so.

Much before I started this Nirvanashatkam of Shankaracharya — which is also known as *Atmashatakam* — I knew that this discourse is not for anyone but myself, because I love to talk about it. If it makes sense to you, well and good, and if it does

not, well…! If you understand, you will be able to make some progress in terms of your *sadhana*. Perhaps you may realise that the goal is still eluding you. It could well be within your grasp; in a way it was, yet it is far.

Talking about the lake, when I reached there, the colour of the lake was turquoise. Slowly it changed into the colour of the sky — light blue. By the time the sun went down it had turned green. After sunset it had turned grayish. At night the water turned black. It was marvellous. As a matter of fact, the colour of the water does not change. But that place is so completely pollution free, that when the sky was blue, the water also appeared blue. When the sky turned dark blue, the water too looked dark blue.

In fact, the sky simply casts its reflection in the lake. After sunset, as the evening settles in, dark shadows begin to lengthen and thousands of fireflies start buzzing around the lake. Because at night it is dark, so the water also appears to be black. Water is neither black nor blue nor green, water is colourless. It seems as if the fireflies are fighting the darkness of the night to illuminate it with their twinkling sparks. When I was living in a small cottage in *Rishikesh*, there were many fireflies there. If a firefly were to come into the room, its burning tail would suddenly illuminate the entire room. It is a very tiny insect and has an even tinier tail, and yet it creates enough light to dispel the darkness in a room.

When the formless fire assumes the form of a flame, it is called light; it dispels darkness. In the same way, God's fire is present in the world in an equitable form; it is omnipresent, even though fire is not present everywhere in the cosmos. God's kingdom exists even where there is no fire. Despite truth being present everywhere in the world, it is only when it assumes the form of the master — *guru*, that 'truth' is revealed and *gyana* is disseminated in the world. How did man know that there is God, that there is *Brahman*?

In fact, *Brahman* just is 'it', was neither born nor does 'it' ever die. I am calling *Brahman* 'it', as it is neither male nor female. *Brahman* is beyond the realm of birth and death. *Brahman* is unchangeable. *Brahman* is beyond all language and debate. It is not the subject of discussion or debate. Then how do we know that 'it' is there? How did man get to know about the existence of something that is beyond the realm of the senses and imagination, that is beyond the comprehension of *buddhi*? We discovered *Brahman* through *Brahman*, i.e. the omniscient is known through the form of *Brahman*, the *guru*, the enlightened one. But only those people know the value of a *satguru* or *guru*, who have tried to look for it, who have sought it.

The search for a master is not easy. In this journey, you may be cheated by dishonest and fraudulent gurus who will claim to be your redeemers. You may fall into their trap and be harassed and tortured by them. Those who have faced such situations know how difficult it is to escape their emotional traps. Those who have fumbled in their search, will know the real worth of a *guru*! Only those who have sought a true master, fallen into the trap of a false one, come out of their trap and finally met a true *guru*, will really know what it means to meet a true master, and how much their true *gyana* is worth! And the one who has not searched, will never know what it means to be in the company of a living God.

Now, there are three types of listeners sitting here. First, the casual visitor who has come here out of sheer curiosity, "Let us go and see what really goes on in a *shivir*!" They have just come to see. Apart from that it means nothing to them. "If others are going, why shouldn't we also go?" — This is their logic. It is more like a situation where a couple of friends tell you that they are going to *Haridwar* for a holy dip and you say, "All right, I will also come along". "If you are going to Anandpur Sahib, why don't you take us along?" "You are going to Nainital for a holiday, we will also accompany you." In the same way you say, "You are going to Gurumaa's *shivir*, I will also get an opportunity to roam around and enhance my image (that I too am a great devotee)". It is just an act of mimicry, nothing more than that.

There are many who come here not out of curiosity but because they have developed an intense affection for me. I will not call it love, but only affection. It is this affection that motivates you to come here, see me and listen to my voice. So they have come with this *bhava*. There are so many who have come here out of sheer devotion for me. They fall in the second category of listeners; a little better than the first.

Tell me, how many of you have come here with the explicit purpose of discovering your real self? How many of you have come with the *bhava* of learning how to discover *Brahman*? How many of you have come to discover what *tattvagyana* is? They are the third type of listeners. If you ask me, then in all honesty I will say that there are two or three such people in this whole gathering, and whatever I am saying is meant only for their benefit. The rest are here to while away their time, just to have good fun.

A yogacharya is also attending this *shivir*. This is his first ever visit. He came to me and said, "I am really enjoying this *shivir*. It is blissful. But there is one thing I find rather strange." I said, "Tell me". Now because he is a naturopath, he said, "The food here is not as *satvik* as it should be". I said, "Yes, I know it is not as *satvik* as it should be". Why? Because the people who make the arrangements also feel that the food should be cooked well. Besides, people have developed the wrong habit of eating thrice a day. He was of the opinion that people should be offered food only once in the afternoon with no regular meal at night — just some sprouts and some fruit or a light soup. He said, "We have come here to meditate, not to enjoy a holiday". I explained, "What can I do? I only get this crowd of fools. After a lot of pruning and weeding, I might ultimately get one or two genuine disciples. So we have to keep their likes and dislikes in mind and arrange for this kind of food. I know, but still I am making this little compromise. Why? Because if I am too strict then you know what will happen."

It is not easy for me to compromise. I have never done it with myself. Here we are discussing something as subtle as this and yet the attention of the people sitting right in front is wandering.

The guru's *gyana* is meant only for the disciples. It is not meant for spectators. They say that when *Bhagwan Krishna* gave the message of the *Gita* to *Arjuna*, there was an image of *Hanuman* embossed on the flag fluttering atop the chariot. They say that it was not just an image, but *Hanuman* present in person in that image. There are some *yogis* like *Hanuman* and *Markandaya* who can assume a gross body at will and give it up as and when they wish to. They are in the league of *Ishwar*. *Markandayaji* is still around. Even Devrishi *Narada* is around and he will continue to be around.

Now, *Hanuman* was sitting atop the chariot. And *Krishna* was busy giving his discourse. He was singing the *Gita* and *Arjuna* was listening intently. And sitting on top of the chariot, *Hanuman* was also listening. And *Krishna* was busy giving his discourse. Someone said, "Now *Arjuna* was the real disciple as he asked all the questions. But didn't *Hanuman* also listen to the *gyana*?" On this question *Krishna* says, "No". "Why?" *Krishna* explains, "He alone deserves to receive *gyana* who sits in front of the *guru* and prays to him saying, '*Gurudev*, give me *gyana*.'" Then, on listening to his prayers, the *guru* has to concede, "Yes, I accept you as my disciple." *Hanuman* did not come in front of *Krishna*. He did not pray for *gyana* the way *Arjuna* said, "I wish to be your disciple. Please take me under your wing." This is something *Hanuman* never uttered.

That is why we accept *Arjuna* and not *Hanuman* as the receiver of the *gyana* enshrined in the celestial song of the *Gita*. It is another matter that *Hanuman* is also a *bhakta* and a *gyani* in his own right. But when it comes to the question of principles, then *Krishna* is the *guru* and *Arjuna* his disciple; *Hanuman* is almost non-existent in this picture.

Even Sanjaya, who was gifted with divine sight, heard the message of the *Gita* and he also saw it. And it was he who communicated the entire message of the *Gita* to Dhritrashtra. Right in the beginning of the *Gita*, Dhritrashtra asks Sanjaya, "Tell me what you see in Kurukshetra?" Then Sanjaya, with the divine sight bestowed upon to him by Sage Vyasa, narrated the events in detail. He described the scene and what *Krishna* and *Arjuna* were talking about. But this discourse could neither liberate Dhritrashtra nor Sanjaya. That only Arjuna's ignorance was dispelled seems strange but is indeed true.

So don't you make any mistake in thinking that all will benefit from the *gyana* of *shivoham*. This process will help only those who are true disciples. And the ones who are not true disciples will not get anything out of it.

God has created a very strange and mysterious system. Though in a way, all of you are present in front of me, yet there is no real gain for all. But if you want, you can take advantage of this opportunity, provided you show the necessary devotion and spirit

of surrender. Otherwise, one may say that this lamp, this mike and other inanimate objects present are also listening mutely to this discourse. It is just not enough to listen to it. In a way, the monkeys sitting outside this waterproof *pandaal* are also listening to it. There are people outside the *pandaal*, and I am sure they are listening too. But will it bring them any gain?

Let me explain another thing here. In fact, living as I do in utter simplicity, it might appear rather odd if I were to even mention this. Nor have I ever encouraged it actively, lest some of you think that I am saying all this for the sake of money. Tradition defines the *guru-shishya* relationship. I might as well tell you what tradition says about how a disciple should approach the *guru*. The *Gita* says:

Tadviddhi Pranipaatena Pariprashnena Sevaya Updekshyanti Te Gyanam Gyaninastattyadarshinaha

When the one who is willing to surrender, devoutly seeks blessings, "*Gurudev*, give me *gyana* which will liberate me and give me true wisdom," only then the *guru* should offer this divine knowledge. Only then can you understand what *tattvagyana* is. This is the first part that must be upheld. The second tradition is that on the completion of this process of imparting *gyana*, the disciple must offer at his guru's feet, whatever he can afford to offer. Someone asked, "What should be the nature of the offering?" The *guru* says, "Whatever you hold most precious in life is what you must part with." What is most precious to anyone? Think! Well! Your own self; so one should offer one's heart and soul to the *guru*.

You are such dishonest people! How will you offer your most precious possession? How will the person who is not even a disciple make an offering? Now that we are talking about it, let me add another thing. In the beginning I used to visit temples and *gurudwaras*, and there would be around two hundred people in the *satsang*. On the last day, people would express their gratitude by offering whatever they wished to offer. Now all kinds of people would come for *satsang*. Suppose I am sitting here and people are offering gifts. It is not really a question of money. Let me say once again that it is not a question of money at all. It is only a

223

matter of feelings and love. I am finding it very difficult to talk about this. I often noticed that the people who otherwise came loaded with gold and diamonds, would pull out the most soiled and rotten currency note from their pocket and offer it. At that time, I would feel…I do not have words to describe it…I would feel revolted deep inside!

When *Janak* went to *Ashtavakra* and said, "Please give me *gyana*," *Ashtavakra* said, "Come tomorrow morning." Now the tradition was that *Janak* should first come and touch his guru's feet and then make an offering. So the next day *Janak* came, placed a tilak on Ashtavakra's forehead, offered a garland of flowers and then asked his *guru* with folded hands, "What do I give you in return for this *gyana*? I just cannot think of anything. Please do tell me." *Ashtavakra* said, "No, the gift is given of one's own volition. I will not say anything. You give me whatever you want to." Overwhelmed, *Janak* said, "*Prabhu*! I offer my body, soul and all the wealth I possess." *Ashtavakra* said, "I accept that."

Then the session started. When *satsang* was over and *Janak* was about to leave for his palace, *Ashtavakra* asked *Janak*, "Where are you going?" "*Gurudev*, back to my palace, my abode!" *Ashtavakra* reprimanded, "I did not know you are a liar, you have changed so soon. Just now you said that you offer me everything, your body, soul and your wealth. When you have offered everything to me, it has ceased to be yours. Now it is mine. And if you have already offered everything to me, you must take my permission to use what now rightfully belongs to me. Now the palace is not yours. How can you go and live in it?"

Janak was shocked, he immediately realised his mistake, "Yes, I am wrong. Now the palace is not mine. So where do I go?" *Ashtavakra* says, "*Janak*, you are being dishonest. You said that you had given your all to me, your body, your *buddhi*, your mind, everything. So how can you decide anything in that mind without my permission? It is not a question of your palace alone. From today onwards, if you choose to entertain some thought in your mind, you must seek my prior permission for it. Go away *Janak*, you have cheated your *guru*. You lied to your *guru*! And I am not going to give *gyana* to a liar." *Janak* stood there stupefied, mind stilled! — When I have given my mind and body to my master, then how can I even think! — He was engulfed in oceanic stillness; this was the moment he experienced his first *samadhi*!

On the one hand, you have *gurus* and *shishyas* like *Ashtavakra* and *Janak*, on the other hand are those who just make tall claims but when the opportunity comes for giving away something, then it's all over…! So finally, I was so tired of it all that I told them not to offer me anything. So I have made it explicitly clear, that under no circumstance should money be offered to me.

Swami Ram Tirath once said in the course of one of his speeches that you should offer to God whatever you cherish the most. Whatever you cherish the most is what you should give away. It is always yourself that you cherish the most and that is what you must give away. This 'I' is now no longer mine; this 'I' is now someone else's.

A few days back, it occurred to me that this time we should celebrate *Gurupurnima* differently. I just thought that tradition is all right as far as disciples coming and offering puja to *guru* is concerned, but this year *Gurupurnima* is going to be a very different affair. On that day I will observe total silence. *Gurupurnima* means a day reserved for worshipping the guru. It is not fair that even on that day you should expect your *guru* to talk. So I will be in silence and whatever you wish to offer will be from the heart and whatever I have to give will also be subtle. There will be no physical offerings or discourses.

The dialogue that often takes place between the *guru* and the disciple goes on all the time. But *Gurupurnima* is a day for the articulation of the guru's rights and the disciple's sentiments. *Guru-shishya* relationship is indeed very different. Only that person knows the value of a *guru* who has genuinely been thirsting for God, and has found a *guru* after a great deal of search.

If someone bad mouths you, you would listen to it even if it means eavesdropping on a conversation, simply because you are eager to know what the other person is saying. One has to have a dying passion in the heart to know and to seek. This is the highest *gyana*, for the sake of which disciples would do everything from chopping wood to sweeping floors, and the master would do

225

everything possible to make the unworthy one's run away. They would make them work like donkeys for no less than twelve years. So much so, that an ordinary person would just take to his heels and run away within a year or so. Renouncing their homes, the seekers would sit at the threshold of their guru's *ashram* without bothering about water, food, sleep or rest.

A seeker has just one urge, one thirst — for *gyana*. The thirst to know and discover *Brahman*. Only such a seeker would be granted *gyana*, after he had passed all the tests. You neither have the thirst nor did you pass any test. I did not put you through a trial either.

Last year during the summer *shivir*, Swami Achalanand Saraswati was here. Yesterday, for some special reason, he sought my permission to leave. As he was observing maun, I did not ask for his reason. Before going he left a letter behind. The letter said, "Honorable Gurumaa! Strange are the ways of time. Though I have been in contact with you for only a little while, yet I seem to have been trapped by the magic of your voice. Now it is difficult for me to get away. Perhaps this is the will of God too. I would like to enter into a long dialogue with you but time is a constraint. Moreover, my silence is another roadblock. So for any kind of sharing, we may have to write to each other. I hope that I continue to receive the prasad (offering) of spirituality from you. And if you choose to guide me along the path, I will feel specially blessed. Now tell me, what should I do? You tell me how to proceed, because I am willing to surrender completely unto you."

The kind of surrender, devotion and love that is required in a *guru-shishya* relationship is all there in him. He has been searching for the last four years or so and is observing strict silence too. You cannot stay silent for even a day, or can you? But he has been observing maun for the past four years. He is searching within, looking for a path, for a destination. Only such a seeker is able to value a *guru*. Only he recognises who a *guru* is? And it is a fact that only such a person can stand to gain through contact with the *guru*.

Chidanandaroopa shivoham shivoham

But this *gyana* does not become accessible to you unless a *guru* opens this door; unlocks it with the key only he possesses. That is why *guru* has been worshipped as *Brahma, Vishnu* and Mahesh. They say you do not have to worship other Gods and Goddesses. If you surrender yourself at the feet of your *guru*, then it means you have touched the feet of all the thirty three billion Gods and Goddesses of *Hinduism.*

If such is the greatness of the *guru*, and such is the devotion of the disciple for his *guru*, then there is no doubt that enlightenment will happen in this very life! A disciple like *Janak* is fortunate enough to get a *guru* like *Ashtavakra*. What transpires between them is magical; one can easily attain *atmabhava*. As soon as you enter the *atmabhava*, you experience the final explosion of *shivoham*. And the moment this event occurs, the *guru* ceases to be a *guru* and the disciple ceases to be a disciple. They merge and a great unison occurs.

The way the distinction between *jiva* and *Ishwar* is obliterated, in the same way the distinction between *guru* and disciple also ceases to exist. Now who is the *guru* and who is the disciple? As long as you are following the path of meditation, the guru's position is venerable. The disciple offers everything to his *guru*: his devotion, his affection, his prayers. He offers all his petitions at the feet of the *guru*, and out of compassion and love, the *guru* shows him the right path. The *guru* gives his disciple the courage to walk on the path of truth.

In other words, the process of mutual exchange goes on. The disciple offers something and so does the *guru*. In the process of this exchange, one day something magical happens, something for which the disciple had come to seek his guru's blessings in the first place. At that moment, he goes into a state of transcendence:

> **Guru Guru Guru — so sings my mind**
> **Without Guru, I am nothing**
> **Guru's blessings are with me day and night**
> **None can take away what he grants**
> **O mind! My only wish is to serve my Guru**
> **I am willing to lay down my life for him**

Only the truly blessed get an opportunity to serve their *guru*. Only the fortunate ones get the *darshan* of their *guru*. And the *guru* offers the ambrosia of *gyana* and awakens the consciousness of the disciple who is prepared to immerse himself in the service of his *guru* with devotion, love and a spirit of surrender. Only on drinking that ambrosia does the disciple realise his atmanswaroopa. Once you have known this atmanswaroopa, you break free of all the chains of worldly attachments.

There is no God comparable to *guru*. Who is like the *guru*? Even God remained hidden from me. He is the one who has lifted the veil of ignorance between God and me. It is the *guru* again, who lights the lamp of knowledge and dispels the darkness of my ignorance. The same God, who once appeared so far away, is now manifesting in the secret chamber of my heart.

Who but the *guru* is responsible for this miracle? He gives me knowledge of my real *swaroopa* — that I am not body, not mind, not senses, neither am I the *panchkoshah* or *saptadhatu*, nor the three stages of wakefulness, dream and deep sleep. 'I' am a conscious, ever blissful witness of this gross spectacle of the world. This is the kind of awareness a *guru* awakens in you.

Once you are able to break the barriers of body, mind and consciousness, you get to see that only *Brahman* exists — it is all pervasive. The veil of ignorance and darkness was the obstacle, but once you pull down this wall, the sun and the moon will come rushing into your eternal being! Then everywhere you will see your own glow reflected. Why is there spring in the garden? Because of me! Whose prayers are being chanted in the temples? Mine, of course! For whom is the azaan being given in the mosques? For me! To whom do all the *raga-raginis* offer their hymns? To me! Where does this world spring from and where does it all go back to? From me and to me! In my Brahmanswaroopa, *Brahma*, *Vishnu* and Mahesh exist! This entire world is just a single tidal wave of my Brahmanswaroopa! All matter and subtle elements exist in me as a mirage exists in a desert!

Immortal, omnipresent is my swaroopa
Brahma, Vishnu, Mahesh are waves
O sage, once you meditate on the all powerful

**You will know, untrue is worldly knowledge
The bliss that this wisdom gives,
is beyond all comprehension and knowledge**

When all the illusions of the mind dissipate, then you know *shivoham*. When all the discrimination of knowledge collapses (*sufis* call it '*An-al-haq*', which means 'I' am *Brahman*), then you know *shivoham*. Before you reach the stage of '*Aham Brahmasmi*', you have to cut through the layers of duality, illusion as well as delusion. Only when illusion and delusion disappear does *gyana* descend. Only that person experiences *gyana*, who is soaked in meditation, detachment and discerning intelligence.

It is not a single day's journey. Not just one day's journey. It is a long journey, but it can be a short one as well. This is the magic of *Vedanta*: when you decide to fill your *chitta* with detachment, the world shall begin to fade away from your horizon. Right now, your mind is not pure, hence you are unable to realise the value and worth of seeing the world as an illusion and nothing more than that. You keep on torturing yourself with attachment, lust and greed. It is important to realise that the world has no pleasures to offer. Only then can you realize the essence of *atman*.

As long as water does not boil at a temperature of a hundred degrees centigrade, it does not turn into steam. At hundred degrees it evaporates. In the same way, your false and impure ego is burnt in the heat of *gyana*. When it is being heated up, the consciousness that 'I' am a witness, 'I' am *Satchidananda* comes. The ego has to go and the individual self to go. The experience is profound; words cannot describe it. The whole experience is death-like; the residue it leaves behind is something that words or language cannot really grasp or comprehend.

Inexpressible, invincible, formless, without beginning or end, invisible — is your true self. It is only when you transcend the barriers of body, mind and consciousness, that you discover the real self. Within the ambit of the body you are either pious or sinful; that is it. Only when you transcend the individual self do you realise your true essence. But this path, my dear, is arduous and challenging.

The path of *gyana* is like the edge of a sword. It is like walking

229

a razor's edge. Now who has the strength to walk on a razor's edge? Who will walk? You do not get anything unless you obliterate yourself and you do not want to do that. There is a beautiful couplet by Swami Nirmalji:

> **I used to think that reality isn't too far**
> **After years I found it within me**

We always think that *Brahman* is not too far away from us. Everyone says, "God is near, God is near." But then why is it so difficult to find him? But once we set out to look for him we discover that it is no mean feat. **"After years I found it within me."**

You must have thought that now that we are going for the *shivir* we will find God, and then return home triumphantly, claiming to have found him. God is not an award that will just fall into your lap. The exploration of the true 'self' is not like receiving an award. You do not want to lose; you do not want to give up your false identity — then how will you find the real one? In *Yoga Vashishta*, *Sage Vashishta* says to *Sri Rama*, "Hey *Rama*, this *gyanamarga* is so simple; the discovery of the *Brahman* is as simple as blinking an eye." In the same breath *Vashishta* says, "Hey *Rama*! It is easy to blink your eyes or to count the stars in the sky, but it is not easy to discover *Brahman*." If you ask an astronomer, he will be unable to tell you the exact number of stars in the sky. This cosmos of ours is not static; it is constantly expanding. There is a constant flow of energy in the world. The people who claim that "God has created this world" are real fools. This world is constantly being created every single day; it is constantly expanding.

So *Vashishta* says, "It is easy to count how many stars there are in the sky, but finding God is even more difficult than that. You can count the stars, but cannot find the God hidden inside you that easily." So *Sri Rama* says, "*Prabhu*! What is this? Just now you said it is easy and now you say it is difficult. Tell me what is correct." Then *Vashishta* answered, "It is simple for the one who has intensity, love, detachment and discerning intelligence, but difficult for those who do not have these attributes."

Waris Shah has composed a beautiful poem; I will give you the gist of it. *Waris Shah* says, "Ranjha wooed Heer by becoming a

cowherd in her house. Farhaad secured the love of Shirin by cutting a tunnel through a mountain, to bring a river to her parched village. Sohni won the affection of Mahiwal by drowning when she tried to cross a river in an unbaked pitcher — she knew that she could lose her life, but it did not deter her — she took the risk. All she thought of was being in the arms of her beloved Mahiwal. She took the risk and jumped straight into a tempestuous Chenab." *Waris Shah* raises the question: "Waris, you say what you will do to propitiate your *guru*? Will you cut through the mountains or jump into the river like Sohni, or will you herd cows and buffaloes like Ranjha? What will you do? They did what they could. Now it is your turn. So why don't you say what you will do?" *Waris Shah* is questioning himself, "What will you do? What are you capable of doing?"

Those who seek shall find — remember this. You must pray devoutly at the feet of the *guru*. And if the *guru* is merciful and compassionate, your duality might change into oneness. That is how Adi Shankaracharya's statement: '*Guru* and *shishya* become one', is realised. Where do you have to go, and where are you now?

**Na bandhur na mitram gurur naiva shishyah
Chidanandaroopa shivoham shivoham**

CHAPTER 14

AMEND THE FOLLY THAT IS YOURS ALONE

The world is a transitory affair
He who understands it is rare
As you sow, so shall you reap
Whether you are a guru or a disciple
With gold and silver
Pearls and diamonds, you played all your life
When the moment of departure arrives
Not even a dime shall accompany you
Built a palace, built a fortress
All your life you cried, it is mine! it is mine!
Kabir says when the last moment comes
They'll all leave you alone
Even if there are twenty or twenty-five baratis
Let us carry the procession through
Kabir says, don't feel bad
This shall be the fate of everyone
In this world, none belongs to you
Neither any close relative nor the distant ones
All your family ties must snap
On this journey, you must walk alone

When people sitting in front are half-asleep, then you have to take recourse in veer *rasa* to wake them up. Veer *rasa* is not meant only for fighting against others. Veer *rasa* is not the trait of the khsatriya alone. It is a very useful *bhava* for every *sadhak* — and

what do you think he kills with veer *rasa*? He kills his own lethargy; his own sleep and his own attachments.

Kabir never lifted a knife in his life, wielding a sword is another matter altogether. *Kabir* never did anything except perform his own *dharma*, that of a weaver. He would weave cloth on a handloom; this is what his ancestors used to do. He never gave up this work. His disciples kept telling him, "Why do you do this work? We will do it for you." He would say, "No! I do not trust my disciples."

I feel disciples are there to make life difficult. Out of a billion people, you hardly find one genuine disciple. You have to trim and prune the ordinary followers and turn them into disciples. Disciples are not available ready-made. If they were, I too would have got them.

They say Ramakrishna Paramhans used to stand on the roof of his house and cry, "Mother! Where are the children whom I can impart this *gyana* to?" You have filled my heart with this wealth, now where do I pour out this *rasa*? Where are those capable people who can be the recipients of this *gyana*, so that I may feel lighter after passing it on to them? Mother, you have made me a cloud charged with love, *gyana*, *yoga* and *tantra*."

Oh! You will not understand the inner state of a cloud, it has to pour down somewhere. It is very much like the fate of a pregnant woman who has completed her term of pregnancy. The child inside the womb is eager to be born, but somehow the birth is not taking place. There could be a hundred and one medical reasons for it. No doubt she loves to carry the child, but still she wants the birth to take place. It is difficult for her to do her daily chores, her health is deteriorating and she is also eager to see the child's face. The mother is eager to see what kind of a child it will be, but if the birth is not taking place, then the pregnant woman would be in the same situation as Ramakrishna and would scream, "Oh, when will I be able to give birth?"

There is one kind of birth that happens through the body. In the language of the *shastras*, a child born thus is called '*bindu bindh santaan*', that is, the child born of the father's semen. And the other kind of child is called '*nadi bindh santaan*', i.e. the child born of the word. *Guru* gives birth to his disciple through the word. That is why the *guru* is both the mother and the father, because he gives birth through his word.

The *guru* is responsible for a kind of rebirth which in *Sanskrit* is called '*dwij*' — twice born. The truth is that unless your total transformation takes place, you do not deserve to be called a disciple. The person who knows no discipline is not a disciple. Discipline is an absolute must.

Discipline is not something imposed by another wielding a stick. If another imposes it through coercive means or by force, it will be called a dictatorship. You do this; you don't do this; get up at this time, so on and so forth. In several *ashrams* there is a fixed time for getting up. Now what can these poor people do? Once they know that they are up against fools, they have to devise rules! At four o'clock when the bell rings, you must get up. When it rings at five, come for prayer. At seven you must come for breakfast. And if it rings at nine, then present yourself for *satsang*. In other words, a bell is rung all the time! I have been frequenting different *ashrams* from time to time and I still do, but most of these *ashrams* appear to be prison-houses, at least from my point of view. I am not saying that all these places were like prisons, but the *gurus* felt necessary to impose all these regulations so that they could bring their good-for-nothing disciples on to the right path. So rules were being imposed to benefit the disciples! Well! Wellbeing does not spring from rules but from understanding and inner awakening.

In fact, you become a disciple in the true sense of the word only when you discipline yourself in accordance with your *viveka* (discerning intelligence) and consciousness. But if the *guru* has to wield a stick to bring you in line, it only means that you are a follower and your so called master is no more than a leader. Followers look good with leaders not with a *guru*. I always say that followers are really dangerous. They go to the extent of claiming the lives of their *gurus* — poor Jesus Christ was killed because of one of his followers! *Buddha* was served poisoned food by his follower!

Do you know what is the root cause of followers killing *gurus* is? The real thing is that you are full of arrogance that makes you feel, "Why should I bow before another person? Why should I call myself agyani and the other person *Brahmangyani*?" Inside

234

your heart you feel challenged and marginalized by the stature of the *guru*. No one wishes to feel inferior to anyone. Followers do entertain these feelings deep in their subconscious. You will say, "No, we have no such thoughts." The most I can say is that you do not know about it. This is the reason that given an opportunity, some followers take revenge.

In college my classmates and professors used to think that I was strange as I would not gossip about movies, films or boys. After my class I would rush out of the campus. I had some secret spots where I would go and enjoy the inner and outer silence. Where is the time to waste! But everyone thought I was abnormal. And well, in a way I was not normal, not from society's point of view. No one had given me orders to remain silent, but silence was happening to me. I used to wear only white clothes, now again it was not a vow or a discipline given to me, but white was the colour I chose for myself. But they found me abnormal. If you like you too can call me abnormal.

It is another matter that when someone falls below the normal level, he is called abnormal, and even when someone is above normal he is called abnormal. If you are below the average level of intelligence, you are not normal. And if you are above the average level of intelligence, even then you are not normal. I do not know which category I belonged to, but they found me strange.

Once, two poets were chatting over a cup of tea. One of them said, "When we go for these poets' meets and get applause from the audience, we feel really good. But when the audience does not respond, we feel bad." The other said, "You talk of no response! When we recite and the audience starts looking at their wristwatches, it is really insulting." A third poet joined in the conversation and said, "Forget that. When they shake their wristwatches and put them time and again against their ears, as if indicating that we should stop, that is the worst!"

I remember the times when I was invited to different temples and everyone found it very strange that a fifteen-year-old girl would speak on *Vedanta*! To become a true seeker is difficult. And if you are one, then you will never develop such a narcissistic behaviour that one day you plot to kill your master, whom you had loved and worshipped. If your love and devotion is genuine then it is a different matter. Otherwise it is so difficult to greet another human being with folded hands. If greeting another is so difficult, then paying obeisance to another and saying, "You mean everything to me, I am an agyani, please pull me out of this darkness, situate me in *gyana*. Hey *satguru*! You are *Brahma*, *Vishnu* and Mahesh to me. Hey *satguru*! You alone can bless me" — is certainly not that easy. Somewhere deep down *ahankara* is reduced to dust, and only then does such humility rise to the lips.

Stotras and chants of the master's glory do not arise in the heart so easily. Any effort at stringing together words does not necessarily result in poetry; all poetry is not shruti (sacred poetry). Shruti is shruti and poetry is poetry. Come to think of it, there haven't been better poets than the sages. But it is quite improbable that every poet is a sage. You tell me, which *guru* taught *Guru Nanak* poetry? *Kabir* learnt his poetic skills from whom?

Once a pair of birds were mating. A hunter's arrow struck the pair and both of them were wounded. On seeing such a tragic scene, sage Valmiki who was meditating on the bank of a river nearby, recited some *shlokas*. These *shlokas* became the basis for the creation of the great epic *Ramayana*. This little incident is behind the story of *Rama* and Sita that he wrote. The act of the mating birds being brutally killed is what prompted him to compose a great epic. The male bird died but the female survived, and seeing the dead body of her mate, she burst into a sad and melancholic wail. Soon she too died grieving over the body of her dead mate. The pain of separation suffered by the birds had the power to stir the deepest recesses of a sage's heart, and it was out of this pain that great poetry was born.

Come to think of it, why should a sage be perturbed by the death of a bird? Or grieve over the sorrow of another? Ordinarily, he should have nothing to do with it! But a genuine *mahatma*, a sage, is not stonehearted. He has a very sensitive heart. That is why *Goswami Tulsi Das* says, "The heart of a saint is as soft as butter." Butter needs fire to melt, but a saint's heart melts with the pain of another.

Why is it that a follower fails to attempt a complete surrender?

The main reason is *ahankara*; deep inside his subconscious carries on a debate with itself. "The *guru* seems so human, why should I consider him a divine incarnation or better than me." Somewhere or the other, you look for a chink in the guru's armour. This is the reason why when someone tells a concocted story about a saint, most people readily agree with the allegations. Why? Because they want to! And if after sometime the accusations are proven to be false, the blame is transferred to the one who told the story, never for a second wondering how on earth you could have doubted your master in the first place! Why do you accept things so easily? Because deep inside, you never recognise any *guru* as a *guru*.

The one who is waiting to escape shall escape either today or tomorrow, on one pretext or the other. The one who is suspicious of the *guru* and the one, who is ashamed of bowing before a *guru*, will sooner or later find a reason for going away. And that is not a bad thing either! Let them believe what they want to believe. And good for him too who does not believe! These rumours cannot be dealt with rejoinders. What kind of a rejoinder will you give to people and for how long can one give such explanations? The worm of doubt is always present in your ego. It is ego that prevents you from surrendering before another.

There is another cause for this ego. Although you are not illumined yet and have not had any realisation so far, the truth is that you are *Brahman* yourself. When I am *Brahman* myself, then why must I bow before another? There is a beautiful scripture in the *Vedanta* called Vichar Sagar which opens with these wonderful lines:

Awadh apaar swaroopa mum lahiri Vishnu Mahesh
Vidhi ravi chanda varun yama, shakti dhanesh ganesh
My true form is expansive, all pervasive.
Shiva, Vishnu, Brahma are just like waves in me.
Destiny, sun, moon, stars, God of death,
Durga, Ganesha are waves in my expansive nature!

Swami Nichaladas is simply incomparable when it comes to his range, the sweep of his imagination and the power of his words and expressions. But when you hear this knowledge it is still information and not realisation. Experience is different from theoretical understanding. Now the question is of how to convert this information into experience. In other words, how do we internalise and incorporate the *gyana* into our experience? The methods are *vairagya* (detachment), *manan* (reflection) and *Nidhdhyasana* (state in which all mental modifications are quietened).

What is *vairagya*? It means detachment from the world and it's so called pleasures. You remember the *bhajan* I started with: 'Duniya do din ka mela, jisko samajh pare *albela*'. The one who understands that this world is a fleeting drama, is a true mystic — *albela*. *Albela* is not one who drowns himself in carnal pleasures or does not care for his parents, nor the one who is self-obsessed. The one who realises that this world is a fleeting affair is *albela* in the true sense of the word. You do not have to be serious or solemn in order to realise this. *Albela* also means ecstatic, joyous, born free.

When the scene of birth takes place you should sing, 'Swagatham Shubhswagatham', and when death strikes you should sing, 'Namaste Namaste, its Vidai'. You laugh only when a birth takes place and start crying over death. What is this? If a boy is born you laugh and if a girl is born you cry. This is absolutely shameless!

I was listening to a very interesting story today. I would like to share it with you. This gentleman had two daughters but no son. On consulting a so called expert he was advised, "You will not be blessed with a son unless you are bitten by a dog." So he would run after every dog he saw in the hope that it would bite him. But the dogs would run away. He would go slinking up to a dog but it would simply scoot. Now ordinarily what happens is that dogs come chasing men, but here it was the other way round. Here a man was chasing dogs who ran away! The dogs must have been scared, wondering why this man was coming after them! "We go to man in search of food, why is he coming after us?"

Now he was really very upset. Sometimes, he would try to lure a dog with a *ladoo* — the dog would eat the sweet and run away — now why would a dog bite the hand that feeds it? When his repeated attempts failed, he would land up at homes of dog-

238

owners and plead, "O dear dog! Please do come and accept my offering. O Maharaja of dogs, please bite me!" For the sake of a son, people are willing to go to any length! Then one day he accepted defeat, thinking that he was not fated to be bitten by a dog. But he refused to accept the fact that he was not destined to have a son. Rather, he thought he was such a degraded being that even stray dogs would not condescend to bite him!

And then one day he was sitting in a friend's house. Though they had a dog, this man was so tired of chasing dogs in the streets that he did not even look at it. He just turned his face away, sure that this insensitive creature would not even look at him, when suddenly out of the blue the dog bit him. The moment he was bitten he started shouting in joy, "Oh, he has bitten me, he has bitten me." He went home and threw a big party — and then within a year, a son was born to him!!! Wow! Indian astrologers are great! They have the stupidest remedies for you. God! Can any sane man understand this method of begetting a son — get bitten by a dog!?

I said he must have had some karmic connection with this dog from his previous birth. And this connection was proved later on, because every time he sits in *dhyana*, he sits with his face up, the way a dog has its snout up! His facial expression is similar to that of a howling dog

When a girl is born you cry. If a girl is born you say, "Thank God, at least she is not lame or blind. All her limbs are intact." The boy may be scrawny, yet you feel overjoyed, "It is a boy!" When someone is born you are overjoyed and when someone dies you cry. But this is not something you should either celebrate or mourn. If you view this from a higher perspective, then 'nothing is born and nothing dies'. Matter manifests and goes back to the state of the unmanifest. The whole world is nothing but an interplay of atoms; it is just a play of atoms integrating and disintegrating.

Each one of you has several worlds in your mind. In a single night you see eight to ten dreams and each dream is of fifteen to twenty minutes duration. The story of each dream is different and yet true. This dream world appears to be so true, but the moment you open your eyes there is nothing! When the eyes open everything vanishes! It is even possible that you think that right now you are seeing a dream in which you are in a *shivir* sitting in front of Gurumaa who is conducting a *satsang*. Can you prove to me that it is not your dream! How can you say that this is not a dream? It can only be a dream!

I have narrated this story many times over. One morning, Zen master Bokoju was feeling rather disturbed, when a disciple who served him with devotion arrived. The disciple said, "*Gurudev*! Why do you look so sad today?" So he told him, "Last night I dreamt that I have become a butterfly. Now the problem is that I wonder: what if the story is vice-a-versa and that a butterfly was dreaming that it is a man, a Zen *guru*?" The disciple said, "So what is the problem?" "The problem is: how far is it true that I am a butterfly and how far is it true that a butterfly can also be me? What is true? What I am now or what I was at night? You tell me, what do you say?" Now he was such a fantastic disciple. He gave a stinging slap to the *guru* and said, "You better come to your senses *gurudev*. Enjoy your cup of tea." Saying this he bowed to the master and both had a hearty laugh! Bokoju said, "Well, you are saved from my blows. Had you said anything else, it would have been insulting."

This is the essence of a *guru-shishya* relationship. In the Indian tradition, such a thing is simply inconceivable, but this story is very popular among the Zen masters and tells us how a disciple slapped his *guru* and said, "*Gurudev*, wake up! Neither your becoming a butterfly was the truth nor your being a man is. It is just a dream."

There is a *mantra* in the *Katha Upanishad*:

Om Sahana bhavatu Sahanau Bhunaktu
Saha veeryam Karavavahai
Tejasvi Naavadhitamastu
Ma Vidwishavahai

Om! May He protect us both together
(by illumining the nature of knowledge)
May He sustain us both (by ensuring the fruits of knowledge)
May we attain the vigour (of knowledge) together

Let what we learn enlighten us
Let us not hate each other

This is an extraordinary prayer which you are not likely to find in any Holy book. In this, both the *guru* and the disciple pray together. They say, "Hey *Brahman*! Make our *buddhi* shine with divine intellect." It is not just the disciple who says, "My *buddhi*...", it is not just the *guru* who says, "My *buddhi*..." — both pray together.

"Both of us are riding in the same boat. He wants to receive something from me and I want to give him something. He has surrendered with total devotion and while placing on his head my compassionate hand, full of blessings, I want to give him the same experience that I have had." Both pray, "Our *buddhi* should shine with divine intellect. Our *buddhi* should be filled with *gyana*." *Guru* says, "Bless me, so that I may be able to give *gyana* as a perfect master. Let me be the medium." And the disciple says, "Bless me, so that I may be able to receive *gyana*."

If the *guru* gives but the disciple is not prepared to receive, then how will it work? It does not work one-way. It has to be a perfect combination — the right giver and the right receiver. Suppose a follower has surrendered himself completely and from a follower has become a true disciple, but the *guru* turns out to be useless, then what will happen? Nothing whatsoever! But soon, if the seeker is lucky, he may realise that he is stuck with a pseudo-*guru* and may be able to rid himself of him. In the past few years I have met thousands of people. I have come across very competent disciples of incompetent *gurus*. And I have also seen very incompetent disciples of very competent *gurus*. But if the *guru* is intelligent and so is the disciple — as in the case of *Ashtavakra* and *Janak* — then it is indeed a wonderful opportunity for both.

The spiritual journey is incomplete without *gyana*. If *gyana* is not fully experienced, then you say, "I am Sohan Lal," "I am Shakuntala," "I am forty-two years old," "I am a man," "I am a woman," "I have so many children." Now, after listening to the stotra of Shankaracharya, you can easily change your statements: "I am *Shiva*," "I am Chidananda." But merely by changing your verbal statements, you cannot expect your consciousness to change.

241

I told you in the beginning that your motive should be to experience *shivoham*. That should be the primary goal of your *sadhana*. You need to put all your energies into it. Mere listening will take you nowhere. You will not enter into that state merely by listening to what I am saying. It can actually happen only if you are a disciple of a very high order. Otherwise like *Ravana*, you will become arrogant. He used to say, "I am God."

Vedanta is a very dangerous enterprise. You can see for yourself that when *Bhagwan Krishna* gives the message of the *Gita* to *Arjuna*, he said in so many words, "Hey *Arjuna*, do not share the secret of this *gyana* with a person who is not worthy of it. You should share it only if he is worthy. Otherwise it is sensible to maintain silence. Do not utter a word, do not share. Let this secret remain a secret. For how long? As long as the seeker does not rise to a level where he proves himself to be worthy of it.

In Krishna's time it was possible to keep knowledge a secret. But these days the *Gita*, the *Upanishads* and the *Gurbani* — and also the works of other sages are printed and people can buy them. What should have been a secret did not remain one. As a result, what happened was that it lead to more loss than gain. People are unable to rise above anger, lust and greed. They could not go deep enough into the process of meditation. They do not get to experience the miracle of the power released by *dhyana*. Even though you have not purified your mind with selfless service; even though you have not achieved any considerable degree of meditativeness or inner stability, you start reciting '*shivoham, shivoham!*' Under these circumstances, reciting '*shivoham*' is nothing more than a petty abuse of this word.

Shivoham is a very pure word. It is not something meant to be spoken or uttered. But if the *guru* has explained it properly and you have followed every word and applied the wisdom of the master, only then will it reveal its worth — you have to work hard. What kind of work do you need to do? Do you have to go on a pilgrimage, do *japa* or *shirshasan*? All these methods can actually become obstacles in the path of a *sadhak* who is striving for *tattvagyana*. *Karmas* such as *yagna*, *mantra japa* etc, are only external aids that help purify and cleanse the *antehkaran*. If you

have heard this *gyana* from the mouth of the *guru*, then it is better not to get involved with all these *karmas*. Then what should one do? For such a person, the guru's service becomes a form of *yagna* and the reflection and contemplation of this *gyana* is meditation enough.

Aham nirvikalpo niraakaarroopo
Vibhurvyapya sarvatra sarvendriyaanaam
Sadaa me samatvam na muktirna bandhah
Chidaanandroopah shivoham shivoham

'**Aham nirvikalpo niraakaarroopo**': 'I' am formless, without any attributes; this is something you must understand. Your mind and intellect are also formless. Have you ever seen your thoughts, feelings, concepts, wisdom, stupidity or knowledge? No one has ever seen his mind; it is subtle and formless. Is it black? Is it white? Is it tall? Is it fat?

Man loves his senses more than he loves his body. If someone hits you, what will you do? Will you not try to protect yourself with your hands, save your eyes, face and head? Suppose someone gives you a choice, "Should I cut off your hand or gouge out your eyes?" You will get your hands chopped off but save your eyes. If someone says, "What should we do, pull out your eyes or drive you mad?" You will say, "Pull out my eyes but spare my mind." The senses are dearer to you than the body. Mind is dearer than the senses. And *buddhi* is dearer than the mind. And dearest of all is you — your self.

All relationships are dear to us, not because of their intrinsic nature, but due to the joy they bring to our lives. The wife is not loved for her own sake; the husband is also not loved for his own sake; they are loved because of the joy they bring to our lives. If I am the recipient of this joy, then what is dear to me, the joy or the object that brings joy? The child is not loved; we love the joy that the child brings to our lives. The house is not loved for its own sake but for the comfort and happiness it brings.

A few days back a gentleman came and said, "A lot of people have told me that my house has not been constructed in accordance with *Vastushastra* and that is why I remain sick and my business

243

is not doing well. So now I am planning to sell it off." In other words, you do not love your own house. You do not like the house that brings you no joy. If the child is not obedient, does not serve the parents, then what do they say? "We have no relationship with you." Sometimes such situations do arise. If the child turns out to be a good-for-nothing and does not mend his ways even when you drill sense into him, there is wisdom in showing him the door. Rather than leaving the house yourself, you should show him the door!

The fact of the matter is that if you do not take a hard decision, then he will pack up your bags and throw you out. "Go, you fuddy-duddy old man!" If both the old man and the old woman are alive, they can always support each other. But if one of them dies and the other is left behind, then he or she faces a very difficult time indeed.

Often such things happen in *ashrams* and pilgrimage centres. Children take their aged parents on a pilgrimage; check into a *dharamshala* and at night the son and daughter-in-law leave quietly. Now the aged parents are sitting and waiting. Poor people, they do not even know their home address. How long will the *dharamshala* people allow them to stay? They also throw them out in a couple of days. Now what will they do? They go around begging, what else? The person who dispensed charity to others has now been reduced to a beggar himself!

Why should you die strangling yourself with the noose of attachment and possessiveness? The one who is hell-bent on ruining his life will do so in any case. A person who refuses to listen to the words of wisdom will learn a lesson only when he suffers the hard knocks of life. Some people do not learn a lesson till the end. So a child is not dear to me for its own sake but because of the pleasure and joy it brings to my life. The house is also not dear for its own sake but only for the comfort it offers. Food is dear to us not for its own sake, but because eating brings satisfaction. So wife, husband, children, shop — all these are dear because they give 'me' happiness. And if they do not give me any happiness, I can easily give up on them!

So I love this body the most. More than the body, I love the

244

senses. More than the senses, I love the mind. And more than the mind, I love the intellect. And more than the *buddhi*, I love the self! The irony is that I do not even know who the real 'I', the real 'self' is! Ignorance drives man to such foolishness, that rather than experiencing *ananda* through his own *anandaswaroopa*, he seeks it through others!

Once a wealthy man told a beggar, "Why don't you work?" The beggar replied very stiffly, "Why should we when you are doing it for us? You earn, and we just call out, 'Shani', and immediately you dole out money!" (Shani is the Demi-God Saturn — a furious God who can be appeased by giving alms on Saturday). "You are scared that Saturn might turn malevolent and make you face its wrath. When Tuesday comes, we ask you for money in the name of Mars. On Monday we remind you of *Shiva*. And you people are so scared that you give us alms for your own sake. So that is how fools like you work for wise men like us! Why should we work?"

When you see others begging for alms you get irritated and start lecturing, "Why don't you work? You do not even respect yourself." But what is it that you do? With the begging bowl of your mind, you go to your wife and say, "Satiate my lust and give me happiness." You spread your hands before your children, before wealth and even before wealthy people. You go around chasing leaders, politicians, actors and whosoever you can, with folded hands. You do not mind being their henchmen or stooges, if it gets you some measure of happiness into the bargain. What a big folly it is! If the folly is mine, then I alone must make amends. The *guru* only shows the path, you must walk on it yourself.

There are many sects which claim that if you are initiated by their *guru* once, then on the basis of his spiritual powers, he will facilitate your *atmasakshatkar*. He will awaken your *kundalini* as well. You do not need to do anything except become his disciple. *Guruji* will take care of the rest! But in return for this, the first thing they do is to get all your property transferred to their name. Realisation can wait; first there should be complete surrender! These people use the story of *Ashtavakra* and *Janak* to their own advantage. I have met so many people who have actually been inveigled into gifting their business and landed property to their *gurus.* The disciple was somewhat reluctant to hand over the entire property and business to the *guru*, so the *guru* said, "All right, let us have a partnership."

Would you like to accept such a person as a *guru*? Look, the disciple may choose to offer everything he has to the *guru*, but if the *guru* starts saying, "You give me everything," then it is a form of thuggery. When I see thousands of people flocking to such *gurus*, it surprises me no end. Then all I have to say is, and it is the bitter truth — that only thugs will go to thugs.

One man came to me and said, "I was with a *guru* for 25 years. He used me as a courier for smuggling and I kept doing it for him. Every time he went to Europe, he would bring diamonds and conveniently slip them into my bag. He was well respected and had an awesome reputation. Even the customs officers stood with folded hands before him." In other words, if you are in trouble you drag others into your mess. The diamonds were smuggled and the landed property was illegally occupied. And if the officers did not listen to him, they were killed by hired assassins. All this was going on. Then for some reason he parted ways with his *guru*. He was really very sad for a long time, thinking that by walking out on his *guru* he had invited a dreadful sin upon his head! O what a pathetic state! It is sheer exploitation.

After listening to me he realized who a real *guru* is; he understood where he had gone wrong. Before he met me, he faxed his entire story without concealing anything. When he came he was in a bad shape; his state of mind was not very good. I asked him, "Today you are saying all this? But did you not feel bad when you were associated with him for twenty-five years? Now that he has turned hostile, you have started speaking against him?" The mind can be so deluded that you know what is wrong, yet are unable to come out of it. The *guru* threatened him with death if he tried to disassociate himself. He did finally part ways but continued to feel very insecure.

The way the position of a *guru* has been misused in India has no parallel. Ordinary people, who do not understand these things and do not know the difference between a genuine and a false *guru* often turn pessimistic; even cynical, and end up as atheists. Then

they also start saying, "You never know they are all alike." So this is how they treat a donkey, a horse and a cow at par.

But all I say is that if you were to go through the *shastras*, you will find the right definition of who a real *guru* is, what kind of a person he should be, what are the signs of a true *guru* and what are the signs of a true disciple. The real *guru* is one who tells the *shishya*: "You should not desire the pleasures of even *Brahmanloka*. You should regard it as no more than a blade of grass. Only when you are truly detached do you know what true *vairagya* is."

Let me now tell you an incident from Baba Farid's life and then I will take you to the next stotra. Once a king came to meet *Baba Farid* and said, "I want to do something for you." Now *Farid* was a *fakir*, with not a care in the world. He said, "Right now I do not need anything." But big people want to show their power and pelf, and most often do not listen to anyone. "No, please tell me what I can do?" At that time *Farid* was stitching his bag with a needle. When the king insisted, *Farid* just took out his needle and threw it into the river flowing nearby. "Go and get me that needle." Now the king started wondering, "What kind of a crazy man is he? Why did I get involved with him?" But because he had given his word, the king went down to the river and started looking for the needle — it was next to impossible to find a needle in the water — he put his hand into the water; of course he did not find the needle but he did see a whole lot of scintillating diamonds and pearls lying at the bottom of the river. *Farid* just wanted to show the king that he was not capable of giving him anything. How could anyone think of giving him anything? If he wanted he could even change the processes of the cosmos — but he had no desire left.

I will tell you something very interesting. As long as you desire, God will not fulfill your desires because he knows you are a fool. You will never talk sense. As long as you keep wishing, none of your wishes will be realised. He says, "The day you stop wishing for things, you will get the power to realise whatever you wish for." Look, once you liberate yourself from all your wishes, then what will you wish for? Then even if you have the power of realising your wishes, will you exercise the power? This is what happens with mystics and devotees.

247

There is a story about *Ravidas*. Once a saint came to visit him and saw that because of abject poverty, he was working as a cobbler. Animal hide was lying in one corner and he was busy drying and cleaning it. The saint said to him, "Give up this dirty job." *Ravidas* answered, "Who says it is a dirty job? Just because it is animal hide it becomes dirty? You think your skin is better? The animal hide can still be put to ten different uses, but my dear, when you die, your skin will not be of any use at all. Animal hide is better than your skin." Who says that we are better than animals? The body of an animal is definitely superior. Their bones are crushed to make gelatin and the same gelatin is used for making capsules. Their hide is used for making shoes and several other things.

The saint refused to listen. While leaving he left a philosopher's stone saying, "This stone is for you. When a piece of iron comes into contact with it, it turns into gold. You can now remove your poverty." After a couple of months he came back thinking that by now *Guru Ravidas* must have constructed a palace. When he came he saw that it was the same hutment, the same broken tools and the same animal hide. He said, "I gave you a philosopher's stone. Why did you not put it to use?" That is when *Ravidas* told him, "When this philosopher's stone touches iron, it converts iron into gold. Iron is dust and so is gold. Ever since my *guru* — who is the real philosopher's stone — has touched me, everything has turned to gold. When a philosopher's stone touches iron it turns into gold, but when the *guru* touches your soul, he changes you into a *guru* and no less. *Guru* gives birth to a *guru*. Now what else do I want? What should I ask for? Gold, silver, iron; all these are different forms of dust. When I was in *agyana* (ignorance), I used to regard this body of flesh and bone as 'I'. Then satguru's blessings elevated me. He has released me from all kinds of bonds, attachments, affections and involvements, and told me who 'I' am. He was the one who told me how I needed to look at myself. I am *Chidanandaswaroopa*."

No one has possibly verbalised a thought more elevating than this ever. The condition that Shankaracharya is talking about is both easy and difficult at the same time. It is easy because 'I' am shivaroopa. I do not have to make *Shiva* out of you. You are

Satchidananda, I do not have to make any special effort to make you one. 'I' am atmaroopa, I do not have to do anything to become atmaroopa. It is the same thing as the ornaments saying, "What should we do now to become gold?" The ornament has to understand and give up the sense of being an ornament. In the same way, what do we do to know that 'I' am *Brahman*? All that you need to understand is that this 'I-ness' is false.

If I were to talk to you in the classical language of the *shastras*, then it will be a problem for you. Well, sometimes people tell me, "You really talk in a simple way." I say, "If I want, I can also use complex language, enough to make you run away. But how will that help? I do not want you to run away, I want you to wake up." So in order to wake you up, it is important to simplify even the most complex philosophies and well, it must be done. Even those who do not, should try to do it.

Once I met a Deputy Shankaracharya — the first time I heard about him, I was rather surprised because Shankaracharya had set up only four centres — *matths*, and had appointed four Shankaracharyas — but these four have multiplied into forty. For a long time now, even this institution has been afflicted by internal politics. We have heard of a Prime Minister and a Deputy Prime Minister, but I do not quite know what this 'Upa' (Deputy) means. So you have Pradhan Mantri and Upa-Pradhan Mantri. Rastrapati (President) and Upa-Rastrapati (Vice-President) which are constitutional positions. But this bit about an Upa-Shankaracharya is beyond my comprehension. It is just dirty politics in a religious body. You are interested in the wealth of your disciple, you are concerned about your growing popularity, you want people to praise you to the skies, but you want to have nothing to do with the disciple's ignorance, misery and lack of knowledge. Such a *guru* sinks to the lowest hell after his death. Bhagwan Shankaracharya has been kind enough to give us this wonderful, unique though dangerous *gyana*, in such beautiful words.

Once the *sadhaks* of this path reflect on the words of Shankaracharya in close association with a *guru*, then all the distinctions in their *buddhi* are destroyed. Only when the false 'I-ness' is killed and the false ego and the impure 'I' removed, shall

'I' be able to enter into this pure *atmabhava*. Only in this pure state can *shivoham* be experienced.

I have already spoken to you about both these things: where we are and where we have to reach. Now if you are caught up in the arrogance of mind, *buddhi, chitta, ahankara*, then where will you reach? You have to attain the consciousness that mind, *buddhi, chitta* and *ahankara* are not 'I'. I have given you an assignment. Now you must do a lot of reflection and contemplation. 'I' am neither body nor mind nor intellect. 'I' am a witness — *sakshi*. 'I' am beyond and above these. Whenever you are entangled in body consciousness, use your *viveka* (discerning intelligence) and snip off all the entanglements. 'I' is not the body. This consciousness of being a body should not chase you, in simple terms it means that: 'I' am not body, this body is not mine. Whenever old conditionings overpower you, you must make an effort to disengage yourself from them.

A gentleman came to meet me in the morning. He offered me a gift and said, "It is my wedding anniversary and I have got this gift for you." I said, "Your anniversary. It is 'your' wedding anniversary." He was somewhat embarrassed and said, "Yes!" I repeated my question, and then in a somewhat serious tone and a little more loudly I asked, "'Your' wedding?" Then he realised and said, "Oh! It was the body that got married. Neither am 'I' a body, nor is it 'my' wedding and she is not 'my' wife either." Repeating 'shivoham' is not going to help you enter Shivaroopa. The rope that you have tied around the body has first to be loosened, and then slowly snipped off.

A child went to buy a balloon. He asked, "How much is this balloon for?" "This is for fifty paisa; this one for one rupee; this one for two rupees; this big one is for five rupees and the one bigger than that is for ten rupees." The child said, "All right, give me this one for two rupees." The seller was about to disentangle it when the child said, "No, give me that five rupee one." He was about to take it off when the child said, "No, give me the biggest one." The seller was about to remove it when the child said, "No, no. Give me that one for fifty paisa."

The balloon seller got irritated and angry, and as he was about to remove the thread of the balloon the child had asked for, the

thread of the biggest balloon slipped out of his hand and it started flying off. Removing the one for fifty paisa and offering it to the child the fellow was exasperated as he spoke, "All right, take it now." The child said, "Why should I take this one? Now I will only take that one. You go your way and I will go chasing that one and somehow get hold of it." He was hiding a branch of a wild bush behind him. He had come with the plan to engage the balloon-seller in a conversation, hoping that in the process one of the balloons would slip away. So sometimes he asked for one and sometimes for the other! He ran after the balloon, wrapped it around the branch and got it free of cost!

As long as the balloon is tied to the pole, it will stay in place. If the knot is loose, then it will fly away. In the same way, you will be able to fly in the sky of spirituality only if you manage to untie the rope of the body, mind, *buddhi*, *chitta* and *ahankara*. The day you are able to do so, you will move in a zone of bliss.

CHAPTER 15

I AM THE SUPREME TRUTH

I will take up a couple of questions I have received. Someone has asked: "When we try to observe the mind with *drashta bhava*, it becomes absolutely calm and still, even stops thinking and re-thinking for sometime. It is just like a thief who stops all of a sudden on being caught in the act of stealing, and then starts all over again. In the same way, after sometime the mind resumes its ebb and tide of thoughts and feelings. This pattern keeps on repeating itself time and again. In spite of being involved in our daily chores, how do we apply the principle of *drashta bhava* to keep a watch on the ebb and flow of the mind? Is this act of watching the mind ultimately transformed into meditation? Please guide us."

The *drashta bhava* you have right now is the product of *buddhi*. There is a very close and intimate relationship between *buddhi* and 'I'. 'I' knows the mind only through the *buddhi*. I am unable to know my mind directly. Initially, in the process of knowing the mind through the *buddhi*, the seeker has to work very hard and has to make a tremendous effort. For instance, if someone is learning to ride a bicycle, he has to work hard in the initial stages. For the learner it becomes difficult to decide which area to pay attention to. Should he keep the handlebar straight so that the cycle does not go left or right, or should he watch the road so that he does not bump into some oncoming vehicle? Simultaneously he has to move the pedals and maintain his balance too!

When someone first learns to ride a bicycle, you will see tension on his face. That is why you expect a child to start with a tricycle. While riding a tricycle, he learns to keep the handle

straight – there is no fear of falling. When he graduates from the three-wheeler to the two-wheeler, he already has some sense of how to hold the handle and how to turn. He has understood the mechanism of handling quite a few things. A child has to use its conscious mind to learn; this is true for every adult too. We learn through our conscious mind and once learning takes place, the same task is done without experiencing any tension — for now the subconscious mind is working. When a child switches from three-wheels to two-wheels, the insecure feeling is still there. Initially, the teacher holds the seat and sometimes even runs along with the child. But gradually, as the child gains confidence, the support is withdrawn. If the child discovers that he is riding on his own, he gets scared and loses his balance and falls down. Slowly the child begins to gain confidence and soon he rides the cycle comfortably. He becomes more daring and now even rides without holding the handles! When someone first learns to ride a cycle or drive a scooter or car, they suffer great personal tension. But once you learn, then there is no tension.

In the same way, when initially you practice *drashta bhava*, you feel it is a laborious task. Because the moment your attention drifts, you cease to be a witness or *sakshi*. It is easier to chant *mantras* or perform a *yagna*, but it is very difficult to distance oneself from one's mind and to be aware. This requires patience and dedication.

It has never been easy to wake up, neither from sleep nor from a state of semi-consciousness. Both require a good deal of labour. We never want to abandon the pleasure of sleep. In the same way, *agyana* (ignorance) has its own strange charm and pleasure. Most people are such that if you tell them to go for *satsang*, they will say, "You go." This is just another way of saying that something is wrong with you and so you need to go there.

Ignorance has a soporific effect. Alcohol has an intoxicating effect and so does sleep. In the same way, ignorance is also very intoxicating. Now you may find it very strange but it is true that ignorance is very intoxicating. It is also intoxicating. The follies we commit in ignorance, never allow us to realise how and in what different ways we inflict harm upon ourselves and our loved ones. The level of ignorance is such that even if someone wishes to guide us, we do not want to listen. People get rude if this is pointed out.

Every packet of cigarettes that a smoker buys carries a statutory warning: 'Cigarette smoking is injurious to health'. Cancer societies insist that the warning should read: 'Cigarette smoking causes cancer too'. Someone has gone to the extent of suggesting that you remove the word 'too' and just write: 'Cigarette smoking does cause cancer'. Right now what they write is, 'Cigarette smoking is injurious to health'. In the USA, authorities have brought a path-breaking ruling and now every pack carries the message: 'Smoking kills you'.

But ask any smoker, or if you smoke then ask yourself, if you know that cigarette smoking increases your propensity for cancer. First bronchitis, then asthma, then patches on the lungs, and then these patches turn into cancer. First bronchitis, then asthma, then patches on the lungs, and then these patches turn into cancer. Despite that, there is no dearth of cigarette smokers. When I went to Canada for the first time, our flight was via Jordan. We had a stop over at Amman, the capital of Jordan. At the hotel near Amman airport where we were to stop for the night, almost everyone had a transparent bag with 'Marlboro' written on it. I kept wondering what 'Marlboro' was. When we reached Toronto airport, it was the same story. By the time I returned I had discovered what it was — it was a brand of cigarettes! While returning to Delhi, again I found that almost every passenger had a 'Marlboro' bag.

In America, when it was first discovered that smoking causes cancer, a patient sued the tobacco company. He won the case and got a lot of money. Now the company was on the back-foot. That is when they decided to write: 'Dangerous for health'. Then they introduced a brand called 'Light', and claimed that this one had less tobacco. The idea was to make regular smokers feel that this brand was less harmful. As a matter of fact, this kind of logic is nothing but a form of entrapment.

Every drunkard knows that an excess of alcohol will damage his liver one day. But everyone thinks that if their father and grandfather who used to drink never had any problem, then it is not going to harm them either. In other words, one goes on looking for cases

where drinking did not actually ruin the person's health, and totally ignores the cases where health was completely ruined. What is this? This is the soporific effect of ignorance. Smoking is a strange act — inhale smoke and exhale smoke! Again inhale smoke and exhale smoke! So those who have nothing better to do are doing this! This is what you call the intoxication of *agyana*. Man lives in this world without discovering his *swaroopa*. The whole world is living in this manner. People feel they do not need *gyana* at all. They think that those who attend *satsang* are crazy, and people like me only contribute to this kind of madness. Such people think, "Gurumaa is driving people mad and people are willing to go mad. But look at us, we are sane; we do not believe in *gurus* — and they think that this too is a sign of their greatness. Well! Everyone has a right to live according to his or her own beliefs."

Those who are obsessed with the body and the senses get a great kick out of pleasures and wish to have more and more of them. The urge to satiate the senses is so strong, that the mind never thinks about the higher planes. Lucky are those whose hearts have been stirred and they can reflect upon life as it is — mortal. It is a great blessing to even think about the reality of life and death. But now when you are trying to shatter this *agyana* and follow the path *gurudev* has recommended, you feel that it is too laborious. Why is it so? Because so far you have not had any direct encounter with the 'self' and your attachment with the senses and the grip of *maya* is very strong.

You have just heard *Brahmangyana*, not known it. At the level of the intellect, you have understood that 'I' am not body, senses, mind or *buddhi*. It is with the *buddhi* that you are trying to maintain your *drashta bhava*. Now whenever your *buddhi* goes off-track, you forget that 'I' am a *sakshi* (witness). Time and again your memory fails you and you have to bring *buddhi* back on the track. Words of *gyana* have to be translated into experience and for that you have to work on eradicating all the seeds of lust, greed and anger, with dispassion, intelligence and *vairagya*. If just intellectual understanding of food cannot satiate your hunger, how can an intellectual understanding of *atman* give you instantaneous *moksha*?

There is another question connected with all this. A lady says, "One thing is definite. Ever since I have met you, the world appears much more beautiful than it ever did. And this body is also experiencing very beautiful things. Sometimes I find myself completely in the present, at least for sometime. Is it not possible to make this temporary feeling permanent?" The lady who has asked this question has been associated with me for eight long years. She is from a *Sikh* family. Despite the fact that she reads the *Gurbani* on a daily basis, she had an insatiable thirst to know what 'truth' is. What is the reality? What is the truth? It was in connection with this quest that she met me. Once she organised a *satsang* at her house and she had loads of questions to ask me. I said, "If you want real answers, then come to me in the *shivir* at *Rishikesh*."

From that day onwards she has been a regular at all the *shivirs*. Even so she felt the need to ask, "When will this state become permanent?" The answer is: It takes time. And why does it take time? Because our sleep is very deep. When a mother wakes up a child in the morning, he fights and cries. When you scold him he says, "Okay mama, I have woken up." No doubt he gets up, but his eyes are still shut as though he is still sleeping. Mama goes out of the room and he goes back to sleep! Again the mother pulls him out of the bed and locks him in the bathroom. Sitting on the toilet seat he again goes off to sleep! When the mother realises that he has gone off to sleep again, she bangs on the door, "Get up!" He gets up from there and again while brushing his teeth goes off to sleep. Now is that not a strange thing? How can anyone fall asleep while brushing his teeth!?

Mornings are really very tough for little children. If you ask me, schools should not start so early. Why do you punish your children? Now because your parents have punished you, so you punish them in turn. If you were to ask an old man to get up at four, he has no problem whatsoever, because as it is he stays awake all through the night. As you get older your sleep becomes lighter. But for a child, even a couple of minutes sleep is very precious. For children, it is a punishment to wake up early. a punishment to wake up early. You must have seen little children sleeping in the vehicle on the way to school. I feel so sorry for them! And their bags are so heavy! With bags on their laps, the children fall asleep, blissfully unaware of their surroundings. If you visit a school in the morning, you will find fifty percent of the children dozing off! The teacher has to slap them time and again to wake them up. So at home parents thrash them and in school it is the teachers. Due to this constant nagging and thrashing, they develop a hatred for elders, parents and teachers — all those who do not allow them to sleep.

Who likes waking up? No one. And why? Because waking up involves labour. If you have just started out on the path of spirituality, then take it that you are still a child in this respect. And for a child, even walking is a labourious act. Have you ever seen a child who is learning to walk? He lifts each foot in a deliberate manner, as though he cannot lift it at all. He lifts one, then the other and then he falls and starts crying. He gets up, walks again and then falls. Even a body has to work hard to learn how to adjust with itself and with its environment. And here I am talking of snapping out of the sleep induced over several years!

You really have to be on your guard. This is new to your intellect, so it will be a time for attentiveness. You have to watch every step of yours, every breath of yours. Every time a thought arises in the mind, you have to learn to keep a distance from it. If your *buddhi* gets a little derailed, no problem; just bring the awareness back. Once you remember, then there is no need to play the guilt game. Simply turn back to *drashta bhava* again. And again you will forget! Initially this is what happens! Do not worry!

This process of forgetting and remembering shall continue in this manner for some time. You will be in the present and the mind may slip back into the past or run towards the future. According to me, it is not important how many times you forget, but how many times you wake up. For this reason, you should not dwell too much on these follies. You just remember how many times you woke up. Because if you remember how many times you woke up, the moments of remembrance will go on increasing. And if you dwell on forgetting, then you will slip into an inferiority complex. "Oh, I am such an ass. I keep forgetting all the time." That is a negative approach and should be avoided at all cost.

Your thinking should not be unproductive; it should be productive and progressive. A negative emotion or thought multiplies with great speed, so never let any negative thought develop in your mind. To do that, you have to remain watchful, always. You must not think how many times you slept and how many times you woke up, but simply be in the moment. To falter is part of *sadhana*; never ever allow this to become a barrier in your path. You must not reflect on how many times you forgot but on how many times you remembered. Prayer and *sewa* (selfless service), is what can pave the way for your steady growth on the path of spiritual practice.

So *drashta bhava* begins with the *buddhi* and as you progress, it becomes more and more real. When you have once learnt how to ride a cycle, you do not have to work hard every time you cycle. But in the beginning it is a lot of hard work; all your attention is focused on the handlebar. All learning happens through the conscious mind. Once the conscious mind has been applied to learning who you really are, soon a moment will come when a quantum leap will take place from mind to no-mind. This will be a very pregnant moment; a window will open up and you will get a glimpse of that which is beyond words, expression and thought.

Initially you have to work really hard to stay in the *drashta bhava*. Slowly, it will become your second nature. Then this is what starts happening, as the *Gita* says:

Indriyaanee indriyartheshu vartanta iti dhaaryan

The senses behave the way senses should — it is their *dharma*, their natural law. But now I am not associating myself with the senses, I am just a witness of the sense activities. The mind is required to do its job of thinking and reflection, *sankalpa-vikalpa*. And when it is not needed, it remains calm. When the *buddhi* is required, it will be used and when it is not required, it stays calm and still. And I know that now I am the one who is watching all the drama of the body, mind and senses. Instill this in yourself, you do not need to verbalise it — just be aware when the senses, mind and intellect function. Know it and remain distant from it — this will pave the way for self-realisation.

When I look at *sadhaks* engaged in meditation, I find that many of you have such an awful expression on the face, as though you are going through something terrible. You have changed meditation into such a stressful activity. Be normal! Bring a little smile to your face. *Buddha* seems serious, but he always has a light smile playing on his lips. Now in your case, this whole thing of becoming aware is something sporadic; it happens one moment, it stops and then it happens again.

One thing is certain, the determination that I should constantly be in the 'present' also becomes an obstacle sometimes. Because you count the number of times you forgot to be aware and fell asleep, but you will not remember the times you remembered and woke up! This is a negative approach. When will it happen…when… when will it happen that I am never unaware? This thought, 'When will it happen?', also becomes an obstacle. So be in the moment, be in the 'now'. Do not analyse, do not judge, do not be your own psychiatrist.

Someone has asked a question: "After listening to you, what I have understood is that the only way to liberation is *gyana*, *dhyana* and annihilation of 'I-ness'. But I have also heard from other people who have come here, that they have met the Almighty in a state of *dhyana*. Now if this is what has happened with them, shouldn't their 'I-ness' be annihilated that very moment?"

Well, if you already have the answer then why bother me! This is a wonderful thing — the blind guiding the blind — they will definitely end up in a ditch. People love giving advice; just ask anyone anything and you will be flooded with advice! Tell someone that you have a stomach ache and you will literally be flooded with suggestions. Someone will say, "Use a hot water bottle." "No, you must take thyme." The third one says, "No, add a bit of castor oil to a spoonful of curd and the pain will disappear miraculously." Another will say, "It must be severe constipation." All kinds of solutions will be offered — take a laxative; allopathic medicine, homoeopathy…this…no that — it goes on and on!

Sometimes when my body is unwell, I make it a point not to tell others. Or else, the moment the word is out, I have people queuing up with medicines. Last year I had a stomach problem and every half hour I was getting a message: now Mr. A has got medicine, now Mr. B has come with some treatment, now so and so has got an allopathic medicine! In a single day, I had no less than six different doctors visiting me. I said, "Now if anyone says that a doctor has come, I am going to thrash him. Do not dare to bring another doctor!"

You have come here to listen to me, so just listen to me. Do not waste your time talking to people who just claim to know — for the simple reason that the one who claims to know definitely does not know. Discussing things with false teachers will only complicate matters further. You say, "Others tell me they have seen the Almighty in a state of *dhyana*." Well, what you see with open or closed eyes is an illusion created by your mind — it is just a projection of your mind. How can you see God with your eyes? Eyes can only see things — is God a thing? The one who is not a sight, a touch, a smell, a sound, a fragrance, cannot be perceived with the senses. Think about this; ponder on it deeply. People live in the fragmentation of their own mind — they hallucinate and see glorious magical forms, which they think is the Almighty.

Now I will take up another question: "Once in a *satsang* you mentioned that if something is too close to your eyes, you are not able to see it clearly. Does it mean that only when *atman* slips out of the body will I experience atambodh (self-realisation)? Is this a pre-condition for self-realisation? You also said that when you say 'I have had food,' or 'I have done service', it is an expression of ignorance. If we do not talk in this manner, then how do we conduct our daily business?"

You have asked two things; now try to understand this. We have three bodies: gross, subtle and causal. At the time of death, the subtle body is released from this gross body. 'I' is separate from all these three bodies. It is not true that in order to know your *swaroopa*, to know who 'I' is, your *atman* has to slip out of the body; well if 'I' slips out then what is left behind? It is not that there are two of which one will remain in the body and the other which will go out and then it will be known. This is a ridiculous statement! Even now 'you' are separate from the body. You are in it but not of it. The body is just a shell, the mind is an inner

layer and the individual self is the core. Have you seen rice which has not been sifted from the chaff? If you want to extract rice, you have to pound it so that the husk is separated from the rice. In *dhyana*, you have to separate the husk of the mind, intellect and body from the *atman*. Though *atman* is inside the body, it is separate from the body. A grain of rice does not get stuck in the husk; you just have to pound it, winnow it and it gets separated. If we look at the husk, the naked eye cannot see that there is rice inside. It is not that it gets separated only when it is winnowed; it is separate even when it is present inside the chaff. In the same way, when you say that 'I' am in the body, it seems as though 'I' and the body are the same. And to see the body and the mind as one, is perhaps the greatest delusion suffered by man. Despite being inside this body, 'I' is separate from the body and is far removed from the body. It is through constant effort that you will see that this is just a delusional state of the mind.

After listening to me you have a new understanding; but this knowledge seems incomplete and something in you wishes to believe and seek. You want to know that if 'I' am not this body, then what am 'I'? Who am 'I'? The individual self, the *jivatman* is separate from the senses, the body, the mind, *chitta*, *ahankara*, and the intellect. Above the mind is the *jivatman*, the unit consciousness, or the soul in its subtlest form. Here is the sense that 'I' know that 'I' am. This individual soul — the *jivatman* is a reflection of the pure self — the *shudhatman*. You need to understand the important difference between the *jiva* and the *shudhatman*, which is the final level.

The *jivatman* is the reflection of the cosmic *atman* on the unit mind. The *atman* is that which witnesses the actions of the mind; it does not partake of the reactions that result — pain or pleasure. It is essential to the existence and activity of the mind, without itself being influenced by the *gunas*. *Atman* and *Brahman* are not two distinct entities — had it not been so, *atman* would have certainly come to know the moment it stepped out of the body. *Atman* is both inside and outside the body — *atman* means 'the pure self'. I will not use the word *Brahman*, but *atman* instead, because you tend to think of these two as different entities. It is almost as though we have only *atman* and *Brahman* is someone else. You or *atman*, or let us say 'I' or *atman*, is one and the same and there is no difference between *atman* and *Brahman*.

Understand that this is like the difference between a forest and trees. Is there a difference between a forest and a tree? A group of many trees is a forest and one unit of a forest is called a tree. Now if I begin to chop off the trees one by one, will the forest survive? If forests are disappearing from the face of our planet, the main reason is that everyone thinks that he is going to cut just a single tree and that is all! Another person thinks, "Oh, I will just cut one tree, how will that change anything."

Brahman is one unit and can be called *atman* too. *Atman* in all its pervasiveness can be called *Brahman*. The 'self' which is in me and in you is *Brahman*. The oneness of existence is an unchangeable phenomenon. I am 'you' is the ultimate statement and to reach this level, you will have to break the barriers created by your mind.

It is extremely important to grasp the separation of the 'I' and the body. The functions of the body are not the functions of 'I'. 'I' simply watches the body perform several functions. Right now your eyes are seeing, but in sleep you will not see anything. Right now my tongue is speaking, but when the body goes off to sleep, it will not speak. Right now, the mind is thinking, but once we are in deep sleep, it will not think anything.

None of the functions of the mind and the *buddhi* are performed in a state of deep sleep. So, is 'I' not present in a state of deep sleep? Even when none of the functions of the mind and *buddhi* are being performed, 'I' is present. In every birth, when the gross body dies, 'I' does not die. 'I' survives because even after the death of the gross body, the subtle and causal bodies carry on their journey. According to its *samskaras*, a new birth happens, and till you break the vicious cycle of 'I am the doer', you will continue to experience the roller coaster ride of births and deaths. Although many births and deaths have happened, yet 'you' never had a birth and neither experienced death!

The identification with the body is so strong, that no matter which body you get, you believe that you are that body. To break this association with the body, use this method: when you eat food, remind yourself that it is the body which is eating and not you — you are only witnessing. You have to bring this awareness to your day to day activities. The body is walking, sleeping, sitting, bathing; in every activity, bring the awareness that you are the witness. This will help you break the identification with the body. 'I am a body' has seeped so deep into your subconscious that you need to employ a tool to break this conditioning.

Therefore I feel that at least for a few days in the beginning, the *sadhak* should consciously speak this language: the body has eaten food, the age of the body is so much. How will it help? As you repeat this, it will sink into your sub-consciousness. You will find it strange that I am harping on the body, but it will be useful for you to know that the functions of the body are not the functions of 'I'.

If someone says, "Are you going to sleep?", then it should occur to you who is it that sleeps? Do not respond unconsciously and reply, "I am going to sleep." Respond in a state of consciousness and say, "This body is going to sleep." Know it, feel it and live it.

If you have a stomach ache and you begin to believe that you are in pain — then the pain becomes unbearable — but the moment you dis-identify yourself from the body, the pain too diminishes. Now this is something very interesting, for this knowledge gives an immense power to the mind. If the pain is there, it is there. What can you do? If you begin to express yourself in this manner, then there will be a world of difference between 'I' am miserable and my 'mind' is miserable.

Once a lady came to meet me who had lost her husband. I said, "I believe your husband died recently." She said, "Yes, his body is dead." She said that he did not die, only his body died. This body will live as long as it has to. This is the magic and miracle of *gyana*. Life will bring different experiences — pleasurable and painful ones! You will experience misery; you will be humiliated, and you will go through several crises, trials and tribulations, but this understanding carries you from the false 'I' to the true 'I'. When misery strikes, you will not say, "I am very sad"; when your body is unwell, you will not say, "I am unwell." You will only say, "My mind is sad." You will not sit and cry, "Oh, my son is dead." You will say instead, "The son of this body is dead." It is not a question of what you will say but of what you will actually experience.

This knowledge has the power to change your perception and thinking totally. Now you can wonder how a person will function if he knows that 'I' am not body, mind or *buddhi*. Well, you do not have to be an ignoramus to do your work. Do you think a *gyani* does not work? In fact, only a *gyani* knows how to work in the right fashion. Only the enlightened ones know how to even indulge correctly. How can a sleeping mind really enjoy this wonderful magical world?

The definitions which you have given to yourself will be shattered to pieces right now. How? Well, you came here with a name, gender, family, address, degrees, achievements etc, and now you have none! All these identifications were of the body and you are not a body. Now you have understood that all your achievements are null and void. You might have the best of houses, men, women, prestige, but you have no identity; you do not know who you really are. These things are part of the temporal *samsara* and you have missed the real thing — the exploration of the self! It is only when life brings unfortunate conditions that people see its fickleness and ask: "What is this life for?" Is it necessary to dig a well only when we feel thirsty? You have to do the digging well in advance.

If you have not heard the discourse of a master or attended a *satsang*, then the chances are that you will not even be aware of such things. It is only your good fortune that brings you in contact with a *guru* and you get a chance to listen to *tattvagyana*. When you listen, then curiosity is awakened in your mind. If this curiosity soon changes into intense search, only then you can move deeply into it.

But the one who just eats, dances, drinks and indulges in sex, would apparently have no time to think of *atman* or *Brahman*. He will say, "We do not know what *atman* is! Why bother about *atman*?" That is why the sages have said, "As long as you are happy with sensual satisfaction, why would you seek this path? But when you are hit by misery, disease or death, you begin to understand the value of such things."

A gentleman once came to attend a *shivir* dragged here by his wife — poor fellow just followed the boss's orders! Though before coming here he had all kinds of apprehensions, once he was here he liked the environment. He thought I would impose a restriction and a curfew on everything! Anyhow, he liked the environment and did some meditation too. Now if you were to ask such a person to do passive meditation, it will be a punishment for him. But luckily that day active meditation was being done and he loved it; the next day it was dance-meditation. So he realised that it was not as boring as he had expected it to be. Rather it was interesting! Only after coming here was his interest aroused.

Now he doesn't just do the meditation himself, but gives meditation cassettes to others too; he gifts my cassettes and books to his friends on Diwali and other festivals. Now he says, "No more sweets. You must have these sweets instead." But as long as he did not know, he used to mock at his wife, "What sort of craziness is this? All the time listen to Gurumaa, Gurumaa, Gurumaa. Don't you ever leave me and this house and go after her." He would keep scolding her and fighting with her, but now that he has enjoyed the bliss of being in the *ashram*, he has himself become an ardent devotee, and practices meditation regularly. He is the one who keeps telling me, "Please allow me to stay in the *ashram* permanently." He, who would not allow his wife to come on a temporary basis, now wants to come on a permanent basis himself!

Only those people know the value of *gyana* who have suffered the miseries of *agyana*. Unless you have a disease, there is no point in administering a medicine. In this assembly, so many of you think that to regard the body as 'I' is no disease. So how can the medicine of atmagyana be administered to you? If you understand that you are a patient, then you look for medicine. But if the patient thinks that his disease is no disease, then why would he seek a cure for it or take any remedial course?

'I' am not a body; 'I' am only a witness, an observer. This entire world is a product of *panchtattvas* and so is this body. But if someone does not want to understand this fact, let him not. Those who have come here only to look at me, just to see the body, do that. But you must remember that this body is going to

265

perish ultimately. The day this body perishes you will cry and feel miserable. Attachment brings pain even if it be with the master; do not ever get attached to the master — love the master and be like the master, that is, enlightened!

Even if you have love for me, you should try to understand who I really am. I am not this body. I am not mind or *buddhi*. This tongue that I am speaking with is not 'I'. What 'I' am is what you are! How does the bond between the *guru* and the disciple become strong? When does this love become strong? Once you discover that the way 'I' am *Satchidananda*, separate from the body, mind and *buddhi*, you too are *Satchidananda*, separate from body, mind and *buddhi* that is when the *guru* and the disciple are united.

You say, "We love to sit at the feet of our *guru*." I say, "If there is so much delight in sitting near the body of the *guru*, then there has to be so much more in recognising the real *swaroopa* of the *guru*." The real love is not for the body. Only that person really loves the *guru* who loves the reality of the *guru*. What is the reality of the *guru*? The body is not the reality for the body is not the *guru*. If you see something in the *guru*, it is only because he has tried to know his *Satchidanandaswaroopa*. It is only because of the *gyana* that the *guru* has, that you feel gurubhava towards him.

Suppose I had had no realization and no *gyana*, then I too would have been an ordinary person like you. What is the difference between the *guru* and the disciple? The only difference is that the *guru* is realized and the *shishya* is not. The *guru* has consciousness of his atmanswaroopa but the disciple does not; *guru* has realized his atmanswaroopa but the *shishya* has not. This is the only difference that is it! *Guru* is devoid of all attachments whereas *shishya* is not.

Of course you say that you love your *guru*, but how will you prove it? When you are devoid of all attachments, when you discover your atmanswaroopa, then you too, will be in the position the *guru* is in right now. This is what love is! Otherwise it will merely be another type of attachment. It is one thing to like a person and quite another to love a person. You must understand this very carefully. Your body is going to perish exactly as your guru's body is going to perish. Guru's real *swaroopa* is *sat*, chit, *ananda*, and is separate from the body, mind and senses in the same way as your real *swaroopa* is *sat*, chit, *ananda*. At the core you and *guru* are one; on the spiritual plane this unity is already there; the art is to feel this at the level of the heart and the mind.

This *gyana* will help you to overcome the fear of death; it has the power to make a man fearless and death merely a play. How does death become a game for a *Brahmangyani*? Because during the course of meditation he experiences death while still being alive. The one who has seen death and experienced that the self is beyond death — well, what fear would he have of death? Only that person fears death, who has not understood the reality of death. But the one who has cracked the code and seen the reality of death knows only too well that it is just a farce. There is nothing more to death than the disintegration of elements! 'I' is beyond the reach of death.

If someone is angry with the sun's rays and wants to slash them with a sword, will he be able to do so? Can you cut light or air? If someone wants to cut fire or kill light, and attacks them with a sword, what will happen? He will only end up hurting his own self. Light cannot be killed, nor can fire be cut. If you hit the light bulb which you use at home with a stick, it is the bulb that will break. The stick cannot hit the light. Just think over it, will the bulb break or the light? The stick only hits the glass shell of the bulb; you cannot hit at the electricity which illuminated the filament.

Let us extend this analogy to the body. A bulb has three things: a shell made of glass; a filament inside the shell; an electric current in the filament. The outer shell is this gross body, the filament that glows is the subtle body and the electricity inside the filament is *atmadev*. When death strikes what does it do? It only breaks the outer glass shell — in other words the gross body. If a bulb gets fused, what do you do? You get a new bulb, is it not so? So the fused bulb is thrown away, a new one got and fitted in. In the same way, the day the bulb of your body gets fused, your family members will lift your body, put it on a wooden plank and dispose it off in the cremation ground.

The only difference is that if a husband dies, most Indian

women do not bring another one home! But husbands are always ready to bring a new wife! Well, they always have one in waiting! Men are really very smart; if the wife dies they will bring home a new wife on the excuse that the children need a mother. But if the husband dies, the wife usually prefers not to remarry. That is why, according to world statistics, there are far more widows than widowers! You can check it out on your own too! You will find more widows than widowers!

A woman was dying; she asked her husband, "O darling! Tell me, will you marry again after my death. My children will be ruined if there is no one to take care of them." He said, "No, no! How is that possible! You are the soul of my life! Though Shakuntala was saying that she will not mind looking after our children," So everything had already been decided!

When the bulb gets fused you get a new one. But if a relative of yours gets fused, do you get another one? What is death? It is like the outer layer of glass shattering to smithereens; the subtle body abides. Now what is the subtle body? Mind, *buddhi*, *chitta*, *ahankara*, the five senses and five *pranas* — all these together constitute the subtle body, and this body survives. According to its *karmas*, the individual soul then gets a new body. In other words, the outer shell changes but the inner content remains the same.

Even after the death of the body, 'I' survives. You do not have to strive for immortality or eternity, you do not have to grab it from anyone — it is always there. You are immortal and eternal — you do not have to strive to attain truth — you are the truth.

CHAPTER 16

I BOW UNTO MYSELF

**Aham nirvikalpo niraakaarroopo
Vibhurvyapya sarvatra sarvendriyaanaam
Sadaa me samatvam na muktirna bandhah
Chidaanandroopah shivoham shivoham**

This is the last stotra, the sixth one. 'Aham' means 'I'. It has
two aspects: pure and impure. Now here I am talking of the pure
'I' and not the impure 'I'. First you must understand very clearly
that we are not talking of the impure 'I' at all. The impure 'I' is
something we have left far behind. The *guru* tells us that you must
'kill' that impure 'I', which introduces you to pain, agony and
anguish. A *Sufi* has put it beautifully in a hymn:

**The moment you are able to kill your ego
You will become a God yourself**

It is your dualism that has separated 'you' from '*Brahman*'.
This couplet is in the Urdu language and it says: **Jab *Khudi* ko
chodega, tu hi *Khuda* ho jayega.** Urdu is a wonderful language.
When you write 'Kh' or 'Ja' in Urdu, they have an almost similar
form — if you add a dot below, it has one meaning, and if you
add a dot above, it has another meaning. In Urdu we call this dot
a '*nukhta*' and in Hindi we call it '*bindi*'. '*Juda*' (separate) could
become *Khuda* (God) and vice versa.

**Khel to sab nukhte ka hai,
Hum yoon hi magaz ghisate rahe**

Khud *Khuda* the hum,
Masjidon me jaa umar yunhi gawate rahe

Brahman was inside but we kept looking outside. I kept on searching for you in temples and mosques and you were right there within me!

Oh! When will you understand that this pure 'I' is God? Only when you give up your attachment to the body will you understand this. And if you refuse to understand, then rest assured that you will always remain '*juda*' — separated from *Brahman*. If you get *gyana*, your 'separation' will be removed. The '*nukhta*' changes its position and khud (self) becomes *Khuda*. The poet says, "It is all a matter of the *nukhta*." Right now your *nukhta* is in the wrong place, and all you have to do is drag it to the right place. That is it! That is all you have to do!

Guru helps you change the vision of seeing things; *Guru* guides you from ignorance to illumination. This morning I was talking to a person who has run away from home. He tells me, "I felt that as the *ashrams* are on the banks of the *Ganga* and many saints live there, so I must also go and live there! It was with these thoughts that I ran away from home at mid-night. And now I will stay here as I do not like my home any more."

What a wonderful state of mind! And here I find people who listen to me year after year and yet their attachment simply refuses to go. And here was a person who had no idea of *guru* or *gyana*, yet had such a strong sense of detachment that he just took the plunge without a thought! What is more, he does not even know what kind of *sadhana* he has to do? Now he will go looking for a *guru* to guide him to the right path. He will look for an *ashram* and offer his prayers, that too with a total sense of abandonment.

Once a gentleman came to a *shivir* and demanded to sit in the front row. He was upset that he would have to sit at the back while saints and *mahatmas* are given front seats. I said, "Well, they are the only ones who deserve to sit in the *shivirs*. Only they deserve to sit as I do not have to lecture them to give up attachment. They have already given it up. You do not have to explain to them to give up attachment for the son or for wealth. They have already given it up. As they have already done half the job, the rest becomes much

easier for me. I also know that when they listen to me, it is not a waste, rather my words shall be valued. Often people ask me, "If we keep thinking all the time that 'I' am not a body, then how will we love our family members?"

What will you get out of the love which is not even love but just attachment? It is just mutual self-interest that continues to govern all relationships. Somewhere there is an apprehension that if the *bhava* that 'I' am not a body gets well entrenched, then how will we run the affairs of our household? In other words, how will the physical relationship between man and woman be established? Somewhere it is the same disease you are stuck with. This 'I' that you are familiar with right now is essentially false and the 'aham' that Shankaracharya is talking of is the real 'I'. You would say, "How can 'I' be of two different types? 'I' is 'I' after all." My dear, it has already happened — you are living with the false 'I'.

Understand this example: On a full moon night there is one moon in the sky and another reflected in the waters below. The reflection is false but the moon in the sky is real compared to the reflection. The moon is always seen in the sky, but minor tremors in the water have the power to disturb the reflection. If the water is muddy the reflection is not clearly seen. Only when the water is still, calm and crystal clear that a reflection is seen. So now we are talking of two things: one is the reflection and the other is the one who is being reflected. The moon is up in the sky and the reflection of the moon is visible in the waters below. In the same manner, 'I' am pure *atman* and the reflection is false. *Aham, Jivabhava*, or *Chidabhaas* are the different names of the same thing.

We only recognise the reflected 'I'; we only accept this 'I' to be true; we are caught in this reflection alone. The reflection of the moon is conditional; it is seen one moment and the next it is not there. When the wind blows, it will shake and move. In the same way, your ego bloats if it experiences happiness and contracts if it experiences misery. If someone respects you, you expand; if someone humiliates you, you shrink.

Your situation is comparable to that of a mechanized toy. If happiness comes, you smile and if misery comes you cry. If the children are serving you then they are angels, and when the same angels refuse to listen to you, you blurt out, "Oh, why did I give birth to these devils?" But how will you kill your own flesh and blood when you have such a strong attachment with them. You would rather die than kill your child!

So 'I' has two forms: true and false. The 'I' you know right now is an impure one. And the 'I' Shankaracharya is talking of is the pure 'I' which is *sat*, chit, *ananda*.

Aham nirvikalpo niraakaarroopo
Vibhurvyapya sarvatra sarvendriyaanaam
Sadaa me samatvam na muktirna bandhah
Chidaanandroopah shivoham shivoham

Aham Nirvikalpo: 'I' am without thoughts; *vikalpa* means counter-thought and thoughts arise in the mind and the mind is not me — it is just a tool which is used by me. Mind is always oscillating, jumping from one object to another, from one emotion to another. When the flow of thoughts is on, all kinds of thoughts such as those of joy and sorrow, respect and humiliation continue to invade the mind. This is good and that is bad; this man is good and that one is bad; he is a friend and he is an enemy; such thoughts of duality continue to bog us down. This is how the needle of our thoughts keeps moving up and down.

Even when you sit down for *dhyana*, the ebb and flow of thoughts does not stop. Even in meditation you think about your near and dear ones. This struggle in the mind exhausts you, and you do not want to meditate as it reminds you of the struggle required. There are some days when the mind is a bit quieter, but this is not a good sign as it takes you into a semi-sleep state which is called tandra in *yoga*. Once meditation ends, the thoughts begin to surface in your mind all over again. That is why those who engage in meditation cry a great deal saying, "Meditation gives us immense joy. But the moment we give up meditation..." Then they start feeling that this world has a corrupting influence upon them. That is why some of you feel that a permanent state of bliss can be experienced by renunciates alone, those who sit on the banks of the *Ganga* with no office work and no children to worry about. Then you tend to believe that you should live in an *ashram*

and focus all your energies on meditation — that this is the only way to empty the mind of all thoughts.

Some people become *sadhus* so that they can experience the emptiness of the mind. But it is the nature of the mind to reflect and think. To insist that the mind should always be free of thoughts is also not good. We have to make a conscious effort to acquire the knowledge which will help us become the sole witnesses of our mind, whether it is silent or thinking. Whatever I am speaking right now is not without applying my mind. If we become 'empty of all thought' then how will we speak? In fact all our activities like eating, drinking and sleeping are governed by thoughts.

There are seven stages of *gyana*, of these the fifth is *padarthabhavini*, which means that the external world is non-existent. This stage precedes the stage of *asanksakti* and the final stage of *turiya*. Once *brahmaveta* (enlightened one), enters the stage of *padarthabhavini*, the entire social behaviour simply drops off, and in this state the body will not live for more than six months.

Let me say one thing: when the body is alive it will feel hunger and thirst; when the body eats, it will also eliminate. I have seen a person who was in such a state that he had to be fed by others and reminded to chew the food in his mouth! Brahmagyani has to eat even if it is a very small quantity or just fruits. Someone will have to peel the fruit, put it in his mouth, and then he has to chew it. So even if you reduce your activity to a minimum, still the basic needs will be there. You have to endure the heat too. It is said about the *Jain Tirthankars* that they never bathed. They were so self-absorbed that only when it rained would the bath take place. They are able to empty the mind of all thoughts to such an extent, that all activities such as eating and bathing are greatly reduced. No one can ever reach a state of zero-activity, but one can always hope to reduce the scale of one's activities.

There are two kinds of *gyanis* in the world — *Jivanmukta* and *Videhmukta*. *Jivanmukta* is one who has attained enlightenment and now wishes to be in total solitude and total detachment from life. Total absorption in inner bliss and a deep dive within, is what he is looking for in the remainder of his life. *Videhmukta* is one who after realisation does not wish to be alienated from the world and continues his worldly activities, but within he is totally detached and aware. Seeing the behaviour of a *Jivanmukta*, people think that a true *Brahmangyani* is one who is not concerned about eating and drinking — others have to bathe him, feed him and change his clothes too. I used to sit with one such *mahatma* and watch him. One of his disciples would come and place food in front of him, and he would just keep sitting. Time and again, she would say, "*Maharaj*! Please have your food!" Then she would start feeding him herself, and the moment she took the spoon of rice close to his mouth, she would remind him, "*Maharaj*! Please open your mouth!" He was so completely silent and immobile, that you virtually had to remind him to chew his food!

The *shastras* say that to have a *darshan* of such a *mahatma* is to have the *darshan* of *Brahman* itself. So after eating his food he got up. And while getting up he forgot all about his clothing, which was nothing more than a long piece of cloth! Someone had wrapped this cloth — a *chaddar* — around his body. Holding his *chaddar*, he walked to the bank of the *Ganga*, let the *chaddar* fall and stepped into the water. He was there for a while, then stepped out, wrapped his *chaddar* and came and sat down. All his acts: getting up, walking up to the *Ganga*, bathing, stepping out, wrapping the *chaddar*, are not happening without any thought. But the thinking is so limited and the thoughts so few that they appear to be almost negligible. In spite of being greatly reduced, the thoughts do endure. In your case if they are a hundred percent, in his case they were probably less than two percent! But thoughts are thoughts after all!

What does 'aham nirvikalpo' mean? Does it mean that a *Brahmangyani* is always in a state of nirvikalpa — thoughtlessness? No action, no *karma*, no movement? No, he does not have to go into that state as he is always in that state. He is 'aham nirvikalpo': 'I' am beyond mind and its thoughts. Right now you have to make an effort to silence your mind, to reach the state of zero-thought. It is only through meditation that you are able to reach the level of zero-thought. If you give up meditation, thoughts begin to invade your mind all over again.

So Shankaracharya says, "Realise the real you, and know that

'you' are not mind, 'you' are away from and beyond the mind."
Your *swaroopa* is 'nirvikalpa'. Such a Brahmanveta does not have to
meditate, he is always meditative. One who is nirvikalpa does not
have to go through the rigours of meditation. The mind of one who
is certain about his nirvikalpa *swaroopa* never has a problem.

Once, a *sadhu* came for a *shivir*. He said to me, "It has been a
long time since I became a *sadhu* and started living with my *guru*.
We were never taught all these methods of meditation. But you
always explain different methods to your disciples." I said, "There
is a reason why I have to explain these procedures. You left your
house because of love and detachment. Your mind is naturally calm,
so it does not have to be calmed through specific procedures. You
are so completely entranced by your love for the *guru* that your
mind does not get restless, so you do not need these methods. But
most of my listeners do not have such a degree of *vairagya* and
love, hence these meditation methods are important."

Meera never felt the need to take recourse to meditation
because she was completely entranced in her love for *Krishna*. She
had become an icon of love; where was the need of meditation?
Guru Gobind Singh has in fact made a mockery of those who
meditate. He says: "Why are you sitting with your eyes shut? You
look like a crane waiting silently for the fish on the bank of a river."
Now so many people have interpreted it to mean that Guru was
opposed to the idea of meditation. Why would Guru say such a
thing? He spent one full year meditating in a place called Vibhor,
and he also said that in his past life he meditated in Hemkund
Sahib. What he meant was that if you just shut your eyes without
purifying and cleansing your mind, then your *dhyana* is nothing
more than pretence.

Look, you must understand why I am often so harsh with
you. Here I am trying my best to teach you all this, to explain
dhyana to you, showering so much love upon you, but despite all
this when I see you fighting with someone, or speaking in a loud
voice humiliating another, I really feel like clubbing your head!
Why? Why should you use bad words for anyone? Why must you
humiliate another? How can you get yourself to do it?

There is one major change that comes about in the life of those who meditate, and come it must, one way or the other. And if this change does not come to you, then you are in the category of false meditators whom Guru has condemned. In giving this analogy of a crane, Guru's purpose is not to oppose *dhyana*. What he means is that if your meditation does not reflect in your behaviour, then you have still not understood what it means to meditate. If you do not see any change, then you are like a crane, but if do, then you shall be like a swan.

When a *sadhak* listens to *Brahmangyana* and moves into the experience, he becomes as pure as a swan. In *Hindu* and Tibetan mythology, the swan Is a symbol of purity and knowledge; the one who is established is called a *paramhans*. Such people are always established in the contemplation of nirvikalpa. This 'I' is nirvikalpa and it is *nirakaar* (formless) too.

Often I am asked this question: Does God have a form or he is formless? And I always say, "Why do you ask whether God has a form or is formless! You look at yourself. Are you with or without form?" Now if you look at the body, it has a form. 'You' are not a body. There is a story about *Devrishi Narada* who once found a king grieving over his dead son. He asked him, "Why do you grieve, death is invincible." King said, "I have lost my only son, how will I live. You have miraculous powers. You can bring him back to life!" *Narada* replied, "How can I violate the law of nature? One who is born must die." But the king insisted, so *Narada* said: "I will summon his *jivatman* and give you the power to converse with it. You can then tell him to come back into his gross body." The king said, "Oh, yes! He is my son after all. He will certainly obey me. You summon him."

With his yogic powers *Narada* summoned the *jivatman* and helped the king converse with his son. The king said, "My son, the sage says that he can bring you back to life with his yogic powers. So you come and enter this gross body." The *jiva* replied, "Which father? You are not my father. I am not your son. I had come into this body due to my *karma*. When my age and my *karma* were over, I left this body. Now why should I go back into this body? Now my *karma* will help me acquire a new body." The king was really surprised; as long as he was alive, his son would not even touch

food without his permission. He was shocked and wondered if he was indeed talking to his son. Then he started pleading, "No, you please come back into this body. You are my son. You have a duty toward me. You cannot leave me like this in my old age." The *jiva* said, "O king! Your relationship with me was just this far. In your previous birth you had me killed. I was born as your son so that in your old age I could avenge my murder. In this life I have died at the age of ten, so that all your hopes are dashed to the ground with the shock of your son's death. This is how I have avenged my death and settled the score."

This *katha* (story) in the Bhagavad tells us that we use this body only to work out our *karmas*. We are adding new *karmas* to out existing Himalayan account. As long as you do not find a *gyani guru*, this vicious cycle does not end. Newer relationships are formed and newer *karmas* are accumulated. You have to accept the rewards and punishments of all your *karmas*, whether you are a *gyani* or an agyani! If you are a doer then you have to be a receiver as well. We are not able to break off old relationships; rather we keep forging new ones. You may wonder how to live otherwise, as this is the way the world goes.

Yes, it definitely does. But let the world go the way it does; you try to correct your perspective. You must look at the entire network of relationships as a play, a *leela*. This body is false, so is the body of the person in front of you. This *leela* goes on; someone meets, someone separates, someone comes and someone departs. Newer relationships of friendship and enmity are formed. You should always be conscious and watchful deep inside.

Enjoy all relationships — but with the knowledge that they are false. Mother-father, brother-sister, all these kinships are false. *Adi Shankaracharya* left home at the age of eight and became a *sanyasi*. His old mother started crying, "You have become a renunciate, now who will take care of me? Who will cremate me? Is it not your duty?" He then gave his word of honour saying, "Ma, when your last moment comes, you just have to think of me and I will be by your side." It is said that he was somewhere near *Badrinath* when he suddenly felt that his mother was summoning him. Look, the mother has been given a very exalted position in life. The moment he felt this deep call, he told his disciples, "I am going back home right away." Now, it is a rule every *sanyasi* has to observe that he cannot ever return home. He is not even supposed to visit his village or his city again. This is strictly forbidden; this is what the law says.

But Shankaracharya went back to his village in Kerala where his mother lived. When he reached he found his mother ailing and bed-ridden. The moment his mother saw him, she was overjoyed. In her last days he served his mother. When the villagers saw that a *sanyasi* had come back home they were very annoyed with him. They felt that he had violated all the laws of sanyasashram. A *sanyasi* has no right whatsoever to return to his home or village.

Do you remember that this is what happened with Gyaneshwar Maharaj's father too? After becoming a *sanyasi*, when his father came back home on the insistence of his *guru*, he underwent untold suffering and misery. Ultimately both husband and wife were driven to suicide. Despite that the scholars refused to forgive them and the local community did not accept their son! So everyone started opposing *Shankar* asking why he had come back and why he was serving his mother? On the one hand you say, "'Pita neva me neva mata na janama', and on the other you come home. This is wrong!" But Shankaracharya was unconcerned; he fulfilled the promise he had made to his mother. When the mother died, no one was prepared to help him with the cremation. No one came from the neighborhood to help him. People just broke off all ties with him. In other words, he was not even allowed access to the cremation ground in the village.

His mother's body was lying there. He took off his sanyasi's dress and wore a white *dhoti*. In the backyard of his own house, he chopped off a couple of trees and made a pyre and performed the last rites of his mother. He finished the ritual, had a bath and wore the dress of a *sanyasi* again. Now some people say that he had removed these clothes whereas others say he did not. I say it really makes no difference!

You will be surprised to know that this incident happened some twelve hundred years ago. How were the villagers to know that this young lad would earn so much respect, honour and glory?

The method he adopted for performing the last rites of his mother are now an accepted social norm in that part of the country. When he was alive, people opposed him, but today they are following his footsteps and emulating him. Why? Because he became famous! He became one of the best custodians, protectors and promoters of the *Hindu* religion.

So *Adi Shankaracharya* knew that 'I' is nirvikalpa, his mind was not disturbed by the flow of thoughts, he was a picture of total detachment, and yet when it came to social behaviour, he did exactly what was expected of him. In a way he was very traditional, but in a way he was also extremely progressive. *Gyana* teaches us right social conduct, to give love to others, to not expect to receive love from others, because one is a source of love and joy — *anandaswaroopa* — oneself. What can a *gyani* expect from others? Nothing! *Brahmangyani* actually shares his own *ananda* with others.

This is the way a *sadhak* should be. Complete in *gyana*, complete in *vairagya*, complete in social conduct too. Shankaracharya was never scared or intimidated. The entire social community was against him, but he did not bother. Because rightful social conduct says, "There is no *guru* greater than the mother!" How could he allow his mother's body to remain uncremated?

Whenever misery strikes — which is bound to happen if you are living in the world — this stotra will relieve you of your turmoil. Social conduct will bring you both joy and misery. If you do a good or bad deed, whether consciously or unconsciously, or someone else does it; if sometime there is heartbreak and you plunge into a deep sorrow, then you must remember this stotra:

Na me mrityushankaa na me jaatibhedaha
Pita neiva me neiva maataa na janm

'I' is *nirakaar* and *anandaswaroopa*. Who is the mother and who the father? Who is the brother and who the sister? Who is a friend and who a foe? Now neither joy remains nor sorrow. Once you become calm and still, then all sorrow and misery is washed away.

Vibhurvyapya sarvatra sarvendriyaanaam
Sadaa me samatvam na muktirna bandhah

Vibhurvyapya sarvatra sarvendriyaanaam: The *atman* is everywhere. The gold is both inside and outside the ornament. Water is both inside and outside a drop. If the drop wants to see itself as separate from water, then it has virtually no existence. If the drop, with the understanding of *gyana*, breaks the barriers of form, then it experiences oneness with the ocean, with its vastness and greatness.

If the drop regards itself as a mere drop, then it will see itself as separate from the ocean. Then the drop is small and the ocean vast. But if the drop realises that it is only water which has assumed the shape of a drop and of the ocean, then the drop will begin to understand the falsehood of its own smallness. And once the drop realises this, it becomes an inseparable part of the ocean. It is still easy to come to terms with the fact that I am *Satchidananda*, but to realise that this *Satchidananda* is also omnipresent is something which is baffling.

Do you remember what I had told you about a *mahatma* I knew from the days of my childhood? One day in his characteristic half-jocular tone, he told me, "Look, I do know how to do *satsang*, but I do not know how to sing." I said, "*Maharaj ji*! How can you say that you do not know how to sing? Just look at yourself. Who are you?" What I was trying to tell him was that you first give up your swami hood and then see who you are. You must also try to see who is singing in this body of mine! He laughingly said, "It is *Brahman* — me who is singing."

It was in this state that *Krishna* proclaimed, "In this entire cosmos, it is only 'I' that is there. Among trees 'I' am a banyan tree; among animals 'I' am Kamadhenu the holy cow; among Gods 'I' am *Indra*; among serpents 'I' am *Sheshnaag*; among the rivers 'I' am *Ganga*." People who could not understand this profound thought started saying, "He is so arrogant. For everything he says 'I'. Even if you allow your imagination to run wild, you will not be able to reach the level at which *Krishna* is speaking. You shall be able to understand this only if you first understand and experience what *atman* is. The *guru* has to present both arguments and evidence in

his support, in order to explain this to you at length. Only then will the *buddhi* understand and blossom.

Right now, even if the *buddhi* is not able to grasp it, let it be. But your *swaroopa* is the same, there is no difference in that. If your *buddhi* fails to grasp it, then you must think that this foolish *buddhi* is unable to grasp, but slowly it will begin to understand. If you listen to the *satsang* of *gurudev* more often, then the *buddhi* will begin to understand. One thing is definite: Vibhur vyapaya sarvatr, means that this pure 'I' is present everywhere.

Every object in the material world has a name and form, it exists, it is likeable and it gives us joy. In *Sanskrit* it is said that every object has five aspects: asti, bhati, priya, *naam* and roopa. These are the only five things in the world! Everything has a name and a shape or form. Asti (truth), Bhati (Consciousness), and Priya (*ananda*) remain unchangeable whereas name and form keep on changing. In this ocean called *Satchidananda*, small waves of *naam* and roopa are constantly being formed, and change is happening continually. Looking at your own atmanswaroopa, you will be overwhelmed!

Let me put it this way, every religious person believes that God is present everywhere. It is the same God who resides in me, you and in everyone. All right, tell me whether God is present in me as a unity or as a duality? Are God and I like two people sitting on the same sofa? He on one side and I on the other? Should I say, "Hello! Hey *Brahman*! How are you?" And *Brahman* answers, "Hey child! How are you?" Do God and I live side by side? God is in everyone and so is he in me as well. How much distance is there between *Govind* and I? One meter? Two meters? Is it one inch, two inches or half an inch? How far are we from God? All right, one centimetre, one millimetre? How far? How close?

The way there is fragrance in a flower and an image in a mirror, both of which are inseparable, in the same way, God and I are enmeshed in each other — neither is separate nor can be separated from the other. The same God who is in everyone is in me too. The devotee says that God is everywhere — in the language of *gyana* it means that 'I' is everywhere. Then who is in the enemy? 'I' is everywhere! Whose light is in the moon? Whose glow is in the sun? Whose sounds are in the ocean? Whose fragrance is in the flowers? Whose sharpness is in the thorns? Whose flight is in the clouds? Whose greenery is in the plants? Whose might blows this wind? It is all because of 'I'.

He himself is the disciple; he himself is the saffron robe; he himself is the *jiva*; he himself is the world; he himself is the God. Your *leela* is strange! You yourself are the disciple! Neither 'I' nor 'You'.

Sadaa me samatvam na muktirna bandhah

'I' always remains the same, only the mind changes or the *buddhi* does. The way the sky does not change, only the clouds float in and out. Sometimes the sun shines brightly and sometimes it grows dim. Sometimes night comes and sometimes it goes. Sometimes you see the sun across the sky, sometimes the moon and sometimes the stars. Sometimes the sky appears blue, sometimes black, sometimes this and sometimes that. But all the colours that we see in the sky are false. If you only look at the sky, you will realise that it never changes; it remains the same.

The 'self' is like the vast unending sky. It never ever changes. No *gyana*, no *agyana*, no bonds and no liberation. When 'I' came into this state of equipoise, then 'I' realised that 'I' never had any bonds, nor do 'I' ever seek liberation. It is the mind that entertains the thought of bondage and it is the mind again that entertains the thought of liberation. If *agyana* afflicts the *buddhi*, *gyana* is also experienced by the *buddhi*. And 'I'? 'I' am always like the virgin sky. 'Vibhuvyaaya Sarvatre Sarvedriyani', also demonstrates this very truth. The disciple asks the *guru*, "Which is the purest water, of the *Ganga* or the *Yamuna*?" The *guru* says, "You are the purest of pure, neither *Ganga* nor *Yamuna*!"

The *guru* says, *"Tatvamasi!"* The disciple says, *"Aham Brahmasmi!"*

Why are you content with being just a body? You are so vast, omnipresent. You are *Satchidananda*, but due to ignorance you regard yourself as a mere mortal. Once I heard a story. A lion's cub was left alone as his mother died after giving birth to him. Somehow a herd of sheep came there and picked up the cub. Now

the cub grew up amongst the sheep. Of course his appearance was that of a lion, but his temperament and nature was that of a sheep. The lion that should ordinarily be roaring would be heard bleating. The moment any wild animal came, he would run the way other sheep did. He had completely forgotten that he was a lion. Who could possibly have told him this? Living amongst the sheep he had become a sheep himself. As he was nurtured on the milk of an ewe, he regarded himself as her son. One day a lion attacked this herd. But when he saw a lion cub amongst the sheep, he was rather amazed.

Forgetting the sheep he ran after the cub. Seeing someone chasing him, the cub ran to save his life. He ran so fast that the other sheep were left behind. Finally when the lion caught up with him, he started crying, "Please don't kill me! I am a poor lamb!" The lion said, "I will not kill you! You are not a lamb but a lion." When he refused to listen, the lion took him to the bank of a river and said, "Now look at yourself in the water! Your face is exactly like mine! Are you convinced, now?" "Yes!" The lion said, "And now look at your teeth in the water. What are they like?" The cub said, "Sharp!" The lion said, "Now you look at mine!" At first he was scared and refused to look. "No, no, you must. I am not going to swallow you. Just look at my teeth," said the lion. "Teeth are also the same." Then the lion showed the cub his tail. The cub said, "Yes, it is just like mine." "Now look at the sheep's tail and tell me what it is like?" The cub found the sheep's tail to be rather strange! "This is what I have been trying to tell you, that you are not a sheep but a lion." Even then he did not understand, so the lion organized a *shivir* and made the lion cub repeat, "I am a lion." But he would end up saying, "I am a sheep." The lion would say, "No, you are a lion."

This is what I have been trying to tell you. You say that 'I' am a *jiva* and I say 'you' are *Shiva*. You wonder how that is possible! You send scores of queries asking how this is possible! "We are just *jiva*." I say, "You are a *Shiva*," but you go about feeling mortally scared. Why fear? Whose fear? Why go far, you are scared of wives, fathers, mothers, school teachers, the police and leaders! It is fear all the way through. Trapped in all kinds of fear! But what are you scared of? Now let us get back to the story… the lion made the cub recognise all the physical signs and then the cub understood. The lion said, "Now I will start roaring." He roared so loudly that the forest shivered, and so did this little cub. "Now you roar." The cub starting bleating, "Ma, ma!" The lion slapped him and said, "Do not speak like this! Speak the way I speak!" It was with great difficulty that he was finally able to roar like a lion. At first he roared rather gently, but soon he gained confidence and roared loudly, "This is the limit! I am a lion after all."

"This is what I have been saying," said the lion. "*Gurudev*! I bow before you! You have made a lion out of a sheep." The lion said, "Child, you were a lion right from the start, but had forgotten this fact. You were never a sheep, always a lion. But because of the company you were in, you had begun to believe that you were a sheep. It was nothing but your *agyana*."

In the same way, you are shivaroopa, formless, devoid of all feelings, devoid of all thoughts, beyond the suspicion of death, beyond the distinctions of caste, beyond all notions of *punya-paap*, beyond all notions of joy and sorrow! Wow! You are shivaroopa! What are you and what had you begun to believe yourself to be! Because you chose to recognise yourself as a body, therefore you were caught in the vicious cycle of joy and sorrow.

Aham nirvikalpo niraakaarroopo
Vibhurvyapya sarvatra sarvendriyaanaam
Sadaa me samatvam na muktirna bandhah
Chidaanandroopah shivoham shivoham

The real greatness of a *guru* lies in the fact that he introduces us to our own reality, our true face and our real self. He introduces me to myself. I was in a state of semi-consciousness. He pulled me back into a state of total awareness. I was in a state of ignorance and he gave me *gyana*. I was in bondage and he liberated me. This is the greatness of a *guru*. *Guru* holds up a mirror of *gyana* to his disciple and says, "Look child! Your real *swaroopa* is *Satchidananda*!"

Unfortunate and condemned are those who fail to come across a Brahmanveta *guru* in their lives! That is how lion cubs continue to live like sheep. He is born with the consciousness of being a body and dies in much the same state.

284

Let me tell you once again, if you have not been able to follow everything I said, you do not have to worry. What is important is that you must have complete trust in and devotion to the guru's word. Whether or not you are able to grasp it, what you must believe in is that the *guru* is speaking the truth. It is the truth because it has the authority of *Adi Shankaracharya* behind it. It is the truth because the *guru* has experienced it within himself. The day you will be able to experience it within yourself, this will become your truth as well. But all said and done, the truth is the truth.

Again and again contemplate every little thing I have said, then you will begin to understand the inherent meaning in what I am saying. Just reflection is not enough to calm down your wandering thoughts, if there are any left. By getting rid of all thoughts, the possibility of *samadhi* increases, which in *Vedanta* is called *Nidhdhyasana*.

I have done what I could, I made you listen to *gyana*. Now your work starts. It is for you to reflect, contemplate, and then accordingly make it a part of your life.

To put it differently, this is not just any talk, this is a talk about inner revolution — a tale of immortality. Once you listen to it, you become immortal yourself. You already are immortal; the only thing is to recognise it. Who told you? With whose blessings and grace did you experience it? Scriptures say, 'Gurbhayo Namah!' O *Gurudev*, I bow before you! You have lifted me beyond the body, senses, mind and *buddhi*. Hey *satguru*! There is none like you! As a *jiva*, we were wandering around restlessly. You made us rest in the shelter of your *gyana*, you sang the song of *gyana* for us and you made us aware of our real self."

Now I do not desire any destination as I have found the shore on the waves themselves. The one who has found a shore in every wave, why should he wait to sail across and find a resting place? Now that there is a shore in every wave, why should I grieve over anything? You have taught me to live. Only those who sorrow over life do not know how to live.

A *sadhak* is never daunted by the sorrows or trials of life. He is not scared of death either. He knows that each 'body' has to die and each 'body' is perishable. If one of your friends or relatives dies, you will naturally feel sad if you do not understand that the dead one was dear to you for your own sake. If you feel, "Now who shall I call mother and in whose lap shall I lay my head? Who will sing a lullaby for me?", then watch your words! For it is the song of 'I' that you are singing. "How will 'I' be happy? Mother is dead, so who will sing a lullaby for me?" I am not saying, "How shall mother get peace and happiness by singing a lullaby for me?" You say, "Who will sing a lullaby for me? Who will love me? Who will guide me?" Mother is dead, but you are not worried about her, you are worried about yourself!

I love everyone for my own sake. And who loves 'I'? My dear, only 'I' loves 'I'. When with the blessings and grace of the *guru* you understand this real, pure 'I', then you understand that the same noor, the same *chaitanya* that illumines the *guru*, illumines you as well. Noor loves noor. If you are able to understand this then tell me: this love for the *guru* — will it give joy or sorrow? Neither joy nor sorrow! To tell you very honestly, people who feel joyous feel sadness too. And those who feel sad feel happy as well — it is such a cycle!

Why do you look to the *guru* for liberation? If the disciple is bogged down by the weight of his own bonds, how can the *guru* liberate him? Look to yourself for help. The fact is that the *guru* will also teach you to look at your own self. And if you look at your own self as it is, then that is good enough. And if you refuse to look, then you can only keep on crying! So if the *guru* is a *gyani*, and the disciple fails to make use of the *gyana* imparted by the *guru*, then despite being a disciple of a *Brahmangyani*, he will remain miserable. It is like saying that swans and frogs live in the same river. But which part of the river does the frog live in? It enjoys the muddy part, the filth. And the swan lives in the clean clear water. Both live in the same river. Now it depends on what you want to do. So take a dip in this ocean of *gyana*.

These are the six *shlokas* of *Atmashatakam* — and they are simply incomparable. *Adi Shankaracharya* has composed several other works too. Sometimes people tell me, "You try to imitate our *guru*." Now this is really the limit! Tell me, who has a copyright over *gyana*? If Shankaracharya, *Kabir*, *Ravidas*, Ramkrishna,

Krishnamurti, Osho and Ramana Maharishi were born before me, is it my fault? What kind of a statement is this? Even so, I will answer this allegation. Several hundred years ago, Shankaracharya said, "Aham nirvikalpo *nirakaar* roopo," and *Ravidas* said much the same thing!

Gyana was the same twelve hundred years ago, five hundred years ago or three hundred years ago. Even today it is the same. When this body of Gurumaa is no longer around, if someone looks inside himself, he will say the same thing that I am saying now. In a way, you could say that *Ravidas* copied Shankaracharya. And *Kabir* copied *Ravidas*. The truth is that no one copied anyone. The truth is one and the same; it does not change with time. Jesus Christ too said the same thing. In a far off land called Jerusalem, Jesus was standing in front of a Roman officer called Pontius Pilot. The Roman officer questioned Jesus, "You say you are the son of God! Are you? Jesus remained quiet. When the officer repeated his question again and again, Jesus said, "I am the eternal truth. I and my father are the same." This is what the Old Testament tells us and this is what Jesus also says.

Tattvagyana is the same; it makes no distinction. The path of *gyana* is simply stupendous and only a fortunate few get to walk on it. This *gyana* knows no limits. You will not be able to comprehend it with the help of *buddhi*. It is beyond the comprehension of *buddhi*. It is limitless; vast and incomprehensible!

For whatever little you have been able to grasp, you must thank *Adi Shankaracharya*. We shall remain eternally grateful to him for composing such beautiful stotras. Whosoever sings these, understands these or listens to these will be liberated. These seeds of *gyana* have sunk deep into your *antehkaran*, and deep impressions have been made; *samskaras* are like seeds, they sprout sooner or later.

The *shastras* have sung panegyrics in honour of this *gyana* and if it seeps into your mind once, then the doors of liberation will open up for you. Whenever you choose to walk on this path, in all sincerity and dedication, you will see the reality; one thing is certain, the doors of liberation will always remain open for you.

GLOSSARY

Acharya: Spiritual preceptor or teacher, used interchangeably with *guru*. (See '*Guru*')

Adi Shankaracharya: First Shankaracharya, propounder of the Advaita philosophy of non-dualism. (See '*Advaita Vedanta*' and '*Vedanta*')

Advaita Vedanta: *Vedanta* of non-duality distinct from monism. (See '*Vedanta*')

Agni: Fire — one of the five primary elements; heat produced by burning; biological fire controlling metabolism; an intermediary between man and God in rituals.

Agyachakra: Command centre of spiritual energies said to be located between the eyebrows.

Agyana: Ignorance; nescience

Aham: I; embodied soul or self; ego

Aham Brahmasmi: The concept or wisdom of being one with *Brahman*. Lit. I am *Brahman*.

Aham Vaishvanaro: Lit. I am the One who resides in the *jiva* and enjoys the world of the senses.

Ahankara: The ego-self; the ego-sense; the illusion of independent identity.

Alaap: Discourse; conversation; prelude to a song; modulation of voice in singing.

Alaknanda: River in North India that falls near Garhwal. (Alak means invisible, not perceived by senses; Nanda is a name for Goddess *Durga*.)

Albela: Unusual; different; frivolous

Amardas (*Guru*): Third of the ten *gurus* of *Sikhism*, he succeeded Guru Angad Dev in 1552. Guru Amardas made many contributions to *Sikh* philosophy and practice. He established the rule that all visitors to *gurudwaras* may have langar - a free meal. He lifted the status

288

of women as equal to men. He created the gift of the prayer called 'Anand Sahib'.

An-al-haq: Islamic term for Allah as the Only Reality.

Ananda: Eternal bliss; spiritual ecstasy; heightened state of bliss.

Anandaroopa: Form or manifestation of bliss.

Anandaswaroopa: See *Anandaroopa*.

Angavastram: Long cotton or silk scarf carried on the shoulder by men, particularly in South India.

Anna: Food grain; that which makes the gross body.

Antehkaran: Instruments of inner perception.

Apana: One of the five vital airs or *pranas*. (See *Prana*)

Arjan Dev (*Guru*) (1563-1606): Fifth of the ten *gurus* of *Sikhism*. Contributed 2218 hymns to the *Guru Granth Sahib*. Author of Sukhmani Sahib, a popular prayer for peace. Compiled and installed the Adi Granth. Built the Golden Temple. First Sikh *Guru* to be martyred by *Jehangir*, the *Muslim* ruler of India. (See *Jehangir*)

Arjuna: Son of *Indra* and third of the five *Pandavas*; skilled and ambidextrous archer; hero of the epic *Mahabharata*; his dialogue with *Sri Krishna* constitutes the *'Bhagavad Gita'* — the song celestial.

Arundhati: *Vedic* sage Rishi Vashishta's wife; name of an asterism.

Asana: Third stage in Patanjali's eight-fold path of *yoga*; physical exercises and postures that lead to control over *prana* and mental activity. Lit. Seat or posture.

Asanksakti: Sixth of the seven stages of realization; it is followed by the final stage of *turiya*.

Asat: Untrue; falsehood; unreal

Ashram: Hermitage; a quiet secluded abode for study and spiritual practice; here a guru instructs disciples in spiritual and religious practices.

Ashtavakra: *Vedic* sage; said to be born realized; *Guru* of King *Janak*, the father of Sita; due to his father's curse he was born with a severely deformed body.

Ashutosh: Name of *Lord Shiva*. Lit. One who is easily pleased.

Ashwathama: Son of *Dronacharya*, the teacher of both the *Kauravas* and the *Pandavas* in the epic *Mahabharata*.

Asura: Anti-God, corresponding broadly to the Greek Titan or the Norse jotun.

Atma: See *Atman*.

Atmabhava: The consciousness of being; state of I-ness.

Atmadev: The God within; the self as God-aspect.

Atmagyani: Self-realised; one who has knowledge of the self.

Atmahatya: Suicide; self destruction. Lit. Killing the self.

Atman: Individual self or soul that is eternal and unchanging; principle of life.

Atmasakshatkar: The realisation of, or unification with, the atman. (See 'Atman').

Atmashatakam: Poem of Adi Shankaracharya expressing the Advaita philosophy of non-dualism as distinct from monism.

Atmavit: A self-realised person.

Avatar: Human incarnation or form taken by a God at a time of crisis to achieve a specific mission. Lit. Descent. (See 'Avataran')

Avataran: To come down or descend. (See 'Avatar')

Avidya: Nescience; ignorance; consciousness of multiplicity.

Ayurveda: Traditional holistic medical science of ancient India, most of it has been preserved in the Charak Samhita. Lit. The knowledge of life.

Baba: Term used to refer to a sage or *sadhu*; respectful address for father, grandfather.

Baba Bulleh Shah (1680-1757): Punjabi Sufi poet, employed the verse form known as the Kafi, a style of Punjabi, Sindhi and Siraiki poetry used by *Sufis* and also by *Sikh gurus*. Bulleh Shah's poetry and philosophy strongly criticises religious orthodoxy.

Badrinath: Pilgrimage site in the *Himalayas* in northern India. Jyoti *matth*, one of the four monasteries of the *Dashanami Sampradaya* founded by Adi Shankara is here.

Bani: Sacred *Sikh* texts. Lit. Voice, sound or word. (See 'Gurbani')

Baraat: The groom's party in a wedding.

Benares: Holiest city of the *Hindus*. It is particularly sacred to *Shiva*, though temples dedicated to all Gods are found here. It is also called *Kashi* (meaning 'shining' or 'splendid') and Varanasi (from the two rivers Varana and Asi); site of one of India's oldest *Sanskrit* University.

Bhagat Singh: Freedom fighter and Indian revolutionary.

Bhagavad Gita: A sacred text of the *Hindus*. It is an exhortation to action; the discourse between Arjuna and his charioteer *Sri Krishna* in the epic *Mahabharata* — it teaches the most effective way to be religious and righteous.

Bhagwan: Blessed; divine; title used for Gods and saints.

Bhai: Brother; Hindi slang term for gangster or hooligan.

Bhairavi (Raga): Late morning raga, usually sung last at a musical session; bhairavi is one of the eight forms of *Devi*. (See *'Devi'*)

Bhaj Govindam: Poem written by Adi Shankaracharya in which he calls *Brahman* as *Govind* and exhorts the seeker to contemplate on *Govind* at all times as no other learning or knowledge is of substance.

Bhajan: Prayer; worship; adoration; anthem; hymn

Bhakta: Devotee; lover of the Divine.

Bhakti: Devotion and love; a discipline in which one dedicates oneself to a meditative path of serving God and *guru*.

Bhaktimarga: The path of *bhaktiyoga*. (See *'Bhaktiyoga'*)

Bhaktisutra: A treatise on *bhakti* which contains the instructions and principles for following *bhaktiyoga*. (See *'Bhakti'* and *'Bhaktiyoga'*)

Bhaktiyoga: A genuine search for the Divine which starts and ends in love. One single moment of the ecstasy of extreme love brings eternal freedom incomparable to any earthly benefit. *Bhakti* is considered greater than *Karma* and *Yoga* because these are intended with an object in view while *bhakti* is its own end, its own fruit and its own means. *Bhaktimarga* is considered to be not very different from *gyanamarga*. (See *'Gyanamarga'*)

Bhava: Feeling or sense of being in a particular state.

Bhavna: Continued meditation or steady concentration of mind. Lit. Feeling or intention.

Bhoomih: Earth; of the earth; one of the five basic elements.

Bindi: Lit. Dot, spot or point.

Bindu bindh santaan: Offspring of the gross body.

Brahma: Creator aspect of the supreme Divine; the first of the *Hindu* trinity of Brahma-Vishnu-Mahesh; embodiment of *Brahman* — the Ultimate reality.

Brahmabhava: State of residing in *Brahma*; oneness with *Brahma*. (See *'Brahma'*)

Brahmachari: Celibate; renunciate; student, in the first stage of life as prescribed by *Hindu* scriptures; one who practices *brahmacharya*. (See *'Brahmacharya'*)

Brahmacharya: Conduct in accord with *Brahman*; first of the four stages of life; student life. (See *'Brahmachari'*)

Brahman: Sacred power; ultimate reality; absolute; one besides whom there is nothing else existent.

Brahmangyana: Realization of *Brahman*; the ultimate reality as a universally pervasive force.

Brahmangyani: One who has attained knowledge of *Brahman*. (See '*Brahman*')

Brahmanloka: The field or world of *Brahman*. (See '*Brahman*')

Brahmasutra: A text attributed to the sage Badarayana. It presents in summary, the essential doctrines of the *Upanishads*, especially the Chandogya, a key text of all Vedantic schools.

Brahmaveta: One who has realised *Brahman*. (See '*Brahman*')

Brahmin: Member of the highest cast in the *Hindu* social order; priest in a *vedic* ritual, hence master of all four *Vedas*.

Buddha: Title of Siddhartha Gautam, founder of *Buddhism*. (See '*Buddhism*')

Buddhi: Wisdom; intellect; one of the four aspects of the internal organs.

Buddhism: Religion founded by Gautam Buddha; an unorthodox philosophy that rejects *vedic* authority. (See '*Buddha*')

Buddhist: Follower of *Buddhism*. (See '*Buddhism*' and '*Buddha*')

Bullah: See '*Baba Bulleh Shah*'

Chaddar: Protective veil or covering; a sheet.

Chaitanya: Consciousness; awareness; awakening

Chakor: Red legged Indian partridge, said to be enamoured of the moon, and to eat fire.

Chandaal: Traditionally, the caste that handled dead bodies.

Charvaka: Founder of the materialist tradition of Indian philosophy which goes by his name; all reality is explained in material terms with no spiritual component.

Chetan: Conscious; aware; manifestation of that which is hidden.

Chidabhaas: Reflected consciousness

Chidanandaswaroopa: Form or manifestation of truth-bliss-consciousness.

Chitta: Mind-stuff; mental consciousness; that aspect of the mind where impressions are stored.

Chittaroopa: Form or manifestation of consciousness.

Dadu Dayal (1544-1603): Poet-saint from Gujarat, India, who was found by an affluent business man, floating on the river Sabarmati. He later moved to Rajasthan where he preached his teachings. Much of the imagery used in his songs is similar to that used by *Kabir*.

His compositions are known as the 'Dadu Anubhav Vaani' which is a compilation of 5,000 verses.

Dafli: Percussion instrument played with a single hand.

Dama: Self control

Dana: Donation; ritual of giving alms.

Darshan: Sighting; viewing; usually used for a glimpse of a God or a deity.

Dashanami Sampradaya: Monastic order founded by Shankaracharya in the 9th century C.E. He established four *matths*, one in each corner of India: Sringeri in Tamil Nadu is the HQ of the order, Puri in the East, *Badrinath* in the *Himalayas* and Dwarka in the West.

Dasharatha: Father of *Sri Rama*, hero of the epic *Ramayana*.

Dehoham: State of associating with the body; materialism; belief that 'I' the self is just the body; state of denial of *Brahman*.

Dehoham bhava: The feeling of *Dehoham*. (See '*Dehoham*')

Dera: Ashram; dwelling; abode; residence; pavilion; tent; camp

Dev: Shining; divine; celestial being; term used to refer to any male deity.

Devi: Divine mother; term used to refer to any female deity but especially to the absolute feminine divine in the form of *Durga*. (See '*Durga*')

Deviji: Respectful form of address to *Devi*; an angel; Goddess; any form of Goddess; feminine aspect of the supreme Divine. (See '*Devi*')

Devpurusha: God-man; man with divine attributes.

Devstri: God-woman; woman with divine attributes.

Dharamraj: King of righteousness; master of ethical behaviour; title given to *Yudhishtira* in the *Mahabharata* and also to his celestial father Yamraj, the God of death.

Dharamshala: House for pilgrims; hospice; inn

Dharana: Sixth stage in Patanjali's eight-fold path of *yoga*; contemplation or fixed inner awareness.

Dharma: Religious and social duty; spirituality; ethical action; intrinsic nature; inherent qualities

Dharti: Field; ground; sphere of action

Dhatu: Primary substance; a humour of the body; any constituent element of the body; mineral, metal etc; various dhatus in the human body are: Rasa (Lymph), Rakta (Blood), Maans (Muscle), *Meda* (Fat), Asthi (Bones), Majja (Nervous System), Shukra (Reproductive Cells).

Dhatur: Of Dhatu (See 'Dhatu')

Dholak: Percussion instrument similar to drum.

Dhoti: Unstitched garment worn around the waist by men and women, popular in India and many Asian countries.

Dhyana: Seventh stage in Patanjali's eight-fold path of *yoga*. Involves prolonged concentration and leads to *samadhi*, a state of non-dualistic realization; meditation; absorption; attention; contemplation

Drashta: Witness; one who sees with awareness but without judgment.

Drashta bhava: Attitude or awareness of being a *Drashta*.

Draupadi: Wife of the *Pandavas*, heroes of the epic *Mahabharata*.

Dronacharya: Spiritual and warfare *guru* of both the *Pandavas* and the *Kauravas* in the epic *Mahabharata*. He sided with the *Kauravas* in the war.

Dukha: Sorrow; pain; suffering; distress; grief; annoyance; unhappiness

Dukharoopa: Manifestation of the negative nature of man; form of *Dukha*. (See '*Dukha*')

Durga (*Devi*): *Hindu* Goddess; mother aspect of the supreme Divine; created from the combined fiery energy of all the Gods. She can take the ferocious form of *Kali* to combat evil as mother is always protective.

Durvasa (*Rishi*): Ancient sage; son of Atri and Anasuya. He is considered an incarnation of *Shiva*. Said to be the only *rishi* whose penance increases instead of decreasing when he curses someone. Known for his short temper, he was equally generous when granting a boon. It was through his blessing that Kunti, mother of the mighty *Pandavas*, was blessed with her five sons.

Duryodhana: Son of the blind king Dhritrashtra and Gandhari; cousin of the *Pandavas*. He cheated *Pandavas* out of their kingdom in a game of dice, thus setting the stage for the great battle of Kurukshetra. Before the battle, he chose Krishna's army in preference to *Krishna* himself.

Dvesha: Hostility; jealousy; revulsion; repulsion

Dwij: Twice born; term used for those, whose investiture with the sacred thread makes for a second birth.

Fakir: Islamic term for religious mendicant.

Farid: *Baba* Sheikh Farid, a *Sufi* and *Sikh* saint; a common Arabic name.

Fatuhi: Hand stitched cotton sleeveless undershirt, often worn in hot weather, instead of, or as a shirt.

Gandhi: Indian nationalist leader. He was called the father of the nation and given the title of *Mahatma*. Used satyagraha — insistence on truth and ahimsa — as tools in political activism. He fasted often for personal discipline, to mobilise public support and as a tool in satyagraha to get others around to his way of thinking.

Ganga: River in North India sacred to Indians. Remover of bad *karma* and purifier of sins.

Gangotri: Himalayan source of the *Ganga*.

Ghee: Clarified butter

Ghraan: Nose

Gita: See '*Bhagavad Gita*'

Goonda: Hooligan; gangster

Gopi: Cowherdess; women of Braja whose love for *Krishna* is considered the ideal of selfless devotion that one can have for God.

Govind: Cowherd; cow-finder; name of *Krishna*

Govindapada: *Guru* of Shankaracharya. A learned *sanyasi*, he lived in a cave on the banks of the Narmada river. Under his inspiration, Shankara re-interpreted the three great scriptures.

Granth: Book; tome; Lit. Composition.

Guna: Three fundamental qualities, tendencies or stresses (*sattva*, rajas and *tamas*) which underlie all manifestation.

Gurbani: The Guru's words. (See '*Bani*')

Guru: Spiritual preceptor; commonly used to mean teacher, guide or master. Lit. Remover of ignorance and darkness.

Guru Granth Sahib: *Sikh* religious text composed by *Guru Nanak* with additions by later *Gurus*. Now considered the living *Guru* and guide of *Sikhs* everywhere. (See 'Granth')

Gurudev: Respectful form of address for the *guru*, in which he is revered as divine. (See '*Guru*')

Gurudwara: *Sikh* temple or house of worship. Gateway to *guru* and therefore to knowledge and liberation.

Guruji: Respectful form of address for *Guru*.

Gurupurnima: The full moon day in the *Hindu* month of Ashad (July-August) is observed as the auspicious day of *Gurupurnima*, a day sacred to the memory of the great sage Vyasa. All *Hindus* are indebted to this ancient saint who edited the four *Vedas*, wrote the eighteen puranas, the *Mahabharata* and the Srimad *Bhagavad Gita*. Vyasa even taught Dattatreya, who is regarded as the *guru* of all *gurus*.

Gyana: Wisdom derived from meditative insight or direct perception of reality transcending form and formless.

Gyanaganga: Sea or flood of realisation and wisdom.

Gyanamarga: Path of knowledge; discipline leading to liberation from rebirth.

Gyanasutra: Text and instructions for the path of wisdom. (See 'Gyanamarg').

Gyani: Self realized; knowledgeable

Gyanindriyan: The five organs of cognizance or sense.

Haji: *Muslim* who has performed the pilgrimage to *Mecca* and *Medina*.

Halwai: Cook who makes sweetmeats. Owner of a sweetmeat shop.

Hanuman: Devotee of *Rama*. He is regarded as the model devotee and has tremendous powers attributed to celibacy; son of *Vayu* (God of wind).

Hari: Name of *Krishna* or *Vishnu*. Lit. Green or verdant.

Haridwar: Town where the *Ganga* leaves the *Himalayas* to traverse the plains; site of the famous *Kumbh Mela* every twelve years; Major pilgrimage site and sacred city for *Hindus*. Lit. Gateway to *Vishnu*.

Harmandir Sahib: *Gurudwara* of historical, spiritual and emotional significance in Punjab, India. Maharaja Ranjit Singh had the structure plated with gold in the early 19th century and it came to be popularly called 'The Golden Temple'. In 1604, the newly compiled Adi Granth was housed here for the first time by the fifth *guru, Guru Arjan Dev*. Lit. 'Temple of God'.

Himalayas: Mountain range in North and North-east India, said to be the home of several saints and sages. Mount Kailash, the abode of *Shiva*, is in this range, as is Mount Everest.

Hindu: Member or race of Hindustan. People living along the banks of the Sindhu river.

Hinduism: The religion and culture of the *Hindus*.

Hiranyakashipu: *Asura* king who requested Lord *Brahma* for immortality, and then forced everyone to worship him instead of God. When his son *Prahlada* refused, he tried to have him killed but failed. *Hiranyakashipu* was ultimately killed by Narsimha, an incarnation of *Vishnu*.

Indra: *Vedic* God of rain; king of the devatas.

Ishwar: Supreme lord of the worlds; the aspect of God which governs and regulates the cosmos.

Jagat: World; material or gross realm

Jain: Follower of *Jainism*. (See '*Jainism*')

Jain Tirthankars: Twenty-four prophets of *Jainism*, considered worthy of worship. In the Rigveda there are clear references to Rishabhdev, the first tirthankar, and to Aristanemi, the twenty-second. The Yajurveda also mentions the names of three tirthankars, viz. Rishabhdev, Ajitanath and Aristanemi. Lord Mahavira was the twenty-fourth and last tirthankar.

Jainism: Religion founded by Vardhamana Mahavira in about sixth century. A spiritual path of radical asceticism, *Jainism* does not admit to the existence of God but affirms the reality of consciousness.

Jalaluddin (Hazrat) (1207-1273): A 13th century Persian poet, Islamic jurist and theologian. He is commonly known as Rumi, which means the 'Roman' as he lived most of his life in Anatolia or 'Rum', now located in Turkey.

Janak: King of Videha and father of Rama's wife Sita. Lit. Source or progenitor.

Japa: Mental repetition of a *mantra* or prayer.

Jara: Non-sentient

Jataka tales: A voluminous body of folklore-like literature, concerning the previous births (jti) of the *Buddha*. Jataka also refers to the traditional commentary in this book.

Jehangir: After the death of the Mughal Emperor Akbar in 1605, Jehangir became the leader of India. Unlike his father, Jehangir was a fundamentalist obsessed with turning the country into an Islamic state. Concerned with the rapid increase in the popularity of *Guru Arjan Dev*, Jehangir had him tortured and his followers persecuted.

Jinn: Jeanie

Jiva: Ego; life; an individual person; often used as a compound term *jivatman*, to refer to self or individual soul. (See '*Jivatman*')

Jivabhava: Feeling or state of being a *jiva*. (See '*Jiva*')

Jivanmukta: One who is liberated from rebirth while still living or one who has realised the supreme identity while still in the body.

Jivatman: The collective divine manifested as the individualised self or spirit of the created being. (See '*Jiva*')

Jivoham: State of associating with the ego; belief that 'I' the self is just the soul; state of denial of unity with *Brahman*.

Jnana: See '*Gyana*'.

Juda: Separate; distinct from; distant

Kabir: North Indian saint claimed by both *Hindus* and *Muslims* as one of their own. A weaver by profession, he rejected organised religion and is best known for his simple yet profound poetry.

Kali: The ferocious form taken by the Divine feminine to counter evil; the form of nature that destroys evil; Shiva's energy

Kama: Desire; pleasure; name of the God of love.

Kama bhava: Lust; feelings or thoughts of lust.

Kamandal: Water vessel carried by *sanyasis* and wandering *sadhus*.

Kamdhenu: Cow belonging to *Indra*, believed to yield whatever is desired from her; a cow that gives plenty of milk. Lit. Wish-fulfiller.

Kamsa: Half-brother of Devaki, the birth mother of *Sri Krishna*; the ruler of the Vrishni kingdom. *Kamsa* was told in a prophecy that the eighth son of Devaki would kill him. The eighth son of Devaki and Vasudeva was *Krishna* who was raised by a cowherd couple, Nanda and Yashoda. *Kamsa* was eventually killed by *Krishna*.

Kapha: Phlegm; rheum; one of the humours in the body.

Karamindriyan: Organs of action

Karma: Action; ritual act; action without attachment; accumulated fruits of past action; destiny; principle of cause and effect. *Hinduism* believes in rebirth according to one's *karma*. *Moksha* is said to be the elimination of all *karma*, good and bad.

Karmakanda: Religious ceremony; cult; science of rituals

Karmamarga: The path of rituals, religious duties and right action; the *yoga* that teaches man to do his duty without attachment to its result.

Kartahmiti Manyate: Assertion that 'I' am the doer.

Kashi: City of *Benares*; also called Varanasi. (See '*Benares*')

Katha: Story; narrative; recital; religious discourse; a saying (See '*Katha Upanishad*')

Katha Upanishad: One of the older, primary *Upanishads* commented upon by Shankara and is associated with the Taittiriya school of the *Krishna* Yajurveda. It has some passages in common with the *Gita*. The Katha Upanishad tells the story of Naciketa, who is offered to *Yama*, the God of death by his father. *Yama* tests his suitability to seek wisdom and eventually leads him to enlightenment. While including both theistic and non-theistic perspectives, the text emphasises the need for moral understanding and achievement in order to attain enlightenment. It expounds the doctrine of *karma* and rebirth. It

also presents an analysis of the self in its empirical dimensions and eternal form. (See 'Katha')

Kauravas: Descendant of Kuru — cousins and opponents of the Pandavas in the epic Mahabharata.

Kaushalya: Mother of Rama, hero of the epic Ramayana.

Kedarnath: The most remote of the four Char Dham sites, it is located in the Himalayas, near the head of the Mandakini river, in Uttarakhand state of India. Kedarnath hosts one of the holiest Hindu temples and is a popular destination for Hindu pilgrims from all over the world. (See 'Kedarnath temple')

Kedarnath temple: One of the holiest Hindu temples dedicated to Shiva. Due to extreme weather conditions, the temple is open only between May and October. The temple is believed to have been built by Adi Shankaracharya and is one of the twelve Jyotirlingas, the holiest Hindu shrines of Lord Shiva. An older temple existed from the times of the Mahabharata, when the Pandavas are supposed to have pleased Shiva by doing penance in Kedarnath. (See 'Kedarnath')

Kevala Advaita: Absolute monism; absolute oneness

Kheer: Rice and milk pudding, often served on auspicious occasions.

Khuda: Islamic name for God.

Khudi: Pride; self

Khwaja: Title used in Middle East and South Asia; also used as a family name.

Kirtan: Devotional songs

Klesha: Misfortunes and sufferings; afflictions which delude and lead you astray. Yoga recognises five

Kaleshas: avidya (ignorance), asmita (ego), raga (attachment), dwesha (hostility) and abhinivesa (attachment to your own conception). Lit. Pain.

Koel: Indian Cuckoo bird

Koshah: Covering or sheath. In the human body it is said to be of five types: annamaya — the physical body, pranamaya — the cosmic energy, manomaya — mind-body, vigyanamaya — the intellect or ego and anandamaya — the causal blissful body.

Krishna: Avatar of Vishnu, the preserver aspect of the holy Hindu trinity. Lit. Black or dark.

Kshetra: A sacred place of pilgrimage; a shrine; in yoga, field of the body. Lit. Field or sphere of activity.

Kshetragya: The conscious principle in the field of the body. The absolute witness, aware of the three states of the self — waking, dream and sleep.

Kumarila Bhatta: Eighth century *Buddhist* scholar, who gave up *Buddhism* to become a great exponent of the Mimansa school which taught ritualism as the only way to liberation. A great debater, when defeated by Shankara, he was convinced that Shruti was God-given and self-authoritative. He decided to expiate for his earlier beliefs and referred Shankara to his pupil *Mandana Mishra*, who was as formidable an exponent of ritualism as he himself had been.

Kumbh Mela: Religious festival held every three years at one of the four places: *Haridwar*, Nasik, Ujjain and Allahabad.

Kundalini: Poetic reference to the yogic principle of serpent power. Feminine energy is seen as a mystic coiled force at the base of the spine. Awakening the *kundalini* and raising it to meet the male or *Shiva* principle at the top of the head leads to liberation from rebirth. Lit. Coiled.

Ladoo: Sweetmeat balls served on auspicious occasions.

Lake Mansarovar: Highest fresh water lake in the world situated in Tibet. To the west of the lake is Lake Rakshastal and to the north is Mount Kailash, which is said to be the Himalayan abode of *Shiva*. According to *Hindu* religion, the lake was first created in the mind of *Brahma*. *Mansarovar* is made up of the *Sanskrit* words: manas (mind) and sarovara (lake). The lake is said to be the summer abode of swans, which are considered wise and sacred. It is believed that Gods descend to bathe in the lake between 3 and 5 am, the time of day known as *Brahma* muhurta. *Buddhists* also associate the lake with the legendary Anotatta lake, where Queen Maya is believed to have conceived the *Buddha*.

Lalu, Pilu, Tilu: Ordinary human beings, Hindi equivalent of Tom, Dick and Harry.

Leela: Divine or cosmic play — the world is said to be God's leela.

Lobh: Greed; avarice

Ma: Mother, used in reference to the divine mother especially when regarded as the absolute or ultimate reality.

Madhav: A name for *Krishna*.

Magneto (and his team of evil mutants): The villain in the popular X men series.

Mahabharata: *Hindu* epic, said to be the world's longest poem, contains the classic '*Bhagavad Gita*'- the discourse between Arjuna and *Krishna*.

Mahabhuta: The five gross elements, so called because the whole universe is based on them. They are: prithvi (earth), jala (water), tejas (fire), *vayu* (air) and akasha (ether).

Mahadev: Name of *Lord Shiva*; the great lord. (See '*Shiva*')

Mahamantra: A great or super *mantra*

Maharaas: The great cosmic show, Sri Krishna's *leela*. (See '*Leela*')

Maharaj: Respectful form of address meaning 'great' or 'revered' master.

Mahatma: Great soul; title given to individuals regarded as saintly; master in tune with the infinite.

Manan: Introspection; reflection; contemplation; the second of the three stages of Vedantic realisation.

Mandaleshwars: Title used by some *Hindu swamis* of the Dashanami order founded by Shankaracharya. A high level of traditional, spiritual guardianship. Lit. Superior or chief of a religious district or province ('Mandala' means district, '*Ishwara*' is a name for the sovereign).

Mandana Mishra: Disciple of *Kumarila Bhatta*. He was a great debater and a formidable exponent of ritualism. When defeated by Shankaracharya in a religious debate, his wife and he became disciples of Shankaracharya. (See '*Kumarila Bhatta*')

Manjire: Bells used as musical accompaniment to devotional songs.

Mann: Mind; the instrument of thought.

Mansarovar: See '*Lake Mansarovar*'.

Mantra: From the root words *manan* (awareness, possessing complete knowledge) and trana (complete protection including from ignorance), therefore that knowledge by which we are protected; incantation; cosmic sound or words used for prayer or as an aid to meditation. Repeated recitations still the mind and breath. Some *mantras* have a clear and obvious meaning while others are a sequence of seed letters, the sound of which is said to be beneficial. However, all *mantras* have meaning.

Mantra japa: Repetition or recitation of a *mantra*.

Manu: Ancient *Hindu* law-giver, his treatise '*Manusmriti*' details social and religious conduct. (See '*Manusmriti*')

Manusmriti: Doctrine of correct social and religious behaviour outlined by the ancient law-giver *Manu*.

Mardana: Disciple of *Guru Nanak*, founder of the *Sikh* religion.

Margs: Paths or roads

Markandaya: A *Brahmin* sage and ascetic. Bhrigu, his ancestor, is celebrated in the Rigveda for having received fire from heaven. One of the eighteen major Puranas is named after him.

Matth: A meeting place and abode of *sadhus*. (See '*Sadhu*')

Maulvi: An honorific Islamic religious title, often given to Sunni religious scholars or Ulema. Similar to the titles viz. Maulana, Mullah or Sheikh. Maulvi generally means any religious cleric who has completed some studies in a madrassa. Maulvi is also associated with formal degrees for those who have passed the course of Maulvi (basic), Maulvi Alim (intermediate) or Maulvi Fazil (advanced). Lit. Master or lord.

Maya: Illusion; false appearance; manifestation or illusion personified

Mecca: Islam's holiest city and home to the Kaaba shrine. The city is known for the annual Hajj pilgrimage.

Meda: Fat — one of the five elements that make up the body. (See 'Dhatu')

Medina: A city in the Hejaz region of Western Saudi Arabia, capital of the Al Madinah Province. It is the second holiest city in Islam and the burial place of Muhammad.

Meerabai: Female saint, princess of a powerful Rajput clan, she was a devotee of *Sri Krishna*. Her songs of love and devotion for *Krishna* are sung to date.

Menaka: Celestial nymph sent to earth by the Gods to prevent *Vishwamitra* from completing his austerities. From their union Shakuntala was born.

Moh: Love; affection; attachment; ignorance; delusion; materialism

Moksha: Salvation, liberation from transmigration — the goal of every *Hindu* tradition. *Advaita Vedanta* regards moksha as union with *Brahman*. Vaishnav traditions regard it as being in the presence of *Krishna*. Shaivism sees moksha as being equal to but not one with *Shiva*.

Mrityudhyana: A form of meditation on the perception of one's own death.

Mukti: Liberation; freedom; emancipation

Mumukshutva: Resolute will

Munna bhai: See '*Bhai*'.

Muslim: Follower of Islam

Naam: The name by which one chooses to refer to one's own preferred deity. Lit. Name.

Naam Yagna: A ritual in which the name of God — as chosen by one — is repeatedly pronounced or written as a method of concentrating the mind to lead to higher awareness.

Nadi bindh santaan: Offspring of the mind — that which the mind has created.

Nambudari Brahmin: A lineage of *Brahmins* in Kerala, South India. They are distinctive for recognising only three *Vedas*.

Namdev (Sant) (c.1270-c.1350 CE): A prominent religious poet of India who wrote in Marathi, Hindi and Punjabi. Sixty-one of his hymns are a part of Sikhism's holy scripture, the *Guru Granth Sahib*. His devotional compositions ('abhangas') are compiled in 'Namdev's Gatha' and his work — 'Teerthavalee' contains compositions concerning his travels in the company of Sant Dyaneshwara.

Nanak (Guru) (1469-1539): Founder of *Sikhism*, he adopted some aspects of *Hinduism* like *karma* and *moksha*, but rejected the authority of the *Vedas* and *Brahmins*. His poems are preserved in the Adi Granth.

Narada: Learned Brahmin sage, often serves as a messenger of the Gods.

Nasruddin (Mullah): A legendary satirical *Sufi* figure who lived in the Middle Ages. Many nations of the Near, Middle East and Central Asia claim Nasruddin as their own. He was a populist philosopher and wise man, and is remembered for his witty stories and anecdotes. 1996-1997 was declared 'International Nasruddin Year' by UNESCO. Lit. 'Victory of the Faith'.

Neem: A species of Indian tree with leaves of bitter taste which have great medicinal properties, especially of purifying the blood.

Neti Neti: *Hindu* philosophy of the world being transient. Lit. Not this, not this.

Nidhdhyasana: A state in which all the modifications of the mind have quietened; uninterrupted contemplation or perpetual meditation; the last of the three stages of *vedic* realisation.

Nirakaar: Without form(s)

Nirguna: Without attribute(s)

Nirvana: Extinction of ego, desire and egoistic action and mentality.

Nirvikalpa Samadhi: The highest state of concentration in which the soul loses all sense of differentiation from the universal self. It is a temporary state from which there is a return to ego consciousness.

Niyama: Second stage in Patanjali's eight-fold path of *yoga*. The don'ts of the spiritual path; religious duties as ordained in the scriptures. Lit. Discipline.

Nukhta: A dot used in the Arabic scripts to indicate the vowel sound. Lit. A point.

Om: The first sound. It represents all sounds and is said to be the key to the *Vedas*.

Om Namah Shivai: The *mahamantra* of Shiva. (See '*Mahamantra*')

Padarthabhavini: State or stage of transgressing matter.

Padmasana: Also called lotus pose. Posture for seated meditation in which the spine is straight, the head upright and the legs crossed. It is suitable for long periods of meditation.

Panchkoshah: Five sheaths or coverings that enclose or hide our true self. These are: annamaya (physical body), pranamaya (cosmic energy), manomaya (mind-body), vigyanamaya (intellect or ego) and anandamaya (causal blissful body).

Panchtattvas: The five gross elements also known as the panchmahabhutas. (See '*Mahabhutas*')

Pandaal: Tent; enclosure; canopy

Pandavas: Descendentants of Pandu; the five brothers who are the heroes of the great *Hindu* epic, *Mahabharata*.

Pandit: Brahmin scholar learned in the sacred *Sanskrit* texts.

Panipado: Hands and feet; organs of locomotion

Paramatma: The supreme self; the universal *Brahman*

Paramgyani: Highly knowledgeable person

Paramhans: Free soul — no longer limited by *karma* or illusions.

Parsi: Follower of Zoroastrianism, the religion and philosophy based on the teachings of the prophet Zarathustra.

Patanjali: Composer of the *Yogasutras*.

Pipal: The Sacred Fig (Ficus religiosa) is a species of the banyan fig. The plant is considered sacred by *Hindus*, *Jains* and *Buddhists*.

Prabhu: Master; owner; God; proprietor

Prahlada: Character from the Puranic texts, he is known for his exclusive devotion to *Vishnu*. Most of the stories in the Puranas are based on Prahlada, and in the Bhagavad Puraana he describes the process of loving worship to *Vishnu*. (See '*Hiranyakashipu*')

Prana: Cosmic energy, vital life force which runs the body and the mind. Five types of prana circulate through channels in the body. Their departure from the body is said to cause death. (See 'Prana, types of')

Prana shakti: The driving force of the pranas.

Prana, types of: Prana is of five types. Prana governs the area between the larynx and the top of the diaphragm and is associated with the organs of respiration, gullet and speech, together with the muscles and nerves that activate them. It is the force by which the breath is drawn in. Five types of Prana are Prana, *Apana, Samana, Udana* and *Vayana*. *Apana* is located below the navel region and provides energy to the large intestine, kidneys, anus and genitals. *Samana* is located between the heart and the navel. It activates and controls the digestive system, the liver, intestines, pancreas and stomach. It also activates the heart and circulatory system and is responsible for the assimilation and distribution of nutrients. *Udana* controls the area above the neck, activating all the sensory receptors such as the eyes, nose and ears. It harmonises and activates the limbs and all their associated muscles, ligaments, nerves and joints. *Vayana* pervades the whole body regulating and controlling all movements. It acts as a reserve force for the other pranas. (See 'Prana')

Pranam: Respectful salutation to an elder.

Pranayama: Fourth stage in Patanjali's eight-fold path of *yoga*; breathing exercises that lead to command over *prana* energy and mental activity. Lit. Energy control.

Prani: A living being

Prarabdha: The part of destiny due to past *karmas* which bear fruit in and has to be worked out in the present birth.

Pratyahaar: Fifth stage in Patanjali's eight-fold path of *yoga*. It involves withdrawal of the senses from objectivity and practice of intense concentration. Lit. Interiorisation.

Prayaga: Ancient city of Allahabad in North India, it is the site of the confluence of the holy rivers *Ganga, Yamuna* and the invisible Saraswati. It is considered the site of *Brahma's* first sacrifice and thus is sacred to *Hindus* as a pilgrimage centre. It is often called as 'Tirtha Raja' or king of pilgrimage centres.

Punya: Good *karma*; actions that are ethical, beneficial and generate merit; virtue

Puris: Deep fried Indian wheat bread

Qur'an: Religious text of the *Muslims.*

Raag: Attachment

Rabab: Stringed musical instrument (of the lute family), native to Afghanistan, used in ancient court music, as well as modern day entertainment music.

Rabia: Female *Muslim Sufi* saint, born between 95 and 99 Hijri in Basra Iraq. Much of her early life is narrated by Farid al-Din Attar based on earlier sources and therefore not verified. Rabia herself did not leave any written works.

Radha: Consort of *Sri Krishna*

Raga-ragini: In Indian classical music, raga is a series of five or more musical notes on which a melody is based. Ragini is an archaic term for the feminine counterpart of a raga. Raga-ragini is an old classification scheme and usually consists of 6 male ragas, each with 6 female raginis. Ragas and raginis were often pictured as *Hindu* Gods, Rajput princes and aristocratic women in an eternal cycle of love, longing and fulfillment. Lit. Colour or mood

Rajoguna: One of the three primal qualities, the principle of activity. (See '*Guna*')

Ram Tirath (Swami) (1873 — 1906): Born in Punjab, India, he was a teacher of the *Vedanta* and amongst the first notable *Hindu* spiritual leaders to lecture and teach in the west. A professor of Mathematics, he was inspired by Swami Vivekananda to become a *sanyasi*. In the late 19th century, he became well known in Punjab for his speeches on worship of *Krishna* and later through lectures and essays on *Advaita Vedanta*.

Rama: Prince of Ayodhaya and hero of the epic *Ramayana*, considered an incarnation of *Vishnu*, the preserver of the holy *Hindu* trinity.

Rama Naam: Repetition of the name of *Rama* chanted as a *mantra*.

Ramayana: An epic written about 2nd century by sage Valmiki. It is the story of prince Rama's exile and subsequent return home after vanquishing the demon king *Ravana* who abducted his princess Sita.

Rasa: A theory of aesthetics first articulated in the Natya Shastra of Bharata in regard to drama and later applied to poetry as well. According to Bharata, eight rasas are: Shringar (love or/and beauty), Hasya (Joy), Adbhuta (Wonder), Veer (Courage), Shanta (Peace), Karuna (Sadness), Raudra (Anger), Bhayanaka (Fear), Vibhatsa (Disgust). Later theorists added a ninth rasa: spiritual peace. Lit: Essence.

Rasakatini: A herb found in the upper reaches of the *Himalayas* which when placed on the tongue makes it insensate to all and any taste.

Ravana: Demon king of Lanka; villain of the epic *Ramayana*

Ravidas (Guru): *Hindu* reformist leader, born in 1376 CE. Founder of the 'Ravidasi' sect and revered as a saint by *Hindus* and Nirankaris,

and as a bhakt (devotee) by *Sikhs*. Forty-one of his writings have been included in the *Guru Granth Sahib*, in addition to a large volume of hymns passed on independently. (See *'Guru Granth Sahib'*)

Rishi: *Vedic* sage

Rishikesh: Holy city in central India. Lit. The rishi's hair.

Rooh: Arabic for breath of life, soul, spirit, the vital principle of life; inspiration; revelation; essence; angel

Rudra: Shiva in one of his five aspects, as that of destroyer.

Rudraroopa: Form of *Rudra*. (See *'Rudra'*)

Sadhak: The one who is engaged in the practice of *sadhana* or *yoga*; seeker; aspirant

Sadhana: A path towards liberation; spiritual discipline; practice of *yoga* by which perfection (*siddhi*) is attained; spiritual self-training and exercise

Sadhu: Ascetic; holy man; saint; one who has reached the goal; one who has renounced the world in search of liberation.

Sakshatkar: Realisation of the ultimate reality.

Sakshi: Witness

Salwar-kameez: Dress worn by women in North India, long shirt with type of loose trousers and sash.

Sama: Equanimity

Samadhi: Eighth and last stage in Patanjali's eight-fold path of *yoga*. State in which union with *Brahman* is achieved, *karma* is eliminated and liberation from rebirth is attained; spiritual trance; complete absorption; also tomb of a saint.

Samana: One of the five vital airs or *pranas*. (See *'Prana'* and *'Prana, types of'*)

Samosas: Deep fried cutlets filled with vegetables, a popular snack in North India.

Samsara: World; worldly life; wheel of life, death and rebirth.

Samskara: Mental impressions; perceptions of experiences that impress the mind and are retained as memories.

Sankalp: Volition; mental activity; thought; tendencies; attachment

Sankalpa-vikalpa: Thought-counter thought

Sanskrit: Language of ancient India, prevalent in *Vedic* times and still in use by scholars. The Sanskrit alphabet is considered to be a *mantra* which contains the seed frequencies of creation. Every sound (shabda) has a power (*shakti*) which conveys the sense related to that sound. Almost a hundred Indo-European languages are derived from it. Recently it has been declared the most mathematically sound language and the best suitable for computer applications. Lit. Perfected.

Sanyas: Asceticism; voluntary surrender of worldly ties and responsibilities.

Sanyasi /Sanyasin: One who has renounced the world.

Saptadhatu: The seven tissues that form or flow in the physical body. These are: Rasa: Fluid, plasma that is digested and then nourishes cells. Rakta: Blood cells that are the foundation of life. Maans: Muscle tissue or flesh that provides strength. *Meda*: Fat that lubricates the body. Asthi: Bones and cartilage that provide support. Majja: Marrow that supports Asthi Dhatu. Shukra: Tissue that helps reproduction.

Saraswat Brahmins: Descendents of a Brahmin caste mentioned in ancient *Hindu* scriptures as inhabiting the mythical Saraswati river valley, the geographic location of which is unknown. An ancient legend mentions that Parashuram, an *avatar* of *Vishnu* is said to have carved the community out of the five sons of Raja Ratten Sen.

Sari: Unstitched garment worn by Asian women.

Sarson: Mustard

Sat: Existence; pure being; luminosity. Lit. Truth.

Satchidananda: Blissful truth; Being-Consciousness-Bliss

Satchidanandaswaroopa: Form or manifestation of Truth — Consciousness — Bliss.

Satguru: The great master; a true or perfect *guru*

Satsang: Religious discourse. Lit. Association with truth.

Sattva: Tendency to purity; one of the three *gunas*. (See '*Guna*')

Satvik: One that has the qualities of *sattva*. (See '*Sattva*')

Satyaswaroopa Atman: The individual self that is a reflection or manifestation of the ultimate reality.

Saundryalahiri: One of the major hymns composed by Shankaracharya in which he accords *Devi* — the feminine principle of divinity — the supreme position among Gods, even above *Brahma*, *Vishnu* and her own consort Shiva.

Sewa: Service; religious service

Shabri: A symbol of total devotion, she waited years for *Sri Rama* to visit her humble cottage, sweeping and cleaning it every day in anticipation of his visit.

Shakti: Power personified as the Goddess Parvati who is the consort of

Shiva, the third God of the holy *Hindu* trinity; manifestation of primal energy. Lit. Power, strength, or force.

Shankar: One of the names of Shiva; Shankaracharya's childhood name.

Shankarbhava: See '*Shivabhava*'.

Shastra[s]: Scriptures; classic *Sanskrit* texts of organised knowledge.

Shastrarth: Religious debate; a common socio-religious practice since *Vedic* times.

Sheshnaag: The serpent on whose head the earth rests according to the Puranas. Lit. Thousand-headed serpent.

Shirshasan: Inverted yogic posture. It reverses the action of gravity taking the physical and spiritual attention to the head. It is said to sublimate sexual energy into spiritual energy.

Shishya: Disciple

Shiva: God of destruction and rejuvenation; third in the holy *Hindu* trinity.

Shiva Tattva: The essence of Shiva. (See 'Shiva')

Shivabhava: The feeling of unity with Shiva.

Shivaswaroopa: Like Shiva; in the image of Shiva

Shivir: Camp or congregation for instruction or training, usually of a religious, spiritual or political nature.

Shivoham: The incantation: 'I am Shiva'.

Shloka: Verse

Shoonya: Absolute void; zero; without any attributes; sky

Shraddha: Faith; earnestness; regard; acquisition of the knowledge of truth that is based on faith.

Shradh: Religious ceremonies held in honour of and for the benefit of dead relatives.

Shri: Prosperity; auspiciousness; Goddess who embodies prosperity.

Sri Rama: Respectful form of address to *Rama*. (See '*Rama*')

Shringar rasa: One of the nine essences in human life described in *Hindu* religious texts, Shringar means love or/and beauty, and rasa means essence. The others are: Hasya (Joy), Adbhuta (Wonder), Veer (Courage), Shanta (Peace), Karuna (Sadness), Raudra (Anger), Bhayanaka (Fear), Vibhatsa (Disgust).

Shrotra: Ears

Shudhatman: The pure form of atman; state in which all but atman ceases to exist. (See 'Atman')

Shukdev: Ascetic son of *Veda Vyasa*. He was the founder of the pre-eminent monastic order into which Shankaracharya was ordained.

Siddhi: Attainment; accomplishment, control, especially of *tantric* powers. It is used as a term for spiritual power or psychic ability. Lit. Perfection.

Sikh: Follower of the *Sikh* religion.

Sikhism: Religion of the *Sikhs* founded by *Guru Nanak*.

Sri Vishwanath: Name of *Vishnu*. Lit. Lord of the Universe.

Srikrishnasharnam: To the refuge and protection of *Sri Krishna*, the preserver. (See '*Krishna*')

Sthir: Unmovable; stable; unchanging

Sufi: *Muslim* mystic

Surahi: A narrow necked pot usually made of baked clay and used to store water.

Surdas (1479-1586): A *Hindu* devotional poet, singer and saint who followed the Shuddhadvaita school of Brahmavada. He was born blind and spent most of his life in *Vrindavan*. He created the epic literary work 'Sur Sagar' which means 'Ocean of melody'. Originally it contained 1, 00,000 poems but approximately 5,000 remain today.

Swa: The self

Swami: A member of the ancient monastic order founded by Adi Shankaracharya; one who is in control of self.

Swaroopa: The form taken by a divinity manifesting itself.

Tamas: Ignorance; darkness; one of the three *gunas*.

Tantra: A system of ritual practice or spiritual discipline encoded in *Sanskrit* texts called Tantras. The language of these texts can be deciphered only by those who have received initiation. *Tantric* practices are found in all major branches of *Hinduism*, *Buddhism* and *Jainism*. Some regard Tantra to be an extension of the *Vedic* heritage, whereas others feel it is extra *Vedic* and esoteric.

Tantric: Of *Tantra*; practitioner of *Tantra*.

Tat: *Brahman*; reality. Lit. That.

Tattva: Reality; truth; principle

Tattvagyana: Knowledge of *Brahman* or atman.

Tattvagyani: One who has acquired *tattvagyana*. (See '*Tattvagyana*')

Tatvamasi: Lit. 'That Thou Art'.

Teertham (Or tirath): Crossing point of a river; the term is used commonly for places of pilgrimage where one can cross over to

liberation in the after-life. Visits to such places are said to wipe out bad *karma*.

Titiksha: Endurance; will power

Tulsi Das (Goswami) (1532-1623): North Indian poet and saint, regarded by some as the incarnation of Valmiki, the first poet (Adi Kavi) and composer of the *Hindu* epic *Ramayana*. He composed the Ramcharitmanas, a poetic rendition of the *Ramayana* in Hindi.

Turiya: The fourth state of consciousness, recognised by *Hinduism* as equivalent to *Brahman* and beyond waking, sleeping and deep sleep. Lit. Fourth.

Tvam: Lit. You.

Udana: One of the five vital airs or *pranas*. (See '*Prana*, types of')

Upanishad: Late *Vedic* texts of unknown authorship, about 250 in number, considered to be the closing chapters of the *Vedic* tradition, taught orally by teachers to select students.

Upareti: Detachment

Upastha-payuh: Organs of excretion and procreation.

Vairagya: Detachment from sense objects; freedom from worldly desires; dispassion

Vaka: Speech; pronouncements

Vanaprastha: Third stage in the life of a *Hindu* when he retires to the forest to live a life of simplicity, free from family and career responsibilities.

Vanaprasthi: Forest dweller. One who is in the third stage of life. (See '*Vanaprastha*')

Vashishta: One of the saptarishis (seven great *rishis*), *Guru* of *Sri Rama*, Rajaguru of the Suryavansha (Solar Dynasty), he is considered the human son of *Brahma*. He is also the owner of the divine cow Kamadhenu, who could fulfil any wish. Vashishta is the chief author of Mandala 7 of the Rigveda, and of a treatise (the 'Vashishta Samhita') on the *Vedic* system of astrology. 'Yoga Vashishta' is another ancient scripture — narrated by sage Vashishta to Rama — containing innumerable insights and secrets to the inner world of consciousness.

Vastushastra: Ancient Indian science of materials, it deals with the various aspects of architecture, designing and building environments that are in harmony with physical and metaphysical forces. Vastu is conceptually similar to Feng Shui.

Vayana: One of the five vital airs or *pranas*. (See '*Prana* and '*Prana*, types of')

Vayu: *Vedic* God of wind. The father of *Hanuman* in the *Ramayana* and Bhim in the *Mahabharata*. *Hanuman* and Bhim inherited his incredible strength; one of the five elements.

Veda: Revealed or directly perceived knowledge. Term applied to the entire *Sanskrit* literature that constitutes the knowledge of ancient India in four sacred books: Rig, Yajur, Sama and Atharva. It extends to cover medical knowledge (*Ayurveda*) and knowledge of weaponry (Dhanurveda). Lit. Knowledge. (See '*Vedanta*')

Veda Vyasa: Title of the Brahmin sage *Krishna* Dvaipayana and the author of the epic *Mahabharata*. He was the father of Dhritrashtra and Pandu in the epic *Mahabharata*. He divided the *Vedas* into four parts and later composed the *Mahabharata* and the Purana collection as historical works of religious significance. He thus represents all the anonymous authors who contributed to India's sacred Brahminical literature. (See '*Veda*')

Vedanta: The Absolute Truth as established by the *Upanishads*, *Brahmasutras* and *Bhagavad Gita* and as interpreted by *Veda Vyasa*; concluding part or consummation of the *Vedas*.

Vedic: Of the tradition of, or pertaining to the *Vedas*. (See '*Veda*')

Videhmukta: A liberated being after he has left the body.

Vigyana: Knowledge; discriminating the real from the unreal. Lit. Science.

Vikalpa: Counter-thought

Vishnu: Second God of the holy *Hindu* trinity, Vishnu is the preserver aspect of the divine ultimate reality, most popularly worshipped in his incarnations as *Rama* and *Krishna*.

Vishnubhava: The state or knowledge of being one with *Vishnu*. (See '*Vishnu*')

Vishwamitra: Seer of the Rigveda. Unique for being born a kshatriya and having transformed himself through austerities into a brahmin. The Gods tried to divert him by sending the celestial nymph *Menaka* who broke his concentration. (See '*Menaka*')

Vithal: Name for *Vishnu* (See '*Vishnu*')

Viveka: Right discrimination

Vrindavan: City in central India associated with *Sri Krishna*.

Vyapak: Omnipresence; present; evident; manifested

Vyom: Sky

Waris Shah (1706-1798): Punjabi *Sufi* poet best known for his seminal work 'Heer Ranjha', which is considered one of the quintessential works of classical Punjabi literature. His other famous books are

'Ibrat Nama' and 'Ushtar Nama'. Waris Shah's mausoleum is today a pilgrimage site, especially for those in love.

Yagna: *Vedic* ritual presided over by a learned *pandit* in which sacrificial offerings are made to appease various Gods.

Yajna: See '*Yagna*'.

Yama: First stage in Patanjali's eight-fold path of *yoga*. The do's of the spiritual path. Lit. Control.

Yamloka: The abode of *Yama*, the God of the dead.

Yamuna: Himalayan river regarded as sacred by the *Hindus*. It merges with the *Ganga* at Allahabad (Prayag).

Yashodha: Foster mother of *Sri Krishna*.

Yog Ashram: Hermitage where the precepts of *yoga* are taught and practiced.

Yoga: One of the six orthodox schools of *Hindu* philosophy; an eightfold discipline of Indian tradition; science that joins the individual with the eternal or divine. Lit. To join or yolk together.

Yoga Vashishta: Ancient scripture narrated by sage *Vashishta* to Rama. A unique and extremely profound discourse, it provides innumerable insights and secrets to the inner world of consciousness and covers all the topics that relate to the spiritual study of a seeker. Yoga Vashishta propounds that everything from a blade of grass to the universes is all but consciousness alone. There is nothing else but consciousness. It expounds the non-dual approach to this creation.

Yogamarga: The path of *yoga*. (See '*Yoga*')

Yogasutra: Text on the discipline of yoga, compiled by Patanjali. (See '*Yoga*')

Yogi: Practioner of yoga. (See '*Yoga*')

Yudhishtira: Eldest of the five Pandava princes. Embodiment of Dharma or righteousness.

Gurumaa Ashram
Come to evolve your consciousness

Gurumaa Ashram is a living Buddhafield where a great evolution is taking place - where personalities are being carved out, polished and groomed from raw unconscious states to gracious, aware and enlightened beings. The Master is the magnetic pull that attracts seekers from all over. When this call of love is made, its strength is such that one cannot miss it, but only truly fortunate ones can hear this call. Gurumaa Ashram is one such place where this magic is unfolding.

Every year Gurumaa Ashram welcomes thousands of seekers from all over the world to be part of serene environment of the Ashram. Under the guided presence of Anandmurti Gurumaa they learn and practice different methods of meditation, participate in different activities of ashram, learn self discipline, expand their capacities to create and realize evolution of highest order.

Gurumaa Ashram is a place brimming with the presence of the master where Gurumaa shares the enduring wisdom of life with the seekers. It offers a perfect climate to explore the vastness of inner world and realize the true essence of life. It is a place which must be visited by every individual longing to walk the divine path.

All are invited to be a part of the harmonious environment of Gurumaa Ashram.

Meditation Retreat with Anandmurti Gurumaa

Every year Gurumaa conducts meditation retreats in the ashram and also at various places across the globe. It is usually a five day retreat and offers a wonderful opportunity to learn meditation from Gurumaa and experience the ultimate transformation triggered by the presence of the enlightened master.

The ashram is located on the G. T. Karnal Road (N.H. 1) in Gannaur, Distt. Sonepat Haryana, India. For details you are welcome to visit www.gurumaa.com

Books of Wisdom
By Anandmurti Gurumaa

These books are transcriptions of the extempore talks given by Gurumaa from time to time at various places. Books are one of the many ways of chronicling the wisdom that flows from the master and serves as a beacon for seekers.

Books	Language
1. Anhad Ki Dhun Pyari	Hindi
2. Antar Drishti	Hindi
3. Antar Ke Pat Khol	Gujarati, Hindi
4. Aatm Bodh	Hindi, Marathi, Telugu
5. Ath Kahe Narad	Hindi
6. Bhaj Govindam	Hindi
7. Chinmaya Ki Aur	Hindi
8. Dhamm- Jivan Aadhar	Hindi
9. Going Beyond The Mind	English
10. Govind Naam Mere Pran	Hindi
11. Govind Rasdhara	Hindi
12. Gyan Kshitij	Hindi
13. Kabira Ram Yu Sumiriye	Hindi
14. Karun Hridya	Hindi
15. Naame Ke Swami Har Ghat Base	Hindi
16. Prema Bhakti Ek Utsav	Hindi
17. Prem Ka Chhalakta Jaam	Hindi
18. Quotes of the Unquotable	English
19. Rumi Aur Main	Hindi
20. Satguru Pura Payo	Hindi, Punjabi, Gujarati
21. Shakti	English, Gujarati, Hindi, Telugu
22. Shivoham	Hindi
23. Swar Madhushala	Hindi
24. The Awakening	English
25. Truth Exposed	English
26. Yuktahaar	Hindi, Telugu
27. Prem Deewani Meera	Hindi
28. Mind & Sex	English

To know more about the books or to buy them online, visit: www.gurumaa.com
Or place your order on call: 09896263821 / 0130 - 2216500 / 0130 - 2216501

Audio & Video Collection of Discourse/Meditation/Sufi/Devotional

By Anandmurti Gurumaa

Discourses A.C.Ds & V.C.Ds - Hindi

1.	Anand Ki Khoj (VCD)	Rs. 125
2.	Buddha Sutra (ACD)	Rs. 125
3.	Jeene Ki Kala (VCD)	Rs. 125
4.	Krodh Se Karuna Tak (ACD)	Rs. 99
5.	Mann Ke Paar (VCD)	Rs. 125
6.	Neend Nishaani Maut Ki (VCD)	Rs. 125
7.	Shankracharya (28 VCD SET)	Rs. 2,000
8.	Shivoham (28 VCD SET)	Rs. 2,000
9.	Shivoham (2 ACD SET)	Rs. 195
10.	Vichar Se Nirvicharita Tak	Rs. 125
11.	Shrimad Bhagavad Gita (Set of 71 DVDs)	Rs. 11,000
12.	Jeene Ki Kala (VCD)	Rs. 125

Discourses A.C.Ds & V.C.Ds - English

1.	God: Mystery or Reality	Rs. 150
2.	Know Your Mind	Rs. 150
3.	Shakti - An Ode to Women	Rs. 199

Meditation A.C.Ds & V.C.Ds

1.	Beyond Boundaries (Hindi & Eng)	Rs. 150
2.	Mudra (Hindi & Eng)	Rs. 150
3.	Pranav (Hindi & Eng)	Rs. 150
4.	Ram Ras	Rs. 150
5.	Sacred Spaces	Rs. 195
6.	Stuti Sutra	Rs. 150
7.	Tratak	Rs. 195
8.	Urja (Hindi & Eng)	Rs. 150
9.	Yoga Nidra - Part 1 (Hindi & Eng)	Rs. 195
10.	Yoga Nidra - Part 2 (Hindi)	Rs. 195
11.	Zikr	Rs. 295

12.	Shwason Ka Vigyan (VCD)	Rs. 150
13.	Sparsh (VCD)	Rs. 150
14.	Yog Nidra for Youth (Hindi)	Rs. 195

Devotional A.C.Ds & V.C.Ds

1.	Chamkan Taare	Rs. 95
2.	Fragrance of Love	Rs. 100
3.	Rangi Re	Rs. 100
4.	Sajda	Rs. 100
5.	Shiva's Ecstasy	Rs. 295
6.	Odyssey of Love	Rs. 295
7.	Saajanra (VCD)	Rs. 150
8.	Waheguru Jaap	Rs. 95
9.	Ishq Hi Maula	Rs. 195
10.	Chants of Krishna	Rs. 150
11.	Saanwal Saanwal	Rs. 150
12.	Waheguru	Rs. 99
13.	Mool Mantra	Rs. 99
14.	Maha Mrityunjaya	Rs. 99
15.	Saanwal Saanwal	Rs. 150
16.	Shoonya	Rs. 295
17.	Baawari Jogan	Rs. 295

Poetry A.C.D

Rumi – Love at its Zenith	Rs. 295

MP-3

1.	Rehras Sahib	Rs. 250
2.	Shankaracharya	Rs. 350
3.	Shivoham	Rs. 350
4.	Jaap Sahib	Rs. 245
5.	Japji Sahib	Rs. 245
6.	Shalok Mahalla Novan	Rs. 195

For more information and comprehensive collection, Please logon to www.gurumaa.com.
Or place your order on call: 09896263821 / 0130 - 2216500 / 0130 - 2216501

FULL CIRCLE publishes books on inspirational subjects, religion, philosophy, and natural health. The objective is to help make an attitudinal shift towards a more peaceful, loving, non-combative, non-threatening, compassionate and healing world.

FULL CIRCLE continues its commitment towards creating a peaceful and harmonious world and towards rekindling the joyous, divine nature of the human spirit.

Our fine books are available at all leading bookstores across the country.

FULL CIRCLE *PUBLISHING*

Editorial Office

J-40, Jorbagh Lane, New Delhi-110003
Tel: 24620063, 24621011 • Fax: 24645795
E-mail: fullcirclebooks@gmail.com • website: www.atfullcircle.com

Bookstores

23, Khan Market, 1st & 2nd Floor
New Delhi-110003 Tel: 24655641/2/3

N-8, Greater Kailash Part I Market
New Delhi-110048 Tel: 29245641/3/4

Number 8, Nizamuddin East Market
New Delhi-110013 Tel: 41826124/5

www.atfullcircle.com fullcirclebooks@gmail.com

FullCircle@Chamiers, New # 85, Chamiers Road
R A Puram, Chennai-600028 Tel: 044-42030733 / 42036833
www.chamiersshop.com

Join the
WORLD WISDOM
BOOK CLUB

GET THE BEST OF WORLD LITERATURE IN THE COMFORT OF YOUR HOME AT FABULOUS DISCOUNTS!

Benefits of the Book Club

Wherever in the world you are, you can receive the best of books at your doorstep.

- Receive FABULOUS DISCOUNTS by mail or at the **FULL CIRCLE** Bookstores in Delhi.

- Receive Exclusive Invitations to attend events being organized by **FULL CIRCLE**.

- Receive a FREE copy of the club newsletter — The World Wisdom Review — every month.

- Get UP TO 25% OFF.

Join Now!

It's simple. Just fill in the coupon overleaf and mail it to us at the address below:

FULL CIRCLE
J-40, Jorbagh Lane, New Delhi-110003
Tel: 24620063, 24621011 • Fax: 24645795
E-mail: fullcirclebooks@gmail.com

Yes, I would like to be a member of the

World Wisdom Book Club

Name ☐ Mr ☐ Mrs ☐ Ms..

Mailing Address..

....

....

City................................. Pin...

Phone............................... Fax...

E-mail...

Profession............................. D.O.B...............................

Areas of Interest...

....

Mail this form to:
The World Wisdom Book Club
J-40, Jorbagh Lane, New Delhi-110003
Tel: 24620063, 24621011 • Fax: 24645795
E-mail: fullcirclebooks@gmail.com

KNOW THYSELF